ISBN 0-8373-2738-5
C-2738 CAREER EXAMINATION SERIES

This is your PASSBOOK® for...

Transportation Supervisor

Test Preparation Study Guide

Questions & Answers

EAST NORTHPORT PUBLIC LIBRARY
EAST NORTHPORT, NEW YORK

NATIONAL LEARNING CORPORATION

Copyright © 2014 by

National Learning Corporation

212 Michael Drive, Syosset, New York 11791

All rights reserved, including the right of reproduction in whole or in part, in any form or by any means, electronic or mechanical, including photocopying, recording, or by any information storage and retrieval system, without permission in writing from the Publisher.

(516) 921-8888
(800) 645-6337
FAX: (516) 921-8743
www.passbooks.com
sales @ passbooks.com
info @ passbooks.com

PRINTED IN THE UNITED STATES OF AMERICA

PASSBOOK®
NOTICE

This book is SOLELY intended for, is sold ONLY to, and its use is RESTRICTED to *individual*, bona fide applicants or candidates who qualify by virtue of having seriously filed applications for appropriate license, certificate, professional and/or promotional advancement, higher school matriculation, scholarship, or other legitimate requirements of educational and/or governmental authorities.

This book is NOT intended for use, class instruction, tutoring, training, duplication, copying, reprinting, excerption, or adaptation, etc., by:

(1) Other publishers

(2) Proprietors and/or Instructors of "Coaching" and/or Preparatory Courses

(3) Personnel and/or Training Divisions of commercial, industrial, and governmental organizations

(4) Schools, colleges, or universities and/or their departments and staffs, including teachers and other personnel

(5) Testing Agencies or Bureaus

(6) Study groups which seek by the purchase of a single volume to copy and/or duplicate and/or adapt this material for use by the group as a whole without having purchased individual volumes for each of the members of the group

(7) Et al.

Such persons would be in violation of appropriate Federal and State statutes.

PROVISION OF LICENSING AGREEMENTS. — Recognized educational commercial, industrial, and governmental institutions and organizations, and others legitimately engaged in educational pursuits, including training, testing, and measurement activities, may address a request for a licensing agreement to the copyright owners, who will determine whether, and under what conditions, including fees and charges, the materials in this book may be used by them. In other words, a licensing facility exists for the legitimate use of the material in this book on other than an individual basis. However, it is asseverated and affirmed here that the material in this book *CANNOT* be used without the receipt of the express permission of such a licensing agreement from the Publishers.

NATIONAL LEARNING CORPORATION
212 Michael Drive
Syosset, New York 11791

Inquiries re licensing agreements should be addressed to:
The President
National Learning Corporation
212 Michael Drive
Syosset, New York 11791

PASSBOOK® SERIES

THE *PASSBOOK® SERIES* has been created to prepare applicants and candidates for the ultimate academic battlefield — the examination room.

At some time in our lives, each and every one of us may be required to take an examination — for validation, matriculation, admission, qualification, registration, certification, or licensure.

Based on the assumption that every applicant or candidate has met the basic formal educational standards, has taken the required number of courses, and read the necessary texts, the *PASSBOOK® SERIES* furnishes the one special preparation which may assure passing with confidence, instead of failing with insecurity. Examination questions — together with answers — are furnished as the basic vehicle for study so that the mysteries of the examination and its compounding difficulties may be eliminated or diminished by a sure method.

This book is meant to help you pass your examination provided that you qualify and are serious in your objective.

The entire field is reviewed through the huge store of content information which is succinctly presented through a provocative and challenging approach — the question-and-answer method.

A climate of success is established by furnishing the correct answers at the end of each test.

You soon learn to recognize types of questions, forms of questions, and patterns of questioning. You may even begin to anticipate expected outcomes.

You perceive that many questions are repeated or adapted so that you can gain acute insights, which may enable you to score many sure points.

You learn how to confront new questions, or types of questions, and to attack them confidently and work out the correct answers.

You note objectives and emphases, and recognize pitfalls and dangers, so that you may make positive educational adjustments.

Moreover, you are kept fully informed in relation to new concepts, methods, practices, and directions in the field.

You discover that you are actually taking the examination all the time: you are preparing for the examination by "taking" an examination, not by reading extraneous and/or supererogatory textbooks.

In short, this PASSBOOK®, used directedly, should be an important factor in helping you to pass your test.

TRANSPORTATION SUPERVISOR

DUTIES
Establishes routes to be followed by various drivers; prepares time schedules for buses; supervises service, maintenance, and repair of all school district vehicles; writes specifications for all new vehicles and equipment; gives road tests to and trains new drivers; assigns substitute bus drivers for all extracurricular trips; supervises loading and recommends stopping places for buses; assists in the preparation of state transportation reports and maps of bus routes; keeps a daily record of mileage and number of pupils carried; makes out periodic reports which include cost of operating each bus on the basis of expenses for gasoline, oil, grease, anti-freeze, parts, labor wages, storage or rental, and other expenses; approves all purchases of parts and materials; arranges for all special trips including those for athletic teams; maintains time records of bus drivers for payroll purposes.

SCOPE OF THE EXAMINATION
The written test will be designed to test for knowledge, skills, and/or abilities in such areas as:
1. Bus driving practices, techniques and traffic laws;
2. Bus driver recordkeeping and scheduling;
3. School bus driving practices, techniques and traffic laws;
4. School Transportation management;
5. Supervision;
6. Maintenance and repair of motor vehicles, including tools and test equipment; and
7. Preparing written material.

HOW TO TAKE A TEST

I. YOU MUST PASS AN EXAMINATION

A. *WHAT EVERY CANDIDATE SHOULD KNOW*

Examination applicants often ask us for help in preparing for the written test. What can I study in advance? What kinds of questions will be asked? How will the test be given? How will the papers be graded?

As an applicant for a civil service examination, you may be wondering about some of these things. Our purpose here is to suggest effective methods of advance study and to describe civil service examinations.

Your chances for success on this examination can be increased if you know how to prepare. Those "pre-examination jitters" can be reduced if you know what to expect. You can even experience an adventure in good citizenship if you know why civil service exams are given.

B. *WHY ARE CIVIL SERVICE EXAMINATIONS GIVEN?*

Civil service examinations are important to you in two ways. As a citizen, you want public jobs filled by employees who know how to do their work. As a job seeker, you want a fair chance to compete for that job on an equal footing with other candidates. The best-known means of accomplishing this two-fold goal is the competitive examination.

Exams are widely publicized throughout the nation. They may be administered for jobs in federal, state, city, municipal, town or village governments or agencies.

Any citizen may apply, with some limitations, such as the age or residence of applicants. Your experience and education may be reviewed to see whether you meet the requirements for the particular examination. When these requirements exist, they are reasonable and applied consistently to all applicants. Thus, a competitive examination may cause you some uneasiness now, but it is your privilege and safeguard.

C. *HOW ARE CIVIL SERVICE EXAMS DEVELOPED?*

Examinations are carefully written by trained technicians who are specialists in the field known as "psychological measurement," in consultation with recognized authorities in the field of work that the test will cover. These experts recommend the subject matter areas or skills to be tested; only those knowledges or skills important to your success on the job are included. The most reliable books and source materials available are used as references. Together, the experts and technicians judge the difficulty level of the questions.

Test technicians know how to phrase questions so that the problem is clearly stated. Their ethics do not permit "trick" or "catch" questions. Questions may have been tried out on sample groups, or subjected to statistical analysis, to determine their usefulness.

Written tests are often used in combination with performance tests, ratings of training and experience, and oral interviews. All of these measures combine to form the best-known means of finding the right person for the right job.

II. HOW TO PASS THE WRITTEN TEST

A. NATURE OF THE EXAMINATION

To prepare intelligently for civil service examinations, you should know how they differ from school examinations you have taken. In school you were assigned certain definite pages to read or subjects to cover. The examination questions were quite detailed and usually emphasized memory. Civil service exams, on the other hand, try to discover your present ability to perform the duties of a position, plus your potentiality to learn these duties. In other words, a civil service exam attempts to predict how successful you will be. Questions cover such a broad area that they cannot be as minute and detailed as school exam questions.

In the public service similar kinds of work, or positions, are grouped together in one "class." This process is known as *position-classification*. All the positions in a class are paid according to the salary range for that class. One class title covers all of these positions, and they are all tested by the same examination.

B. FOUR BASIC STEPS

1) Study the announcement

How, then, can you know what subjects to study? Our best answer is: "Learn as much as possible about the class of positions for which you've applied." The exam will test the knowledge, skills and abilities needed to do the work.

Your most valuable source of information about the position you want is the official exam announcement. This announcement lists the training and experience qualifications. Check these standards and apply only if you come reasonably close to meeting them.

The brief description of the position in the examination announcement offers some clues to the subjects which will be tested. Think about the job itself. Review the duties in your mind. Can you perform them, or are there some in which you are rusty? Fill in the blank spots in your preparation.

Many jurisdictions preview the written test in the exam announcement by including a section called "Knowledge and Abilities Required," "Scope of the Examination," or some similar heading. Here you will find out specifically what fields will be tested.

2) Review your own background

Once you learn in general what the position is all about, and what you need to know to do the work, ask yourself which subjects you already know fairly well and which need improvement. You may wonder whether to concentrate on improving your strong areas or on building some background in your fields of weakness. When the announcement has specified "some knowledge" or "considerable knowledge," or has used adjectives like "beginning principles of…" or "advanced … methods," you can get a clue as to the number and difficulty of questions to be asked in any given field. More questions, and hence broader coverage, would be included for those subjects which are more important in the work. Now weigh your strengths and weaknesses against the job requirements and prepare accordingly.

3) Determine the level of the position

Another way to tell how intensively you should prepare is to understand the level of the job for which you are applying. Is it the entering level? In other words, is this the position in which beginners in a field of work are hired? Or is it an intermediate or advanced level? Sometimes this is indicated by such words as "Junior" or "Senior" in the class title. Other jurisdictions use Roman numerals to designate the level – Clerk I, Clerk II, for example. The word "Supervisor" sometimes appears in the title. If the level is not indicated by the title, check the description of duties. Will you be working under very close supervision, or will you have responsibility for independent decisions in this work?

4) Choose appropriate study materials

Now that you know the subjects to be examined and the relative amount of each subject to be covered, you can choose suitable study materials. For beginning level jobs, or even advanced ones, if you have a pronounced weakness in some aspect of your training, read a modern, standard textbook in that field. Be sure it is up to date and has general coverage. Such books are normally available at your library, and the librarian will be glad to help you locate one. For entry-level positions, questions of appropriate difficulty are chosen – neither highly advanced questions, nor those too simple. Such questions require careful thought but not advanced training.

If the position for which you are applying is technical or advanced, you will read more advanced, specialized material. If you are already familiar with the basic principles of your field, elementary textbooks would waste your time. Concentrate on advanced textbooks and technical periodicals. Think through the concepts and review difficult problems in your field.

These are all general sources. You can get more ideas on your own initiative, following these leads. For example, training manuals and publications of the government agency which employs workers in your field can be useful, particularly for technical and professional positions. A letter or visit to the government department involved may result in more specific study suggestions, and certainly will provide you with a more definite idea of the exact nature of the position you are seeking.

III. KINDS OF TESTS

Tests are used for purposes other than measuring knowledge and ability to perform specified duties. For some positions, it is equally important to test ability to make adjustments to new situations or to profit from training. In others, basic mental abilities not dependent on information are essential. Questions which test these things may not appear as pertinent to the duties of the position as those which test for knowledge and information. Yet they are often highly important parts of a fair examination. For very general questions, it is almost impossible to help you direct your study efforts. What we can do is to point out some of the more common of these general abilities needed in public service positions and describe some typical questions.

1) General information

Broad, general information has been found useful for predicting job success in some kinds of work. This is tested in a variety of ways, from vocabulary lists to questions about current events. Basic background in some field of work, such as sociology or economics, may be sampled in a group of questions. Often these are principles which have become familiar to most persons through exposure rather than through formal training. It is difficult to advise you how to study for these questions; being alert to the world around you is our best suggestion.

2) Verbal ability

An example of an ability needed in many positions is verbal or language ability. Verbal ability is, in brief, the ability to use and understand words. Vocabulary and grammar tests are typical measures of this ability. Reading comprehension or paragraph interpretation questions are common in many kinds of civil service tests. You are given a paragraph of written material and asked to find its central meaning.

3) Numerical ability
Number skills can be tested by the familiar arithmetic problem, by checking paired lists of numbers to see which are alike and which are different, or by interpreting charts and graphs. In the latter test, a graph may be printed in the test booklet which you are asked to use as the basis for answering questions.

4) Observation
A popular test for law-enforcement positions is the observation test. A picture is shown to you for several minutes, then taken away. Questions about the picture test your ability to observe both details and larger elements.

5) Following directions
In many positions in the public service, the employee must be able to carry out written instructions dependably and accurately. You may be given a chart with several columns, each column listing a variety of information. The questions require you to carry out directions involving the information given in the chart.

6) Skills and aptitudes
Performance tests effectively measure some manual skills and aptitudes. When the skill is one in which you are trained, such as typing or shorthand, you can practice. These tests are often very much like those given in business school or high school courses. For many of the other skills and aptitudes, however, no short-time preparation can be made. Skills and abilities natural to you or that you have developed throughout your lifetime are being tested.

Many of the general questions just described provide all the data needed to answer the questions and ask you to use your reasoning ability to find the answers. Your best preparation for these tests, as well as for tests of facts and ideas, is to be at your physical and mental best. You, no doubt, have your own methods of getting into an exam-taking mood and keeping "in shape." The next section lists some ideas on this subject.

IV. KINDS OF QUESTIONS

Only rarely is the "essay" question, which you answer in narrative form, used in civil service tests. Civil service tests are usually of the short-answer type. Full instructions for answering these questions will be given to you at the examination. But in case this is your first experience with short-answer questions and separate answer sheets, here is what you need to know:

1) Multiple-choice Questions
Most popular of the short-answer questions is the "multiple choice" or "best answer" question. It can be used, for example, to test for factual knowledge, ability to solve problems or judgment in meeting situations found at work.
A multiple-choice question is normally one of three types—
- It can begin with an incomplete statement followed by several possible endings. You are to find the one ending which *best* completes the statement, although some of the others may not be entirely wrong.
- It can also be a complete statement in the form of a question which is answered by choosing one of the statements listed.

- It can be in the form of a problem – again you select the best answer.

Here is an example of a multiple-choice question with a discussion which should give you some clues as to the method for choosing the right answer:

When an employee has a complaint about his assignment, the action which will *best* help him overcome his difficulty is to
  A. discuss his difficulty with his coworkers
  B. take the problem to the head of the organization
  C. take the problem to the person who gave him the assignment
  D. say nothing to anyone about his complaint

In answering this question, you should study each of the choices to find which is best. Consider choice "A" – Certainly an employee may discuss his complaint with fellow employees, but no change or improvement can result, and the complaint remains unresolved. Choice "B" is a poor choice since the head of the organization probably does not know what assignment you have been given, and taking your problem to him is known as "going over the head" of the supervisor. The supervisor, or person who made the assignment, is the person who can clarify it or correct any injustice. Choice "C" is, therefore, correct. To say nothing, as in choice "D," is unwise. Supervisors have and interest in knowing the problems employees are facing, and the employee is seeking a solution to his problem.

2) True/False Questions

The "true/false" or "right/wrong" form of question is sometimes used. Here a complete statement is given. Your job is to decide whether the statement is right or wrong.

SAMPLE: A roaming cell-phone call to a nearby city costs less than a non-roaming call to a distant city.

This statement is wrong, or false, since roaming calls are more expensive.

This is not a complete list of all possible question forms, although most of the others are variations of these common types. You will always get complete directions for answering questions. Be sure you understand *how* to mark your answers – ask questions until you do.

V. RECORDING YOUR ANSWERS

Computer terminals are used more and more today for many different kinds of exams.
For an examination with very few applicants, you may be told to record your answers in the test booklet itself. Separate answer sheets are much more common. If this separate answer sheet is to be scored by machine – and this is often the case – it is highly important that you mark your answers correctly in order to get credit.

An electronic scoring machine is often used in civil service offices because of the speed with which papers can be scored. Machine-scored answer sheets must be marked with a pencil, which will be given to you. This pencil has a high graphite content which responds to the electronic scoring machine. As a matter of fact, stray dots may register as answers, so do not let your pencil rest on the answer sheet while you are pondering the correct answer. Also, if your pencil lead breaks or is otherwise defective, ask for another.

Since the answer sheet will be dropped in a slot in the scoring machine, be careful not to bend the corners or get the paper crumpled.

The answer sheet normally has five vertical columns of numbers, with 30 numbers to a column. These numbers correspond to the question numbers in your test booklet. After each number, going across the page are four or five pairs of dotted lines. These short dotted lines have small letters or numbers above them. The first two pairs may also have a "T" or "F" above the letters. This indicates that the first two pairs only are to be used if the questions are of the true-false type. If the questions are multiple choice, disregard the "T" and "F" and pay attention only to the small letters or numbers.

Answer your questions in the manner of the sample that follows:

32. The largest city in the United States is
    A. Washington, D.C.
    B. New York City
    C. Chicago
    D. Detroit
    E. San Francisco

1) Choose the answer you think is best. (New York City is the largest, so "B" is correct.)
2) Find the row of dotted lines numbered the same as the question you are answering. (Find row number 32)
3) Find the pair of dotted lines corresponding to the answer. (Find the pair of lines under the mark "B.")
4) Make a solid black mark between the dotted lines.

VI. BEFORE THE TEST

Common sense will help you find procedures to follow to get ready for an examination. Too many of us, however, overlook these sensible measures. Indeed, nervousness and fatigue have been found to be the most serious reasons why applicants fail to do their best on civil service tests. Here is a list of reminders:

- Begin your preparation early – Don't wait until the last minute to go scurrying around for books and materials or to find out what the position is all about.
- Prepare continuously – An hour a night for a week is better than an all-night cram session. This has been definitely established. What is more, a night a week for a month will return better dividends than crowding your study into a shorter period of time.
- Locate the place of the exam – You have been sent a notice telling you when and where to report for the examination. If the location is in a different town or otherwise unfamiliar to you, it would be well to inquire the best route and learn something about the building.
- Relax the night before the test – Allow your mind to rest. Do not study at all that night. Plan some mild recreation or diversion; then go to bed early and get a good night's sleep.
- Get up early enough to make a leisurely trip to the place for the test – This way unforeseen events, traffic snarls, unfamiliar buildings, etc. will not upset you.
- Dress comfortably – A written test is not a fashion show. You will be known by number and not by name, so wear something comfortable.

- Leave excess paraphernalia at home – Shopping bags and odd bundles will get in your way. You need bring only the items mentioned in the official notice you received; usually everything you need is provided. Do not bring reference books to the exam. They will only confuse those last minutes and be taken away from you when in the test room.
- Arrive somewhat ahead of time – If because of transportation schedules you must get there very early, bring a newspaper or magazine to take your mind off yourself while waiting.
- Locate the examination room – When you have found the proper room, you will be directed to the seat or part of the room where you will sit. Sometimes you are given a sheet of instructions to read while you are waiting. Do not fill out any forms until you are told to do so; just read them and be prepared.
- Relax and prepare to listen to the instructions
- If you have any physical problem that may keep you from doing your best, be sure to tell the test administrator. If you are sick or in poor health, you really cannot do your best on the exam. You can come back and take the test some other time.

VII. AT THE TEST

The day of the test is here and you have the test booklet in your hand. The temptation to get going is very strong. Caution! There is more to success than knowing the right answers. You must know how to identify your papers and understand variations in the type of short-answer question used in this particular examination. Follow these suggestions for maximum results from your efforts:

1) Cooperate with the monitor
The test administrator has a duty to create a situation in which you can be as much at ease as possible. He will give instructions, tell you when to begin, check to see that you are marking your answer sheet correctly, and so on. He is not there to guard you, although he will see that your competitors do not take unfair advantage. He wants to help you do your best.

2) Listen to all instructions
Don't jump the gun! Wait until you understand all directions. In most civil service tests you get more time than you need to answer the questions. So don't be in a hurry. Read each word of instructions until you clearly understand the meaning. Study the examples, listen to all announcements and follow directions. Ask questions if you do not understand what to do.

3) Identify your papers
Civil service exams are usually identified by number only. You will be assigned a number; you must not put your name on your test papers. Be sure to copy your number correctly. Since more than one exam may be given, copy your exact examination title.

4) Plan your time
Unless you are told that a test is a "speed" or "rate of work" test, speed itself is usually not important. Time enough to answer all the questions will be provided, but this does not mean that you have all day. An overall time limit has been set. Divide the total time (in minutes) by the number of questions to determine the approximate time you have for each question.

5) Do not linger over difficult questions

If you come across a difficult question, mark it with a paper clip (useful to have along) and come back to it when you have been through the booklet. One caution if you do this – be sure to skip a number on your answer sheet as well. Check often to be sure that you have not lost your place and that you are marking in the row numbered the same as the question you are answering.

6) Read the questions

Be sure you know what the question asks! Many capable people are unsuccessful because they failed to *read* the questions correctly.

7) Answer all questions

Unless you have been instructed that a penalty will be deducted for incorrect answers, it is better to guess than to omit a question.

8) Speed tests

It is often better NOT to guess on speed tests. It has been found that on timed tests people are tempted to spend the last few seconds before time is called in marking answers at random – without even reading them – in the hope of picking up a few extra points. To discourage this practice, the instructions may warn you that your score will be "corrected" for guessing. That is, a penalty will be applied. The incorrect answers will be deducted from the correct ones, or some other penalty formula will be used.

9) Review your answers

If you finish before time is called, go back to the questions you guessed or omitted to give them further thought. Review other answers if you have time.

10) Return your test materials

If you are ready to leave before others have finished or time is called, take ALL your materials to the monitor and leave quietly. Never take any test material with you. The monitor can discover whose papers are not complete, and taking a test booklet may be grounds for disqualification.

VIII. EXAMINATION TECHNIQUES

1) Read the general instructions carefully. These are usually printed on the first page of the exam booklet. As a rule, these instructions refer to the timing of the examination; the fact that you should not start work until the signal and must stop work at a signal, etc. If there are any *special* instructions, such as a choice of questions to be answered, make sure that you note this instruction carefully.

2) When you are ready to start work on the examination, that is as soon as the signal has been given, read the instructions to each question booklet, underline any key words or phrases, such as *least, best, outline, describe* and the like. In this way you will tend to answer as requested rather than discover on reviewing your paper that you *listed without describing*, that you selected the *worst* choice rather than the *best* choice, etc.

3) If the examination is of the objective or multiple-choice type – that is, each question will also give a series of possible answers: A, B, C or D, and you are called upon to select the best answer and write the letter next to that answer on your answer paper – it is advisable to start answering each question in turn. There may be anywhere from 50 to 100 such questions in the three or four hours allotted and you can see how much time would be taken if you read through all the questions before beginning to answer any. Furthermore, if you come across a question or group of questions which you know would be difficult to answer, it would undoubtedly affect your handling of all the other questions.

4) If the examination is of the essay type and contains but a few questions, it is a moot point as to whether you should read all the questions before starting to answer any one. Of course, if you are given a choice – say five out of seven and the like – then it is essential to read all the questions so you can eliminate the two that are most difficult. If, however, you are asked to answer all the questions, there may be danger in trying to answer the easiest one first because you may find that you will spend too much time on it. The best technique is to answer the first question, then proceed to the second, etc.

5) Time your answers. Before the exam begins, write down the time it started, then add the time allowed for the examination and write down the time it must be completed, then divide the time available somewhat as follows:
   - If 3-1/2 hours are allowed, that would be 210 minutes. If you have 80 objective-type questions, that would be an average of 2-1/2 minutes per question. Allow yourself no more than 2 minutes per question, or a total of 160 minutes, which will permit about 50 minutes to review.
   - If for the time allotment of 210 minutes there are 7 essay questions to answer, that would average about 30 minutes a question. Give yourself only 25 minutes per question so that you have about 35 minutes to review.

6) The most important instruction is to *read each question* and make sure you know what is wanted. The second most important instruction is to *time yourself properly* so that you answer every question. The third most important instruction is to *answer every question*. Guess if you have to but include something for each question. Remember that you will receive no credit for a blank and will probably receive some credit if you write something in answer to an essay question. If you guess a letter – say "B" for a multiple-choice question – you may have guessed right. If you leave a blank as an answer to a multiple-choice question, the examiners may respect your feelings but it will not add a point to your score. Some exams may penalize you for wrong answers, so in such cases *only*, you may not want to guess unless you have some basis for your answer.

7) Suggestions
   a. Objective-type questions
      1. Examine the question booklet for proper sequence of pages and questions
      2. Read all instructions carefully
      3. Skip any question which seems too difficult; return to it after all other questions have been answered
      4. Apportion your time properly; do not spend too much time on any single question or group of questions

5. Note and underline key words – *all, most, fewest, least, best, worst, same, opposite,* etc.
6. Pay particular attention to negatives
7. Note unusual option, e.g., unduly long, short, complex, different or similar in content to the body of the question
8. Observe the use of "hedging" words – *probably, may, most likely,* etc.
9. Make sure that your answer is put next to the same number as the question
10. Do not second-guess unless you have good reason to believe the second answer is definitely more correct
11. Cross out original answer if you decide another answer is more accurate; do not erase until you are ready to hand your paper in
12. Answer all questions; guess unless instructed otherwise
13. Leave time for review

   b. Essay questions
1. Read each question carefully
2. Determine exactly what is wanted. Underline key words or phrases.
3. Decide on outline or paragraph answer
4. Include many different points and elements unless asked to develop any one or two points or elements
5. Show impartiality by giving pros and cons unless directed to select one side only
6. Make and write down any assumptions you find necessary to answer the questions
7. Watch your English, grammar, punctuation and choice of words
8. Time your answers; don't crowd material

8) Answering the essay question

Most essay questions can be answered by framing the specific response around several key words or ideas. Here are a few such key words or ideas:

M's: manpower, materials, methods, money, management
P's: purpose, program, policy, plan, procedure, practice, problems, pitfalls, personnel, public relations

   a. Six basic steps in handling problems:
1. Preliminary plan and background development
2. Collect information, data and facts
3. Analyze and interpret information, data and facts
4. Analyze and develop solutions as well as make recommendations
5. Prepare report and sell recommendations
6. Install recommendations and follow up effectiveness

   b. Pitfalls to avoid
1. *Taking things for granted* – A statement of the situation does not necessarily imply that each of the elements is necessarily true; for example, a complaint may be invalid and biased so that all that can be taken for granted is that a complaint has been registered

2. *Considering only one side of a situation* – Wherever possible, indicate several alternatives and then point out the reasons you selected the best one
3. *Failing to indicate follow up* – Whenever your answer indicates action on your part, make certain that you will take proper follow-up action to see how successful your recommendations, procedures or actions turn out to be
4. *Taking too long in answering any single question* – Remember to time your answers properly

IX. AFTER THE TEST

Scoring procedures differ in detail among civil service jurisdictions although the general principles are the same. Whether the papers are hand-scored or graded by machine we have described, they are nearly always graded by number. That is, the person who marks the paper knows only the number – never the name – of the applicant. Not until all the papers have been graded will they be matched with names. If other tests, such as training and experience or oral interview ratings have been given, scores will be combined. Different parts of the examination usually have different weights. For example, the written test might count 60 percent of the final grade, and a rating of training and experience 40 percent. In many jurisdictions, veterans will have a certain number of points added to their grades.

After the final grade has been determined, the names are placed in grade order and an eligible list is established. There are various methods for resolving ties between those who get the same final grade – probably the most common is to place first the name of the person whose application was received first. Job offers are made from the eligible list in the order the names appear on it. You will be notified of your grade and your rank as soon as all these computations have been made. This will be done as rapidly as possible.

People who are found to meet the requirements in the announcement are called "eligibles." Their names are put on a list of eligible candidates. An eligible's chances of getting a job depend on how high he stands on this list and how fast agencies are filling jobs from the list.

When a job is to be filled from a list of eligibles, the agency asks for the names of people on the list of eligibles for that job. When the civil service commission receives this request, it sends to the agency the names of the three people highest on this list. Or, if the job to be filled has specialized requirements, the office sends the agency the names of the top three persons who meet these requirements from the general list.

The appointing officer makes a choice from among the three people whose names were sent to him. If the selected person accepts the appointment, the names of the others are put back on the list to be considered for future openings.

That is the rule in hiring from all kinds of eligible lists, whether they are for typist, carpenter, chemist, or something else. For every vacancy, the appointing officer has his choice of any one of the top three eligibles on the list. This explains why the person whose name is on top of the list sometimes does not get an appointment when some of the persons lower on the list do. If the appointing officer chooses the second or third eligible, the No. 1 eligible does not get a job at once, but stays on the list until he is appointed or the list is terminated.

X. HOW TO PASS THE INTERVIEW TEST

The examination for which you applied requires an oral interview test. You have already taken the written test and you are now being called for the interview test – the final part of the formal examination.

You may think that it is not possible to prepare for an interview test and that there are no procedures to follow during an interview. Our purpose is to point out some things you can do in advance that will help you and some good rules to follow and pitfalls to avoid while you are being interviewed.

What is an interview supposed to test?

The written examination is designed to test the technical knowledge and competence of the candidate; the oral is designed to evaluate intangible qualities, not readily measured otherwise, and to establish a list showing the relative fitness of each candidate – as measured against his competitors – for the position sought. Scoring is not on the basis of "right" and "wrong," but on a sliding scale of values ranging from "not passable" to "outstanding." As a matter of fact, it is possible to achieve a relatively low score without a single "incorrect" answer because of evident weakness in the qualities being measured.

Occasionally, an examination may consist entirely of an oral test – either an individual or a group oral. In such cases, information is sought concerning the technical knowledges and abilities of the candidate, since there has been no written examination for this purpose. More commonly, however, an oral test is used to supplement a written examination.

Who conducts interviews?

The composition of oral boards varies among different jurisdictions. In nearly all, a representative of the personnel department serves as chairman. One of the members of the board may be a representative of the department in which the candidate would work. In some cases, "outside experts" are used, and, frequently, a businessman or some other representative of the general public is asked to serve. Labor and management or other special groups may be represented. The aim is to secure the services of experts in the appropriate field.

However the board is composed, it is a good idea (and not at all improper or unethical) to ascertain in advance of the interview who the members are and what groups they represent. When you are introduced to them, you will have some idea of their backgrounds and interests, and at least you will not stutter and stammer over their names.

What should be done before the interview?

While knowledge about the board members is useful and takes some of the surprise element out of the interview, there is other preparation which is more substantive. It *is* possible to prepare for an oral interview – in several ways:

1) Keep a copy of your application and review it carefully before the interview

This may be the only document before the oral board, and the starting point of the interview. Know what education and experience you have listed there, and the sequence and dates of all of it. Sometimes the board will ask you to review the highlights of your experience for them; you should not have to hem and haw doing it.

2) Study the class specification and the examination announcement

Usually, the oral board has one or both of these to guide them. The qualities, characteristics or knowledges required by the position sought are stated in these documents. They offer valuable clues as to the nature of the oral interview. For example, if the job involves supervisory responsibilities, the announcement will usually indicate that knowledge of modern supervisory methods and the qualifications of the candidate as a supervisor will be tested. If so, you can expect such questions, frequently in the form of a hypothetical situation which you are expected to solve. NEVER go into an oral without knowledge of the duties and responsibilities of the job you seek.

3) Think through each qualification required

Try to visualize the kind of questions you would ask if you were a board member. How well could you answer them? Try especially to appraise your own knowledge and background in each area, *measured against the job sought*, and identify any areas in which you are weak. Be critical and realistic – do not flatter yourself.

4) Do some general reading in areas in which you feel you may be weak

For example, if the job involves supervision and your past experience has NOT, some general reading in supervisory methods and practices, particularly in the field of human relations, might be useful. Do NOT study agency procedures or detailed manuals. The oral board will be testing your understanding and capacity, not your memory.

5) Get a good night's sleep and watch your general health and mental attitude

You will want a clear head at the interview. Take care of a cold or any other minor ailment, and of course, no hangovers.

What should be done on the day of the interview?

Now comes the day of the interview itself. Give yourself plenty of time to get there. Plan to arrive somewhat ahead of the scheduled time, particularly if your appointment is in the fore part of the day. If a previous candidate fails to appear, the board might be ready for you a bit early. By early afternoon an oral board is almost invariably behind schedule if there are many candidates, and you may have to wait. Take along a book or magazine to read, or your application to review, but leave any extraneous material in the waiting room when you go in for your interview. In any event, relax and compose yourself.

The matter of dress is important. The board is forming impressions about you – from your experience, your manners, your attitude, and your appearance. Give your personal appearance careful attention. Dress your best, but not your flashiest. Choose conservative, appropriate clothing, and be sure it is immaculate. This is a business interview, and your appearance should indicate that you regard it as such. Besides, being well groomed and properly dressed will help boost your confidence.

Sooner or later, someone will call your name and escort you into the interview room. *This is it.* From here on you are on your own. It is too late for any more preparation. But remember, you asked for this opportunity to prove your fitness, and you are here because your request was granted.

What happens when you go in?

The usual sequence of events will be as follows: The clerk (who is often the board stenographer) will introduce you to the chairman of the oral board, who will introduce you to the other members of the board. Acknowledge the introductions before you sit down. Do not be surprised if you find a microphone facing you or a stenotypist sitting by. Oral interviews are usually recorded in the event of an appeal or other review.

Usually the chairman of the board will open the interview by reviewing the highlights of your education and work experience from your application – primarily for the benefit of the other members of the board, as well as to get the material into the record. Do not interrupt or comment unless there is an error or significant misinterpretation; if that is the case, do not hesitate. But do not quibble about insignificant matters. Also, he will usually ask you some question about your education, experience or your present job – partly to get you to start talking and to establish the interviewing "rapport." He may start the actual questioning, or turn it over to one of the other members. Frequently, each member undertakes the questioning on a particular area, one in which he is perhaps most competent, so you can expect each member to participate in the examination. Because time is limited, you may also expect some rather abrupt switches in the direction the questioning takes, so do not be upset by it. Normally, a board member will not pursue a single line of questioning unless he discovers a particular strength or weakness.

After each member has participated, the chairman will usually ask whether any member has any further questions, then will ask you if you have anything you wish to add. Unless you are expecting this question, it may floor you. Worse, it may start you off on an extended, extemporaneous speech. The board is not usually seeking more information. The question is principally to offer you a last opportunity to present further qualifications or to indicate that you have nothing to add. So, if you feel that a significant qualification or characteristic has been overlooked, it is proper to point it out in a sentence or so. Do not compliment the board on the thoroughness of their examination – they have been sketchy, and you know it. If you wish, merely say, "No thank you, I have nothing further to add." This is a point where you can "talk yourself out" of a good impression or fail to present an important bit of information. Remember, *you close the interview yourself.*

The chairman will then say, "That is all, Mr. _____, thank you." Do not be startled; the interview is over, and quicker than you think. Thank him, gather your belongings and take your leave. Save your sigh of relief for the other side of the door.

How to put your best foot forward

Throughout this entire process, you may feel that the board individually and collectively is trying to pierce your defenses, seek out your hidden weaknesses and embarrass and confuse you. Actually, this is not true. They are obliged to make an appraisal of your qualifications for the job you are seeking, and they want to see you in your best light. Remember, they must interview all candidates and a non-cooperative candidate may become a failure in spite of their best efforts to bring out his qualifications. Here are 15 suggestions that will help you:

1) Be natural – Keep your attitude confident, not cocky

If you are not confident that you can do the job, do not expect the board to be. Do not apologize for your weaknesses, try to bring out your strong points. The board is interested in a positive, not negative, presentation. Cockiness will antagonize any board member and make him wonder if you are covering up a weakness by a false show of strength.

2) Get comfortable, but don't lounge or sprawl

Sit erectly but not stiffly. A careless posture may lead the board to conclude that you are careless in other things, or at least that you are not impressed by the importance of the occasion. Either conclusion is natural, even if incorrect. Do not fuss with your clothing, a pencil or an ashtray. Your hands may occasionally be useful to emphasize a point; do not let them become a point of distraction.

3) Do not wisecrack or make small talk

This is a serious situation, and your attitude should show that you consider it as such. Further, the time of the board is limited – they do not want to waste it, and neither should you.

4) Do not exaggerate your experience or abilities

In the first place, from information in the application or other interviews and sources, the board may know more about you than you think. Secondly, you probably will not get away with it. An experienced board is rather adept at spotting such a situation, so do not take the chance.

5) If you know a board member, do not make a point of it, yet do not hide it

Certainly you are not fooling him, and probably not the other members of the board. Do not try to take advantage of your acquaintanceship – it will probably do you little good.

6) Do not dominate the interview

Let the board do that. They will give you the clues – do not assume that you have to do all the talking. Realize that the board has a number of questions to ask you, and do not try to take up all the interview time by showing off your extensive knowledge of the answer to the first one.

7) Be attentive

You only have 20 minutes or so, and you should keep your attention at its sharpest throughout. When a member is addressing a problem or question to you, give him your undivided attention. Address your reply principally to him, but do not exclude the other board members.

8) Do not interrupt

A board member may be stating a problem for you to analyze. He will ask you a question when the time comes. Let him state the problem, and wait for the question.

9) Make sure you understand the question

Do not try to answer until you are sure what the question is. If it is not clear, restate it in your own words or ask the board member to clarify it for you. However, do not haggle about minor elements.

10) Reply promptly but not hastily

A common entry on oral board rating sheets is "candidate responded readily," or "candidate hesitated in replies." Respond as promptly and quickly as you can, but do not jump to a hasty, ill-considered answer.

11) Do not be peremptory in your answers

A brief answer is proper – but do not fire your answer back. That is a losing game from your point of view. The board member can probably ask questions much faster than you can answer them.

12) Do not try to create the answer you think the board member wants

He is interested in what kind of mind you have and how it works – not in playing games. Furthermore, he can usually spot this practice and will actually grade you down on it.

13) Do not switch sides in your reply merely to agree with a board member

Frequently, a member will take a contrary position merely to draw you out and to see if you are willing and able to defend your point of view. Do not start a debate, yet do not surrender a good position. If a position is worth taking, it is worth defending.

14) Do not be afraid to admit an error in judgment if you are shown to be wrong

The board knows that you are forced to reply without any opportunity for careful consideration. Your answer may be demonstrably wrong. If so, admit it and get on with the interview.

15) Do not dwell at length on your present job

The opening question may relate to your present assignment. Answer the question but do not go into an extended discussion. You are being examined for a *new* job, not your present one. As a matter of fact, try to phrase ALL your answers in terms of the job for which you are being examined.

Basis of Rating

Probably you will forget most of these "do's" and "don'ts" when you walk into the oral interview room. Even remembering them all will not ensure you a passing grade. Perhaps you did not have the qualifications in the first place. But remembering them will help you to put your best foot forward, without treading on the toes of the board members.

Rumor and popular opinion to the contrary notwithstanding, an oral board wants you to make the best appearance possible. They know you are under pressure – but they also want to see how you respond to it as a guide to what your reaction would be under the pressures of the job you seek. They will be influenced by the degree of poise you display, the personal traits you show and the manner in which you respond.

ABOUT THIS BOOK

This book contains tests divided into Examination Sections. Go through each test, answering every question in the margin. We have also attached a sample answer sheet at the back of the book that can be removed and used. At the end of each test look at the answer key and check your answers. On the ones you got wrong, look at the right answer choice and learn. Do not fill in the answers first. Do not memorize the questions and answers, but understand the answer and principles involved. On your test, the questions will likely be different from the samples. Questions are changed and new ones added. If you understand these past questions you should have success with any changes that arise. Tests may consist of several types of questions. We have additional books on each subject should more study be advisable or necessary for you. Finally, the more you study, the better prepared you will be. This book is intended to be the last thing you study before you walk into the examination room. Prior study of relevant texts is also recommended. NLC publishes some of these in our Fundamental Series. Knowledge and good sense are important factors in passing your exam. Good luck also helps. So now study this Passbook, absorb the material contained within and take that knowledge into the examination. Then do your best to pass that exam.

EXAMINATION SECTION

EXAMINATION SECTION
TEST 1

DIRECTIONS: Each question or incomplete statement is followed by several suggested answers or completions. Select the one that BEST answers the question or completes the statement. *PRINT THE LETTER OF THE CORRECT ANSWER IN THE SPACE AT THE RIGHT.*

1. Which of the following types of services is MOST likely to involve overtime pay for operators?   1._____

    A. Special education
    B. Extracurricular
    C. Regular home-to-school service
    D. Desegregation

2. In making cost estimates, it is important to separate mechanics' wages and other mechanical, fuel, and repair costs in terms of the _____ each type of service.   2._____

    A. individual personnel conducting
    B. number of miles for
    C. overall monthly departmental consumption of
    D. individual vehicle used for

3. Which of the following is most likely to be used as a measure of the efficiency of the use of buses by a transportation department?   3._____

    A. Percentage of vehicle capacity used at each route's peak period
    B. Stops per 1,000 vehicle miles
    C. Number of students transported by each bus per route
    D. Ratio of students transported to miles driven

4. Performance measures among transportation departments are typically used for each of the following EXCEPT as a(n)   4._____

    A. objective yardstick for evaluating the service being provided
    B. basis for comparison with other departments with similar variables
    C. basis for monitoring a contractor's compliance with the terms of a contract
    D. basis for recognizing or sanctioning employees

5. Which of the following is an example of a direct cost that would be calculated by route or type of service?   5._____

    A. Cost of capital   B. Bus depreciation
    C. Collision insurance   D. Fuel costs

6. If a contractor is responsible for the operation of transportation services, it is customary to require that the contractor maintain fleet records for a minimum of _____, at no cost to the district or school.   6._____

    A. 90 days   B. 6 months   C. 1 year   D. 5 years

7. If a district decides to increase the maximum time spent on buses by students, the most likely effect would be a(n)
   A. increase in operating costs
   B. shortening of the walking radius
   C. increase in the number of bus routes
   D. increase in the size of the service area

8. If a transportation department purchases buses outright or lease-purchases them, the cash expense is typically realized in _____ year(s).
   A. 1   B. 1-2   C. 3-5   D. 5-10

9. If more than one educational agency wants to enter into an interagency agreement that will allow each organization to make capital investments, the best form of administration for their transportation services would be
   A. in-lieu payments
   B. a joint power authority
   C. a loose consortium
   D. a cooperative

10. Each of the following is an example of a direct cost to the transportation department that cannot be identified directly with a particular type of route or service EXCEPT
    A. operators' overtime premiums
    B. liability insurance
    C. purchased vehicle maintenance services
    D. bus lease costs

11. A filing system on bus operators should usually include a tickler file that indicates those drivers who should be evaluated within the next
    A. 14 days   B. 30 days   C. 3 months   D. year

12. In order to accurately estimate the costs of a transportation department, costs data should be collected for a period of at LEAST
    A. 3 months   B. 6 months   C. 1 year   D. 2 years

13. Which of the following is generally NOT true of a school or district which provides all of its own transportation services?
    A. Costs are minimized by the profit motive.
    B. The school or district is the agency with sole legal liability.
    C. Procurement and personnel processes are lengthy and demanding.
    D. Service quality is flexible.

14. Which of the following is a fixed and allocated indirect cost to a transportation department?
    A. Costs of central school services used
    B. Fire/property insurance
    C. Cost of capital
    D. Utilities for terminal and shop

15. In school or district transportation departments, preventive maintenance inspections are typically performed on vehicles every 15.____

    A. 30 days
    B. 3,000 miles or 45 days, whichever comes first
    C. 5,000 miles
    D. 7,500 miles or 6 months, whichever comes first

16. Which of the following is NOT considered to be a general performance measure used by a transportation department? 16.____

    A. Compliments or complaints
    B. Percentage of vehicle capacity used
    C. Vehicle downtime
    D. Stops or runs missed

17. A district decides to transfer the responsibility for operating its transportation services to an outside contractor. In order to be fair to its current operators and to the contractor, the district should require 17.____

    A. a lump-sum buyout by the contractor of any of the district's current bus drivers who are not hired by the contractor
    B. that the contractor agree to interview for bus driver positions all drivers currently serving the district who request interviews
    C. a reduction in the overall number of drivers used to meet the requirements of newly-designed routes
    D. that the contractor hire all drivers currently serving the district who request to be hired

18. In measuring the performance of a particular bus route, most departments consider a bus to be *late* 18.____

    A. if it shows up within any period, however, small, past the scheduled arrival
    B. if it arrives at a stop more than 15 minutes after it was scheduled to arrive
    C. *only* if it arrives at its final destination with a margin of fewer than 15 minutes remaining before the start of the first scheduled class or activity
    D. *only* if students miss a portion of the activity or class to which the bus is delivering them

19. Cooperatives, consortiums, or multilateral interagency agreements for providing transportation services are likely to involve 19.____

    A. a strict interagency hierarchy
    B. more economical insurance coverage
    C. greater accountability to school or district administrators
    D. a higher level of managerial oversight

Questions 20-21.

DIRECTIONS: Questions 20 and 21 refer to the following information. A personnel department can determine the total hours worked by bus operators, but does not know the separate wage cost for each type of service.

20. What is the cost category that should be used in the above problem? 20.____

   A. Ratio of operators' wages to miles driven
   B. Operators' wages for hours worked
   C. Miles driven
   D. Hours of bus service

21. What is the allocation factor in the above problem? 21.____

   A. Ratio of operators' wages to miles driven
   B. Operators' wages for hours worked
   C. Miles driven
   D. Hours of bus service

22. When used as a performance measure, statistics on non-collision injury incidents associ- 22.____
    ated with transportation services are typically calculated in incidents corresponding to

   A. 1,000 miles driven per bus
   B. 1,000 wage hours per operator
   C. 1,000 pupils transported per month
   D. one million vehicle miles

23. Schools or districts considering a contracting arrangement for transportation services 23.____
    are most likely to overlook

   A. management and labor costs of writing a request for proposals (RFP) and contract
   B. avoidable costs of school or district delivery
   C. salary and benefit costs of a contract administrator position
   D. material costs of writing a request for proposals (RFP) and contract

24. Which of the following is NOT a necessary factor in computing the training wage costs for 24.____
    a transportation department?

   A. The number of drivers attending
   B. Number of non-training hours worked
   C. Hourly wages
   D. The number of training hours received

25. Which of the following is/are summary measures of the overall efficiency of a pupil trans- 25.____
    portation operation?
     I.   Direct variable costs to the department per mile for all types of services
     II. Full cost per mile, including both live and deadhead miles
     III. Transportation department overhead costs per pupil transported
     IV. Full cost per pupil transported each way, each day
    The CORRECT answer is:

    A. I, II   B. II, IV
    C. II, III, IV   D. I, II, III

KEY (CORRECT ANSWERS)

1.	B	11.	B
2.	D	12.	C
3.	A	13.	A
4.	B	14.	A
5.	D	15.	B
6.	C	16.	C
7.	D	17.	B
8.	C	18.	C
9.	B	19.	B
10.	C	20.	B

21. D
22. C
23. C
24. B
25. B

———

TEST 2

DIRECTIONS: Each question or incomplete statement is followed by several suggested answers or completions. Select the one that BEST answers the question or completes the statement. *PRINT THE LETTER OF THE CORRECT ANSWER IN THE SPACE AT THE RIGHT.*

1. Which of the following credentials would NOT be part of the records needed to satisfy most state requirements for bus drivers?

    A. Driver training record card
    B. Evidence of first aid
    C. Negative tuberculin test evidence
    D. Class C or non-commercial driver's license

    1.____

2. Agencies with students who live in remote areas may choose a payment-in-lieu-of-services arrangement rather than deliver transportation services. An agency engaged in such an arrangement should expect it to involve

    A. strict accountability standards for parents
    B. high day-to-day involvement in managing
    C. continued liability for pupil safety
    D. payment on a per-pupil basis

    2.____

3. The most difficult costs for a transportation department to measure are typically

    A. purchased vehicle maintenance services
    B. rent, lease or depreciation costs for land and buildings used
    C. central school or district services used by the department
    D. depreciation, lease, or rental costs for buses

    3.____

4. The performance measure most often used among transportation departments for workers' compensation claims is the

    A. number of claims per 100 employees per year
    B. number of claims per route per year
    C. number of claims per year in excess of $500
    D. total number of claims per year

    4.____

5. The primary advantage associated with using longer-term contracts for the provision of transportation services is

    A. greater flexibility
    B. fewer disagreements with contractor
    C. more competitive bidding
    D. liability exposure is usually increased for the district or department

    5.____

6. When used as performance measures in transportation departments, safety-related statistics are usually calculated in units corresponding to

    A. 1,000 miles driven per bus
    B. 1,000 pupils transported per month
    C. 1,000 operator's wage hours
    D. one million vehicle miles

    6.____

7. A school district is considering whether to turn the administration of its transportation services over to an outside contractor. Before any comparison of the district's current cost of services or capital can be fairly compared to those of a contractor, it will be necessary to

    A. consider at least three competitive bids
    B. subtract nonavoidable costs from the full cost of the district's service or item of capital
    C. separate fixed from variable costs and determine whether the contractor's costs are similarly fixed or variable
    D. compare amortization tables used in determining the cost of capital items

8. For a transportation department which makes use of contractors, it is generally most important for the district to retain authority over

    A. routing and scheduling
    B. vehicle maintenance
    C. operations and dispatch
    D. driver training

9. During the process of bidding for the provision of transportation services, it is customary for a proposer to be forbidden from withdrawing his bid for a period of _____ days after the date set for the receipt of bid proposals.

    A. 10   B. 30   C. 60   D. 90

10. Multiplying the book value of an item of transportation-related equipment by the interest rate paid by a school or district when it borrows money will yield the

    A. indirect costs of transportation
    B. cost of capital
    C. variable costs
    D. amortization rate

11. Which of the following is most likely to be true of a bilateral interagency agreement for the provision of pupil transportation?

    A. Service provision involves more direct accountability than with a single provider.
    B. Fixed costs are often duplicated.
    C. Economies of scale are nearly impossible.
    D. More efficient service than with a single provider

12. Which of the following decisions on the part of a school or district would be most likely to improve cost savings?

    A. Increasing walking radius
    B. Changing bell schedules
    C. Increasing the use of in-lieu payments
    D. Increasing the area of a route

13. A district, fielding bids from providers of transportation services, decides to accept bids on the basis of the number of hours of service provided. The MAIN advantage to this approach is that

A. it makes bidding more competitive among proposers
B. proposers do not face a significant risk of unforeseen costs
C. the district will have an easier time monitoring the number of hours of service provided
D. it reduces the number of line-items in a proposal

14. In estimating costs, mechanics' wages for time during shop upkeep, disability, sick leave, or vacation are calculated by

    A. subtracting mechanics' hours per route from total mechanics' wages
    B. adding mechanics' wages for hours worked and total mechanics' wages
    C. dividing total mechanic's wages by the mechanic's hours for each individual route, then adding up the totals, then subtracting from wages for total hours worked
    D. subtracting mechanics' wages for hours worked from total mechanics' wages

15. A school district transports 5,000 students each way daily, on average, over a period of a month. It it receives 10 complaints on bus service during the month of September, what is the *complaint measure* for September?

    A. 2 B. 10 C. 50 D. 500

16. A district has decided to issue an intent to award notice to a contractor who has submitted a bid for the provision of transportation services. Typically, the district will then reserve the right to negotiate changes in the scope of work that do not exceed _____% of the initial price bid.

    A. 5 B. 10 C. 15 D. 20

17. Each of the following is an example of a transportation department's fixed overhead costs EXCEPT

    A. mechanic's overtime premiums
    B. operator's overtime premiums
    C. terminal support staff salaries and benefits
    D. workers' compensation insurance for mechanics

18. In the process of accepting bids for transportation services, a proposer's bond presented by a contractor is typically offered at a rate of _____% of the total bid proposal price.

    A. 5 B. 7 C. 10 D. 15

19. Which of the following decisions on the part of a school or district would be most likely to reduce the number of students served?

    A. Increasing the walking radius
    B. Improving the route design
    C. Increasing the use of in-lieu payments
    D. Redesigning routes

20. Which of the following is/are advantages specific to the administration of transportation services by means of a contract with a private provider?
    I. The ability to make wholesale changes in the provision of services in a short time
    II. The minimization of costs
    III. Reduced need for quality monitoring
    IV. Lower staff turnover
    The CORRECT answer is:

    A. I, II   B. II, III   C. III, IV   D. I, IV

21. Setting different start times for _____ school(s) is NOT a typical way in which a district may coordinate bell schedules to allow an increased number of runs per bus.

    A. elementary schools, middle schools, and high
    B. different programs within individual
    C. specific grade levels within individual
    D. each individual

22. In most jurisdictions, a long-term contract with a provider of transportation services may not exist for a term longer than _____ year(s).

    A. 1   B. 5   C. 10   D. 15

23. Occasionally, a school or district may arrange student transportation with a public carrier. Any agency which engages in such an arrangement should expect it to involve

    A. a good degree of flexibility in routes and scheduling
    B. a high degree of school or district management attention
    C. a generalized lack of parental comfort
    D. high per-pupil costs

24. Schools or districts considering a contracting arrangement for transportation services should keep in mind that writing a new contract and a request for proposals (RFP) will probably require about _____ hours of management time.

    A. 20-60   B. 40-100   C. 50-150   D. 120-200

25. In an arrangement in which a district requires a contractor to use a district-owned terminal, which will typically be easiest for the district to monitor?

    A. Portal-to-portal miles   B. Total miles
    C. Live hours   D. Per-pupil ridership

KEY (CORRECT ANSWERS)

1. D
2. C
3. B
4. A
5. C

6. D
7. B
8. A
9. C
10. B

11. D
12. B
13. B
14. D
15. A

16. B
17. B
18. A
19. A
20. A

21. C
22. B
23. C
24. C
25. A

EXAMINATION SECTION

TEST 1

DIRECTIONS: Each question or incomplete statement is followed by several suggested answers or completions. Select the one that BEST answers the question or completes the statement. *PRINT THE LETTER OF THE CORRECT ANSWER IN THE SPACE AT THE RIGHT.*

1. A successful school transportation operation depends MOST upon the high quality of dedication and performance by the
    A. school administrator
    B. driver
    C. transportation director
    D. supervisor
    E. vehicle maintenance personnel

    1.____

2. It is NOT the driver's responsibility to
    A. conduct pre- and post-trip checks on the vehicle
    B. maintain orderly conduct of passengers
    C. communicate effectively with the public
    D. enforce wearing of seatbelts
    E. complete reports

    2.____

3. The training program for maintenance and service personnel does NOT have to include
    A. procedure for recognizing cause and effect relationship between driving habits and vehicle maintenance
    B. recovery procedures for vehicles involved in accident or breakdown
    C. preparation of maintenance records
    D. establishment of parts inventory control procedures
    E. repair procedures for each type of vehicle in the fleet

    3.____

4. A student's riding privileges may be suspended when
    A. drugs or controlled substances are used on the bus
    B. classroom conduct is not observed on the bus
    C. hazardous materials are brought on the bus
    D. rights of others are jeopardized
    E. safe operation of the bus is jeopardized

    4.____

5. It is recommended that school officials provide
    A. clearly marked walkways through the school bus zones
    B. controlled traffic flow through the school bus zones
    C. clearly marked parking patterns through the school bus zones
    D. adequate space for backing of transportation equipment
    E. all of the above

    5.____

6. What distinguishes a Circular Route? It
    A. is the most economical
    B. enables the first student who boards the bus in the morning to be the first to disembark in the evening

    6.____

C. eliminates the need for students to cross the roadway
D. holds the number of miles a student must ride to a minimum
E. permits one bus to transport more than one load of students

7. Which method for dissemination of information is BEST for informing the public about procedures the schools will follow in cases of severe weather conditions?
    A. Radio
    B. Telephone calls
    C. Public address system
    D. Public press
    E. Bulletins

8. What is the BEST method for communicating with students regarding all forms of safety?
    A. Meetings
    B. Public address system
    C. Bulletins
    D. Conference
    E. Television

9. Insurance agents should be contacted to determine if additional coverage is necessary when the activity trip is scheduled to
    A. another town
    B. another county
    C. another state
    D. any distance greater than fifty miles
    E. any location beyond the school district's boundaries

10. What is the LEAST important factor to be considered in selecting a bus for a trip?
    A. Climate conditions
    B. Parking requirements
    C. Age group of students
    D. Driver familiarity with the route
    E. Miles to be traveled

11. Transportation for handicapped students requires an assessment of their _____ capacities.
    A. physical
    B. social
    C. emotional
    D. intellectual
    E. all of the above

12. Which of the following is NOT a characteristic of a student with a learning disability?
    A. Average or higher intellectual ability
    B. Disorganized in solving problems
    C. Demonstrates extreme emotional behaviors
    D. Friendly and affectionate
    E. Hyperactivity

13. Arrangements for special education students' transportation should be communicated to
    A. parents
    B. school personnel
    C. other students on the bus
    D. the driver
    E. all of the above

14. What must be considered to effect behavior modification?
    A. Ages of the students
    B. Nature of the reward
    C. Clear definition of what constitutes acceptable behavior
    D. All of the above
    E. None of the above

15. What is the driver's PRIME responsibility when a handicapped student has a seizure? To
    A. administer the student's medication
    B. place something in the student's mouth to prevent tongue injury
    C. restrain the student's limbs to avoid broken bones
    D. see that the student rests comfortably afterward
    E. all of the above

16. What is the MOST important preparation for special education student management in an emergency?
    A. Appointing a student to take over
    B. Notifying school and parents
    C. Reassuring the students
    D. Teaching pupils what to expect
    E. Preplanning students' needs

17. Suspension of special education students from the bus is usually MOST appropriate when
    A. there is clear evidence of lack of respect for authority
    B. the safety of other students is threatened
    C. the misbehavior is repeated
    D. behavior is drug or alcohol related
    E. there is alternate transportation available to the student

18. Which of the following is NOT in the best interest for behavior control?
    A. Rearranging seating positions
    B. Relaxing classroom behavioral expectations
    C. Suspension of bus privileges
    D. Allowing students to suggest and enforce rules
    E. Referral to school psychologist

19. Comfort is a HIGH priority when the student has a(n)
    A. visual impairment   B. orthopedic handicap
    C. hearing impairment   D. intellectual impairment
    E. emotional impairment

20. Facial expression and body language are important aspects in communicating with
    A. the emotionally disturbed
    B. the visually handicapped
    C. learning disabled students
    D. mentally retarded students
    E. hearing impaired students

21. A dry run prior to a scheduled trip date is MOST recommended when
    A. night driving may be involved
    B. terrain or road difficulties may be encountered
    C. destination parking is other than students' destination
    D. bridges or tunnels may be encountered
    E. specialized equipment may be used

22. What is the PRIMARY role of the driver transporting handicapped students?
    To
    A. accommodate student's needs
    B. promote successful student management
    C. assess and anticipate the needs of individual problems
    D. give personal attention to each student
    E. drive the bus

23. Who has the FINAL responsibility on an activity bus?
    A. Chaperone
    B. Teacher
    C. Parent supervisor
    D. Senior chaperone
    E. Bus driver

24. The Bureau of Motor Carrier Safety Manual recommends which maximum limit for the driver of an activity bus?
    A. ten hours of duty of which eight are driving time
    B. ten hours of continuous off-duty prior to a long trip
    C. no more than forty hours driving per week
    D. no more than sixty hours driving per week
    E. twelve hours continuous off-duty prior to a long trip

25. Which of the following is NOT an objective of a planned maintenance program?
    A. Preventing road failures
    B. Enhancing appearance of the school bus
    C. Improving the handling and performance characteristics
    D. Conserving fuel
    E. Extending the bus' useful life

KEY (CORRECT ANSWERS)

1. B
2. D
3. A
4. E
5. A

6. B
7. A
8. B
9. C
10. B

11. E
12. D
13. E
14. D
15. D

16. E
17. B
18. B
19. B
20. E

21. B
22. E
23. E
24. D
25. C

TEST 2

DIRECTIONS: Each question or incomplete statement is followed by several suggested answers or completions. Select the one that BEST answers the question or completes the statement. *PRINT THE LETTER OF THE CORRECT ANSWER IN THE SPACE AT THE RIGHT.*

1. Employee personnel records usually do NOT include
    A. causes of absences
    B. criminal records
    C. marital status
    D. confirmed work history
    E. psychological evaluation

    1.____

2. When are alternately flashing red lights used?
    A. When poor visibility conditions exist
    B. When bus is crossing railroad tracks
    C. When bus is stopping to take on or discharge passengers
    D. When bus is stopped to take on or discharge passengers
    E. All of the above

    2.____

3. Which of the following policies are determined by state statute and/or state regulations?
    A. Policy with regard to transportation of non-public school students
    B. Policy relative to supervision of students while loading and unloading at school sites and enroute
    C. Procedure for determining eligibility for student transportation service
    D. Use of special lighting and signaling equipment on the bus
    E. Policy with regard to standees, length of time in transit, and type of supervision required

    3.____

4. Which of the following is NOT a qualification of the director of student transportation?
    A. A record free of criminal convictions
    B. An undergraduate degree or equivalent experience
    C. Ability to work effectively with a broad range of individuals
    D. Ability to provide comprehensive bus driver training program
    E. Ability to manage personnel and resources

    4.____

5. The driver training program SHOULD include instruction in
    A. repair procedures
    B. recovery procedures for vehicles involved in an accident
    C. procedures for performing pre- and post-trip inspections
    D. preparation of maintenance records
    E. all of the above

    5.____

6. All of the following are bus regulations regarding student   6.___
   demeanors EXCEPT:
   A. Students are to remain seated
   B. Students are to place school-related objects in aisles
   C. Students are prohibited from eating on the bus
   D. Students are prohibited from leaving or boarding the
      bus at locations other than assigned home or school
      stop
   E. Students are permitted to pass objects on, from, or
      into buses

7. Students should be instructed on   7.___
   A. proper storage of material that cannot be held on
      their laps
   B. safe eating and drinking procedures on the bus
   C. entering and leaving the bus
   D. passing objects on, from, or into the bus
   E. all of the above

8. Which type route eliminates the need for the student to   8.___
   cross the roadway?
   A. Shoestring route   B. Retracing route
   C. Double routing   D. Emergency route
   E. Circular route

9. A systemic inspection of the bus before each trip is the   9.___
   responsibility of the
   A. bus garage personnel
   B. school administration
   C. transportation supervisor
   D. driver
   E. service and maintenance personnel

10. What is the BEST way to inform parents of all school and   10.___
    state regulations?
    A. Conferences   B. Telephone calls
    C. Letters   D. Meetings
    E. Radio

11. Safety criteria for evaluating the transportation system   11.___
    usually does NOT include
    A. property damage accidents
    B. moving traffic violations
    C. complaints
    D. route and routing procedures
    E. road failures

12. How many days in advance of a trip date should driver   12.___
    assignment take place? ____ day(s).
    A. 7   B. 1   C. 3   D. 2   E. 5

13. Which of the following is NOT a consideration for   13.___
    selecting drivers for trip assignments?
    A. License held
    B. Seniority
    C. Skill
    D. Familiarity with trip vehicle
    E. Familiarity with area to be traveled

14. Which group of students does NOT represent any unusual behavior problems?
    A. Mentally retarded students
    B. Learning disabled students
    C. Hearing disabled students
    D. All of the above
    E. None of the above

15. A lack of stability from day to day in desirable behavior is characteristic of ____ students.
    A. emotionally disturbed
    B. learning disabled
    C. mentally retarded
    D. visually handicapped
    E. hearing impaired

16. What type of student is MOST likely to have few self-care skills? ____ students.
    A. Learning disabled
    B. Mentally retarded
    C. Emotionally disturbed
    D. Orthopedically handicapped
    E. Visually handicapped

17. What is the BEST approach to special education students?
    A. Promptly correct any unsuitable behavior
    B. Tell rather than show pupils what you want them to do
    C. Define rules clearly and enforce them firmly
    D. Allow some latitude because of students' handicaps
    E. Do not expect students to accept responsibility for their own actions

18. Behavior modification when applied to special education students requires
    A. giving a reward after demonstration of appropriate behavior
    B. long-term behavioral goals
    C. liberal amounts of praise to encourage acceptable behavior
    D. establishing rules that can be easily followed
    E. taking appropriate disciplinary action for each rule infraction

19. Which of the following confidential information should the aide on a bus transporting handicapped students have?
    A. Nature of student's handicap
    B. Emergency health care information
    C. Name and phone number of student's parents
    D. All of the above
    E. None of the above

20. It is BEST to seat a young and hyperactive special education student
    A. with a very young student
    B. at the front of the bus
    C. at the rear of the bus
    D. with an older, well-behaved student
    E. with a fragile student

21. All medically-related incidents involving special education students require
    A. summoning professional medical attention
    B. the driver to give medication or medical assistance
    C. reporting to school and parents at earliest possible moment
    D. all of the above
    E. none of the above

22. Visually handicapped students respond BEST when
    A. they are given independence
    B. they are consistently reminded what is expected of them
    C. angry outbursts and punishment is avoided
    D. they are addressed by name
    E. body language is used to reinforce speech

23. What is the LAST consideration in planning for the transportation of special education students? The
    A. group of students on the vehicle
    B. design of the car seats
    C. type of supports needed
    D. type of vehicle required
    E. class placement of students

24. The driver of handicapped children needs to be more
    A. controlled   B. alert   C. flexible
    D. lenient   E. rigid

25. Which of the following is USUALLY necessary when a special trip is planned?
    A. Bus is equipped with radio
    B. Public address system is installed
    C. Driver is provided with cash
    D. Driver is provided with a uniform
    E. Seats are equipped with seatbelts

KEY (CORRECT ANSWERS)

1. E
2. D
3. A
4. D
5. C

6. B
7. C
8. B
9. D
10. C

11. D
12. C
13. A
14. C
15. A

16. B
17. C
18. A
19. D
20. D

21. C
22. D
23. A
24. C
25. C

EXAMINATION SECTION

TEST 1

DIRECTIONS: Each question or incomplete statement is followed by several suggested answers or completions. Select the one that BEST answers the question or completes the statement. *PRINT THE LETTER OF THE CORRECT ANSWER IN THE SPACE AT THE RIGHT.*

1. Pick-up and delivery points in suburban districts should include the following EXCEPT:
    A. Corner pick-ups at traffic-controlled locations should be discouraged
    B. Young passengers should cross streets at locations where protection is a community responsibility
    C. There should be minimum interference with traffic on arterial or collector streets
    D. Area discharge points away from the heavy traffic should be designated
    E. Personalized bus stops should not be permitted

2. The success of safety programs depends on involvement beginning at the ____ level.
    A. county   B. state   C. district
    D. individual   E. national

3. Fleet accidents and costs are MOST affected by
    A. bus selection and equipment
    B. operating maintenance policies
    C. driver attitude
    D. bus routes and fleet utilization
    E. the fleets' public image

4. Which of the following is the LEAST important consideration concerning the hiring of low I.Q. drivers?
    A. Lack of accurate judgment in emergency situations
    B. Difficulty in concentrating while driving a vehicle
    C. Make poor witnesses in cases of accident
    D. Difficult to supervise
    E. Difficulty taking decisive action

5. How does the supervisor evaluate the trainees' progress? By
    A. *evaluating* written test scores
    B. *observing* attitudes and safety awareness
    C. *observing* driver performance over a prescribed course
    D. *observing* driver's performance while transporting pupils
    E. *evaluating* the results of driving simulation tests

6. What type of driver testing is needed to enable the supervisor to help each driver develop the compensating habits needed to drive safely? ____ test.
   A. Reaction time
   B. Distance judgment
   C. Visual
   D. Tunnel vision
   E. Glare recovery

7. *Protection Routes* do NOT usually consider
   A. traffic volume on available alternate routes
   B. railroad crossings
   C. distance to be traveled
   D. sharp curves
   E. narrow pavements

8. Policy statements from the local school board should define all the following EXCEPT:
   A. Minimum requirements for driver selection and training
   B. The extent of school bus service
   C. Factual basis for establishing transportation policies
   D. Equipment replacement schedule
   E. Provisions for extracurricular transportation

9. Driver selection, training, and motivation MUST be designed to
   A. get and keep uniform standards of vehicle operation
   B. transport and supervise students
   C. the principles of defensive driving
   D. prevent accidents
   E. develop responsibility

10. What is the MOST important quality for a school bus driver?
    A. Physical fitness
    B. Congenial personality
    C. High intelligence
    D. Neat appearance
    E. Emotional maturity

11. Drivers who complete an initial training course usually do NOT know
    A. the laws and regulations applicable to school bus fleet operation
    B. how to administer first aid
    C. the flexibility of schedules
    D. how to deal with students who disobey rules
    E. how to operate a fire extinguisher

12. Which of the following motivational methods and techniques are recommended for use by supervisors?
    A. Terminate the employ of any driver involved in a preventable accident
    B. Hold driver responsible for cleanliness of bus
    C. Do not publicly single out individuals for merit
    D. Do not inform drivers of the high degree of skill required before qualifying to drive in the fleet
    E. Defuse any developing spirit of competitiveness

13. Remedial training is PRIMARILY intended to instruct
    A. operation of new equipment
    B. changes in policies, laws, and regulations
    C. problem drivers
    D. older drivers
    E. new drivers with previous driving experience

14. Glare recovery is an important test for anyone who drives when
    A. there is strong sunlight
    B. the roads are snow-covered
    C. headlights must be used
    D. the roads are slick with rain
    E. routes involve tunnels

15. When does driver instruction begin? With the
    A. first training class
    B. introduction to the vehicle
    C. orientation session
    D. first road test
    E. first contact with the supervisor

16. Which of the following factors MOST contributes to triggering accidents?
    A. Weather conditions
    B. Road conditions
    C. Condition of vehicle
    D. Driving errors
    E. Student behavior

17. School bus drivers may continue to drive if they have suffered the loss of
    A. a finger
    B. a hand
    C. a foot
    D. all of the above
    E. none of the above

18. Which of the following would NOT bar a person from driving a school bus?
    A. Impaired use of foot or leg
    B. Any disease likely to interfere with safe driving
    C. Use of alcohol beverages
    D. Impaired use of arm or hand
    E. Addiction of habit-forming drugs

19. What factor determines the safety and efficiency of the school transportation program?
    A. The vehicle
    B. The driver
    C. The maintenance of the vehicle
    D. All of the above
    E. None of the above

20. Violations of traffic laws CANNOT be condoned because they
    A. cause loss of respect by motorists for school vehicles
    B. may result in reduced use of public streets
    C. may expose pupils to serious hazards
    D. increase the cost of school transportation
    E. reflect badly on the school system

21. What state department is MOST directly responsible for student transportation?
    A. Transportation B. Motor vehicles C. Public welfare
    D. Public safety E. Education

22. What is the MOST important consideration to be included in the specifications for new vehicle purchases?
    A. Ages of pupils to be transported
    B. Type of terrain in which vehicle will be used
    C. The pattern of transit operation
    D. The fleets' safety performance
    E. The activities for which the vehicle will be used

23. What MOST motivates drivers to perform safely?
    A. Recognition and appreciation by the school district
    B. Attendance at safety seminars
    C. Policy of rapid dismissal of unsafe drivers
    D. Proper pupil behavior
    E. The operating condition of the vehicle

24. All of the following are responsibilities of the school superintendent EXCEPT:
    A. Show interest in good accident control program
    B. Outline responsibilities of all participants in the transportation system
    C. Provide specific guidelines for driver recruitment and training
    D. Establish standards for bus maintenance
    E. Involve schools and parents in transportation safety program

25. Which of the following is NOT an indication of sub-standard driver performance?
    A. Inadequate maintenance
    B. Errors in the performance of work
    C. Changes in everyday behavior and manners
    D. Near accidents
    E. Changes in simple habits of a routine nature

KEY (CORRECT ANSWERS)

1. A	6. D	11. A	16. D	21. E
2. B	7. C	12. B	17. A	22. B
3. B	8. C	13. C	18. C	23. A
4. B	9. D	14. C	19. D	24. D
5. C	10. E	15. E	20. C	25. A

TEST 2

DIRECTIONS: Each question or incomplete statement is followed by several suggested answers or completions. Select the one that BEST answers the question or completes the statement. *PRINT THE LETTER OF THE CORRECT ANSWER IN THE SPACE AT THE RIGHT.*

1. Who should be responsible for driver selection?   1.___
   A. District superintendent
   B. Transportation supervisor
   C. School office of personnel
   D. School board
   E. Contractor

2. Which of the following is LEAST important regarding the school bus driver?   2.___
   Driver
   A. finds satisfaction in job
   B. gets along well with others
   C. is courteous to pedestrians and motorists
   D. is highly intelligent
   E. has neat appearance

3. What is the MOST important ingredient in an efficient school transportation service?   3.___
   A. Safe driving
   B. Control of students
   C. Safe bus routes
   D. Vehicle maintenance
   E. Compliance with traffic regulations

4. The amount of time needed for initial training depends on the   4.___
   A. person employed   B. selection program
   C. person's experience   D. all of the above
   E. none of the above

5. What is the purpose of refresher training? To   5.___
   A. develop an appreciation of the importance of the job
   B. keep performance efficient and safe
   C. prevent accidents
   D. solves problems
   E. evaluate physical fitness of older drivers

6. What is the key to the success of a safety program?   6.___
   A. Driver selection   B. Supervision
   C. Maintenance   D. Money
   E. Driver motivation

7. What instruction technique is MOST useful for remedial training?
   A. Individual reading material
   B. Classroom lecture
   C. Road instruction
   D. Videotape
   E. Group discussion

8. What is the emphasis of reaction time testing? The
   A. importance of keeping an adequate distance between moving vehicles
   B. time needed to react to an emergency situation or condition
   C. ability to evaluate distance
   D. ability to estimate the speed of approaching vehicles
   E. development of compensating habits

9. Eighty percent of the total number of accidents annually involve
   A. single cars
   B. car/truck collisions
   C. two cars
   D. multiple cars
   E. multiple trucks

10. All of the following are proper backing procedures EXCEPT:
    A. get out of bus before beginning to back
    B. backing from the passenger's side
    C. using a reliable person for guidance
    D. check both sides continually while backing
    E. backing slowly

11. Minimum visual acuity in both eyes with or without glasses should NOT be less than (Snellen)
    A. 15/20   B. 20/20   C. 20/40   D. 20/60   E. 20/200

12. Which of the following is NOT a disqualifying condition for school bus drivers?
    A. Diabetes
    B. Cardiovascular disease
    C. Hernia
    D. Pregnancy
    E. Back injury

13. What MOST determines the size requirement of the driver?
    A. Type of students to be transported
    B. Federal regulations
    C. Configuration of the driver's compartment
    D. Height of bus
    E. Type of bus

14. The catalyst to the safety and efficiency of the school bus transportation program is the
    A. local school board
    B. driver
    C. student
    D. district supervisor
    E. safety supervisor

15. In order to prepare specifications for bus purchases, what should the safety supervisor know?
    A. Knowledge of bus routes
    B. Knowledge of students to be transported
    C. Knowledge of environmental conditions
    D. Knowledge of operational conditions
    E. All of the above

15.___

16. Which of the following necessitates the planning of *Protection Routes*?
    A. Scattered pick-up locations
    B. Inclement weather conditions
    C. Transportation of students outside the community
    D. Unexpected traffic delays
    E. Transportation of special education students

16.___

17. What qualification would MOST recommend a pupil to the position of bus monitor?
    A. Height and weight
    B. Intelligence
    C. Maturity
    D. Lives near start of bus line
    E. Lives near end of bus line

17.___

18. What is the MOST important criteria in adopting management for the special education student?
    A. Selecting the proper driver
    B. Behavior modification
    C. Providing personalized service
    D. Planning for each student's needs prior to placement
    E. Providing comfortable transportation

18.___

19. All activity trips should require the presence of
    A. adult chaperone   B. teacher
    C. school official   D. parent
    E. all of the above

19.___

20. Under what conditions may loose luggage or equipment be transported in the passenger compartment of an activity bus?
    A. When there is no danger of causing injury
    B. When it does not block passageways
    C. When the destination is a league sporting event
    D. When it can be safely secured
    E. None of the above

20.___

21. Which of the following items should be carried on the bus at all times?
    A. Instant camera for scene report
    B. Cards for witness signatures
    C. Portable tape recorder for witness testimony
    D. Radio to summon help
    E. All of the above

21.___

22. An operational plan to provide two-way communication with parents is imperative in the event of
    A. sudden disability of driver
    B. road failure
    C. strikes by school staff or drivers
    D. accident
    E. civil defense drill

23. When are standees permitted while the bus is in motion?
    A. When written permission is obtained
    B. During special activity trips
    C. When safety straps are provided
    D. All of the above
    E. None of the above

24. Statistics show that automobile accidents occur MOST frequently
    A. in the morning rush hours   B. around noon
    C. soon after sunset   D. near midnight
    E. just before sunrise

25. A bus driver is liable under the law to receive a traffic ticket for
    A. double standing when a bus stop is occupied by a car
    B. not taking on all people waiting at a stop
    C. passing a preceding bus on a grade
    D. discharging a passenger at other than a bus stop
    E. none of the above

KEY (CORRECT ANSWERS)

1. B
2. D
3. A
4. D
5. B

6. E
7. E
8. A
9. C
10. B

11. C
12. D
13. C
14. E
15. E

16. C
17. C
18. D
19. A
20. E

21. B
22. D
23. E
24. C
25. D

TEST 3

DIRECTIONS: Each question or incomplete statement is followed by several suggested answers or completions. Select the one that BEST answers the question or completes the statement. *PRINT THE LETTER OF THE CORRECT ANSWER IN THE SPACE AT THE RIGHT.*

1. A transportation director who rides the school bus is NOT required to observe   1.____
   A. the conditions at the school's loading and unloading areas
   B. operation of vehicle in accordance with prescribed regulations
   C. accuracy of driver's route and schedule
   D. driver-student ratio
   E. driver attitude toward other motorists and pedestrians

2. Which of the following would be proper procedure for conducting an emergency drill?   2.____
   A. Student may exit with lunchboxes and books.
   B. The driver should assist the students out of the bus.
   C. Drills should be held on the actual bus route.
   D. Drills should be held more often in the spring and fall.
   E. Students who ride buses on special trips may be excluded.

3. What is the goal in planning the parking of buses at the school loading zone? To   3.____
   A. accommodate the maximum number of buses
   B. exclude the necessity for backing up the buses
   C. inhibit the regular flow of traffic within the school site
   D. achieve the closest proximity to the school building
   E. accommodate student pick-up by parents

4. No portion of the bus may be driven onto railroad tracks if the view in either direction is obstructed for ____ feet.   4.____
   A. 250   B. 100   C. 2000   D. 500   E. 1000

5. A fleet's safety performance should measure the number of accidents per   5.____
   A. vehicle within a year
   B. vehicle mile within a year
   C. vehicle within a month
   D. length route and students carried
   E. vehicle mile within a month

6. Bus drills used to teach students about emergency evacuation procedures should have everyone exit through the   6.____
   A. front entrance door
   B. rear emergency door
   C. emergency window

D. front entrance door or rear emergency door
E. rear emergency door or emergency window

7. What sign or signal may be activated from the bus while it is stopped for a railroad crossing? 7.____
   A. Stop signal arm B. White flashing strobe light
   C. Yellow signal lamps D. Red signal lamps
   E. Turn signal lights

8. The driver must evacuate the bus if in normal traffic conditions the bus is not visible for a MINIMUM distance of ____ feet. 8.____
   A. 1000 B. 50 C. 300 D. 100 E. 500

9. What is the MINIMUM radius on the inner edge of pavement on all road curves within the school site? ____ feet. 9.____
   A. 50 B. 100 C. 60 D. 80 E. 90

10. All of the following are recommended EXCEPT: 10.____
    A. Roads should completely encircle a school
    B. Curbing should be constructed on all roads
    C. Eliminate all crossroads in front of buses
    D. A maximum standard of 5% grade is allowed on all roads
    E. Traffic control devices should be provided at all exits

11. Under what condition may a driver NOT proceed across railroad tracks unless authorized by a law enforcement officer or flagman? 11.____
    A. Tracks at which there is in operation any flashing red lights and/or bell
    B. During wet, stormy, or foggy weather
    C. Tracks controlled by crossing gate or barrier
    D. Tracks at which there is a railroad grade crossing
    E. Tracks not controlled by traffic signals

12. What is the SAFEST way to proceed if a bus stops near a precipice where it could still move and go over the cliff? 12.____
    A. Instruct students to remain in seats
    B. Redistribute carrying weight of students to area of greatest stability
    C. Driver should exit and stabilize bus with emergency equipment
    D. Instruct students to assume *crash* position
    E. Evacuate bus

13. Which of the following would NOT necessitate the evacuation of a school bus? 13.____
    A. Danger of fire B. Behavior control
    C. Unsafe position D. All of the above
    E. None of the above

14. How far from the bus should students go during an emergency drill? ____ feet. 14.____
    A. 100 B. 300 C. 25 D. 50 E. 200

15. Bus canopies have been found to be advantageous in
    A. schools with handicapped students
    B. elementary schools
    C. schools with large enrollments
    D. schools with small enrollments
    E. schools located in cold climates

16. How far from rails nearest the front of the bus must the driver come to a complete stop? ____ feet.
    A. 25   B. 15   C. 50   D. 35   E. 60

17. Which of the following factors pertaining to school bus evacuation must be considered FIRST?
    A. Safety of students
    B. Stability of vehicle
    C. Leadership capacity of driver
    D. Communication of emergency situation to proper authority
    E. Maturity of students

18. What is the SAFEST way to park buses for loading and unloading?
    A. Perpendicular to curb, front end facing
    B. Perpendicular to curb, rear end facing
    C. Diagonal to curb, front end facing
    D. Diagonal to curb, rear end facing
    E. Bumper to bumper, alongside curb

19. Diagonal parking requires a MINIMUM width of paved surface of ____ feet.
    A. 50   B. 60   C. 30   D. 100   E. 40

20. When the bus driver is incapacitated, it is NOT necessary for the appointed student monitor to know how to
    A. turn off ignition switch   B. set emergency brake
    C. use the fire ax   D. set flags and flares
    E. put transmission in gear

21. If it is necessary to load or unload students on the main thoroughfare in front of the school, a paved road should be provided at least ____ feet wide.
    A. 36   B. 24   C. 48   D. 60   E. 40

22. What MINIMUM tangent section should be provided between reverse curves? ____ feet.
    A. 60   B. 50   C. 30   D. 40   E. 75

23. During an evacuation drill, the
    A. ignition should be left off
    B. transmission should be in neutral position
    C. front entrance door should be blocked
    D. emergency doors' folding stirrup step should be used
    E. all of the above

24. What is the MAXIMUM standard of grade allowed for roads on school sites?
    A. 1%   B. 5%   C. 2%   D. 7%   E. 3%

25. School bus safety is BEST achieved when
    A. separate loading zones accommodate two-way bus traffic
    B. intersections within school site are eliminated
    C. trees and shrubbery are not planted or eliminated
    D. island construction in driveways should be avoided
    E. all roads should be of uniform width

KEY (CORRECT ANSWERS)

1. D
2. D
3. B
4. E
5. B

6. D
7. E
8. C
9. C
10. A

11. A
12. E
13. B
14. A
15. A

16. C
17. A
18. C
19. B
20. E

21. E
22. B
23. A
24. B
25. B

EXAMINATION SECTION
TEST 1

DIRECTIONS: Each question or incomplete statement is followed by several suggested answers or completions. Select the one that BEST answers the question or completes the statement. *PRINT THE LETTER OF THE CORRECT ANSWER IN THE SPACE AT THE RIGHT.*

1. An employee under your supervision complains that he is assigned to work late more often than any of the other employees in the garage. You check the records and find that this isn't so.
   You should

   A. advise this employee not to worry about what the other employees do but to see that he puts in a full day's work himself
   B. explain to this employee that you get the same complaint from all the other employees
   C. inform this employee that you have checked the records and the complaint is not justified
   D. not assign this employee to work late for a few days in order to keep him satisfied

   1.____

2. A garage employee has reported late for work several times.
   His supervisor should

   A. give this employee less desirable assignments
   B. overlook the lateness if the employee's work is otherwise exceptional
   C. recommend disciplinary action for habitual lateness
   D. talk the matter over with the employee before doing anything further

   2.____

3. In choosing a man to be in charge in his absence, the supervisor should select first the employee who

   A. has ability to supervise others
   B. has been longest with the organization
   C. has the nicest appearance and manner
   D. is most skilled in his assigned duties

   3.____

4. An employee under your supervision comes to you to complain about a decision you have made in assigning the men. He is excited and angry. You think what he is complaining about is not important, but it seems very important to him.
   The BEST way for you to handle this is to

   A. let him talk until *he gets it off his chest* and then explain the reasons for your decision
   B. refuse to talk to him until he has cooled off
   C. show him at once how unimportant the matter is and how ridiculous his arguments are
   D. tell him to take it up with your superior if he disagrees with your decision

   4.____

5. Suppose that a new employee has been appointed and assigned to your supervision. When this man reports for work, it would be BEST for you to

   5.____

A. ask him questions about different problems connected with a motor vehicle and see if he answers them correctly
B. check him carefully while he carries out some routine assignment that you give him
C. explain to him the general nature of the work he will be required to do
D. make a careful study of his previous work record before coming to the Department

6. The competent supervisor will be friendly with the employees under his supervision but will avoid close familiarity.
This statement is justified MAINLY because

   A. a friendly attitude on the part of the supervisor toward the employee is likely to cause suspicion on the part of the employee
   B. a supervisor can handle his employees better if he doesn't know their personal problems
   C. close familiarity may interfere with the discipline needed for good supervisor-subordinate relationships
   D. familiarity with the employees may be a sign of lack of ability on the part of the supervisor

7. An employee disagrees with the instructions that you, his supervisor, have given him for carrying out a certain assignment.
The BEST action for you to take is to tell this employee that

   A. he can do what he wants but you will hold him responsible for failure
   B. orders must be carried out or morale will fall apart
   C. this job has been done in this way for many years with great success
   D. you will be glad to listen to his objections and to his suggestions for improvement

8. As a supervisor, it is LEAST important for you to use a new employee's probationary period for the purpose of

   A. carefully checking how he performs the work you assign him
   B. determining whether he can perform the duties of his job efficiently
   C. preparing him for promotion to a higher position
   D. showing him how to carry out his assigned duties properly

9. Suppose you have just given an employee under your supervision instructions on how to carry out a certain assignment.
The BEST way to check that he has understood your instructions is to

   A. ask him to repeat your instructions word for word
   B. check the progress of his work the first chance you get
   C. invite him to ask questions if he has any doubts
   D. question him briefly about the main points of the assignment

10. Suppose you find it necessary to change a procedure that the men under your supervision have been following for a long time.
A good way to get their cooperation for this change would be to

    A. bring them together to talk over the new procedure and explain the reasons for its adoption
    B. explain to the men that if most of them still don't approve of the change after giving it a fair try, you will consider giving it up

C. give them a few weeks' notice of the proposed change in procedure
D. not enforce the new procedure strictly at the beginning

11. An order can be given by a supervisor in such a way as to make the employee want to obey it.
According to this statement, it is MOST reasonable to suppose that

   A. a person will be glad to obey an order if he realizes that he must
   B. if an order is given properly, it will be obeyed more willingly
   C. it is easier to obey an order than to give one correctly
   D. supervisors should inspire confidence by their actions as well as by their words

11._____

12. If one of the men you supervise disagrees with how you rate his work, the BEST way for you to handle this is to

   A. advise him to appeal to your superior about it
   B. decline to discuss the matter with him in order to keep discipline
   C. explain why you rate him the way you do and talk it over with him
   D. tell him that you are better qualified to rate his work than he is

12._____

13. A supervisor should be familiar with the experience and abilities of the employees under his supervision MAINLY because

   A. each employee's work is highly important and requires a person of outstanding ability
   B. it will help him to know which employees are best fitted for certain assignments
   C. nearly all men have the same basic ability to do any job equally well
   D. superior background shortly shows itself in superior work quality, regardless of assignment

13._____

14. The competent supervisor will try to develop respect rather than fear in his subordinates.
This statement is justified MAINLY because

   A. fear is always present and, for best results, respect must be developed to offset it
   B. it is generally easier to develop respect in the men than it is to develop fear
   C. men who respect their supervisor are more likely to give more than the required minimum amount and quality of work
   D. respect is based on the individual and fear is based on the organization as a whole

14._____

15. If one of the employees you supervise does outstanding work, you should

   A. explain to him how his work can still be improved so that he will not become self-satisfied
   B. mildly criticize the other men for not doing as good a job as this man
   C. praise him for his work so that he will know it is appreciated
   D. say nothing or he might become conceited

15._____

16. A supervisor can BEST help establish good morale among his employees if he

   A. confides in them about his personal problems in order to encourage them to confide in him
   B. encourages them to become friendly with him but discourages social engagements with them

16._____

C. points out to them the advantages of having a cooperative spirit in the department
D. sticks to the same rules that he expects them to follow

17. The one of the following situations which would seem to indicate poor scheduling of work by the supervisor in a garage is

   A. everybody in the garage seeming to be very busy at the same time
   B. re-assignment of a man to other work because of breakdown of a piece of equipment
   C. two employees on vacation at the same time
   D. two operators waiting to have their vehicles greased and the oil changed

17.____

Questions 18-20.

DIRECTIONS: Questions 18 through 20 are to be answered ONLY on the basis of the information given in the following paragraph.

The supervisor will gain the respect of the members of his staff and increase his influence over them by controlling his temper and avoiding criticizing anyone publicly. When a mistake is made, the good supervisor will talk it over with the employee quietly and privately. The supervisor will listen to the employee's story, suggest the better way of doing the job, and offer help so the mistake won't happen again. Before closing the discussion, the supervisor should try to find something good to say about other parts of the employee's work. Some praise and appreciation, along with instruction, is more likely to encourage an employee to improve in those areas where he is weakest.

18. A good title that would show the meaning of this entire paragraph would be

   A. How to Correct Employee Errors
   B. How to Praise Employees
   C. Mistakes are Preventable
   D. The Weak Employe

18.____

19. According to the above paragraph, the work of an employee who has made a mistake is more likely to improve if the supervisor

   A. avoids criticizing him
   B. gives him a chance to suggest a better way of doing the work
   C. listens to the employee's excuses to see if he is right
   D. praises good work at the same time he corrects the mistake

19.____

20. According to the above paragraph, when a supervisor needs to correct an employee's mistake, it is important that he

   A. allow some time to go by after the mistake is made
   B. do so when other employees are not present
   C. show his influence with his tone of voice
   D. tell other employees to avoid the same mistake

20.____

Questions 21-24.

DIRECTIONS: Questions 21 through 24 are to be answered ONLY on the basis of the information given in the following paragraph.

All automotive accidents, no matter how slight, are to be reported to the Safety Division by the employee involved on Accident Report Form S-23 in duplicate. When the accident is of such a nature that it requires the filling out of the State Motor Vehicle Report Form MV-104, this form is also prepared by the employee in duplicate and sent to the Safety Division for comparison with the Form S-23. The Safety Division forwards both copies of Form MV-104 to the Corporation Counsel, who sends one copy to the State Bureau of Motor Vehicles. When the information on the Form S-23 indicates that the employee may be at fault, an investigation is made by the Safety Division. If this investigation shows that the employee was at fault, the employee's dispatcher is asked to file a complaint on Form D-11. The foreman of mechanics prepares a damage report on Form D-8 and an estimate of the cost of repairs on Form D-9. The dispatcher's complaint, the damage report, the repair estimate, and the employee's previous accident record are sent to the Safety Division where they are studied together with the accident report. The Safety Division then recommends whether or not disciplinary action should be taken against the employee.

21. According to the above paragraph, the Safety Division should be notified whenever an automotive accident has occurred by means of

    A. Form S-23
    B. Forms S-23 and MV-104
    C. Forms S-23, MV-104, D-8, D-9, and D-11
    D. Forms S-23, MV-104, D-8, D-9, and D-11 and employee's accident report

21.____

22. According to the above paragraph, the forwarding of the Form MV-104 to the State Bureau of Motor Vehicles is done by the

    A. Corporation Counsel
    B. dispatcher
    C. employee involved in the accident
    D. Safety Division

22.____

23. According to the above paragraph, the Safety Division investigates an automotive accident if the

    A. accident is serious enough to be reported to the State Bureau of Motor Vehicles
    B. dispatcher files a complaint
    C. employee appears to have been at fault
    D. employee's previous accident report is poor

23.____

24. Of the forms mentioned in the above paragraph, the dispatcher is responsible for preparing the

    A. accident report form
    B. complaint form
    C. damage report
    D. estimate of cost of repairs

24.____

Questions 25-27.

DIRECTIONS: Questions 25 through 27 are to be answered ONLY on the basis of the information given in the following paragraph.

One of the major problems in the control of city motor equipment, and especially passenger equipment, is keeping the equipment working for the city and for the city alone for as many hours of the day as is practical. Even when most city employees try to get the most out of the cars, a poor system of control will result in wasted car hours. Some city employees have a legitimate use for a car all day long while others use a car only a small part of the day and then let it stand. As a rule, trucks are easier to control than passenger cars because they are usually assigned to a specific job where a foreman continually oversees them. Even though trucks are usually fully utilized, there are times when the normal work assignment cannot be carried out because of weather conditions or seasonal changes. At such times, a control system could plan to make the trucks available for other uses.

25. According to the above paragraph, a problem connected with controlling the use of city motor equipment is

    A. increasing the life span of the equipment
    B. keeping the equipment working all hours of the day
    C. preventing the over-use of the equipment to avoid breakdowns
    D. preventing the private use of the equipment

25.____

26. According to the above paragraph, a good control system for passenger equipment will MOST likely lead to

    A. better employees being assigned to operate the cars
    B. fewer city employees using city cars
    C. fewer wasted car hours for city cars
    D. insuring that city cars are used for legitimate purposes

26.____

27. According to the above paragraph, a control system for trucks is useful because

    A. a foreman usually supervises each job
    B. special conditions sometimes prevent the planned use of a truck
    C. trucks are easier to control than passenger cars
    D. trucks are usually assigned to specific jobs where they cannot be fully utilized

27.____

Questions 28-33.

DIRECTIONS: In the paragraph below, some of the underlined words have been purposely changed and spoil the meaning that the rest of the paragraph is meant to give. Read the paragraph carefully, then answer Questions 28 through 33.

The motor vehicle supervisor who is <u>responsible</u> for training drivers in the operation of <u>special</u> equipment cannot expect a man to carry out all of his duties <u>poorly</u> <u>immediately</u> after receiving instruction. The employee may be <u>overwhelmed</u> by all of the details he must master, <u>happy</u> because he is <u>associated</u> with new fellow workers, or fearful that he may not <u>succeed</u> on the job. It is the supervisor's <u>job</u> to make the <u>operator</u> feel at ease and <u>discourage</u> his self-confidence. The supervisor must also vary the speed of the <u>driving</u> according to the operator's <u>capacity</u> to <u>absorb</u> the instruction without undue <u>pressure</u> or confusion. All learners <u>progress</u> through <u>several</u> stages of <u>development</u> <u>unless</u> they become expert in their duties. As the operator's skills <u>increase</u>, he will require <u>more</u> instruction but the supervisor should be available to correct <u>mistakes</u> promptly to prevent wrong <u>habits</u> being formed.

28. Of the following words underlined in the above paragraph, the one that does NOT give the real meaning that the rest of the paragraph is meant to give is

    A. responsible   B. special
    C. happy   D. immediately

29. Of the following words underlined in the above paragraph, the one that does NOT give the real meaning that the rest of the paragraph is meant to give is

    A. overwhelmed   B. happy
    C. associated   D. succeed

30. Of the following words underlined in the above paragraph, the one that does NOT give the real meaning that the rest of the paragraph is meant to give is

    A. job   B. operator
    C. discourage   D. self-confidence

31. Of the following words underlined in the above paragraph, the one that does NOT give the real meaning that the rest of the paragraph is meant to give is

    A. driving   B. capacity   C. absorb   D. pressure

32. Of the following words underlined in the above paragraph, the one that does NOT give the real meaning that the rest of the paragraph is meant to give is

    A. progress   B. several
    C. development   D. unless

33. Of the following words underlined in the above paragraph, the one that does NOT give the real meaning that the rest of the paragraph is meant to give is

    A. increase   B. more   C. mistakes   D. habits

Questions 34-40.

DIRECTIONS: Each of Questions 34 through 40 consists of a word in capital letters followed by four suggested meanings of the word. Select the word or phrase which means MOST NEARLY the same as the word in capital letters.

34. ACCELERATE

    A. adjust   B. press   C. quicken   D. strip

35. ALIGN

    A. bring into line   B. carry out
    C. happen by chance   D. join together

36. CONTRACTION

    A. agreement   B. denial
    C. presentation D. shrinkage

37. INTERVAL

    A. ending   B. mixing together of
    C. space of time D. weaken

38. LUBRICATE

    A. bend back   B. make slippery
    C. rub out   D. soften

39. OBSOLETE

    A. broken-down   B. hard to find
    C. high-priced   D. out of date

40. RETARD

    A. delay   B. flatten   C. rest   D. tally

KEY (CORRECT ANSWERS)

1.	C	11.	B	21.	A	31.	A
2.	D	12.	C	22.	A	32.	D
3.	A	13.	B	23.	C	33.	B
4.	A	14.	C	24.	B	34.	C
5.	C	15.	C	25.	D	35.	A
6.	C	16.	D	26.	C	36.	D
7.	D	17.	D	27.	B	37.	C
8.	C	18.	A	28.	C	38.	B
9.	D	19.	D	29.	B	39.	D
10.	A	20.	B	30.	C	40.	A

TEST 2

DIRECTIONS: Each question or incomplete statement is followed by several suggested answers or completions. Select the one that BEST answers the question or completes the statement. *PRINT THE LETTER OF THE CORRECT ANSWER IN THE SPACE AT THE RIGHT.*

Questions 1-3.

DIRECTIONS: Questions 1 through 3 consist of a word in capital letters followed by four suggested meanings of the word. Select the word or phrase which means MOST NEARLY the same as the word in capital letters.

1. SYNCHRONIZE

   A. draw out
   B. happen at the same time
   C. move at a steady rate
   D. turn smoothly

2. OSCILLATE

   A. attract   B. echo   C. roll   D. swing

3. TERMINAL

   A. last   B. moldy   C. named   D. spoken

4. In a certain garage, when the dispatcher issues gas and oil to a vehicle, he notes on his record the mileage reading of the vehicle.
   This is probably done MAINLY in order to

   A. check gas consumption against distance traveled
   B. compare age of vehicle with economy of operation
   C. decide when the vehicle should be scheduled for a grease job
   D. estimate future life expectancy of the vehicle

5. A supervisor of motor vehicle equipment was asked by the head of the bureau to investigate a certain procedure used in the garage and write a report with a recommendation whether the procedure should be changed. The supervisor, after he finished his investigation, made his report in which he said: *I recommend that you base your decision* to change the present procedure on whether or not the new procedure will improve operations.
   In this case, the supervisor carried out his assignment

   A. *poorly,* because he should have given his recommendation right at the beginning of the report
   B. *poorly,* because his investigation should have brought out whether the new procedure would improve operations
   C. *well,* because he left the final decision about changing the procedure up to the head of the bureau
   D. *well,* because he made an investigation and turned in a report as required

6. When a supervisor writes a report, it is LEAST important that

   A. all paragraphs in the report be of the same length
   B. a summary or list of the recommendations be given at the beginning of the report if the report is long
   C. independent ideas be taken up in separate paragraphs of the report
   D. the report give all the evidence on which the conclusions are based

7. The supervisor who makes a special point of using long words in preparing written reports is, in general, PROBABLY being

   A. *unwise,* because a written report should be factual and accurate
   B. *unwise,* because simplicity in a report is usually desirable
   C. *wise,* because the written report will become a permanent record
   D. *wise,* because with long words he can use the right emphasis in his report

8. The most thorough investigation is of no value if the report written by the person who made the investigation does not help his superior to decide what action to take.
   According to this statement, it is LEAST correct to suppose that

   A. an investigation is of no value unless it is thorough
   B. a purpose of the report turned in after an investigation is to help supervisors decide what action to take
   C. the report on an investigation is usually written by the person who made the investigation
   D. the value of an investigation depends in part on the report turned in

9. Before you turn in a report you have written of an investigation that you made, you discover some additional information that you didn't know about before.
   Whether or not you rewrite your report to include this additional information should depend MAINLY on the

   A. amount of time left in which to submit the report
   B. effect this information will have on the conclusions of the report
   C. number of changes that you will have to make in your original report
   D. possibility of turning in a supplementary report later

10. The advantage of using an *inspection check sheet* when making inspections of premises or equipment is that

    A. fewer inspections are required
    B. the inspection becomes easy and can be done by a subordinate
    C. there is less chance of forgetting some important point of the inspection
    D. there is less paper work

11. Of the following methods for keeping supplies and records of supplies, the one that will MOST quickly tell you at any time how many pieces of any item are on hand in the supply room is

    A. keeping a minimum number of each item on hand
    B. recording each item when it is added to or removed from stock
    C. stocking the same number of pieces of each item and reordering weekly to keep the count even
    D. taking a daily count

12. When a supervisor submits a report on a motor vehicle accident, it is LEAST important for him to include in his report the

    A. addresses of the witnesses to the accident
    B. number of the police precinct where the accident happened
    C. probable cause of the accident
    D. time of the accident

13. The MAIN reason a supervisor in charge of motor vehicle equipment or personnel should make sure that his men obey the safety rules is that

    A. accident prevention is a new program and should be tried out
    B. every accident can be prevented
    C. other safety measures are not needed where safety rules are obeyed
    D. safety rules are based on proven methods of accident prevention

14. When he investigates an accident in which a city vehicle was involved, the MAIN object of the supervisor should be to

    A. complete the investigation as fast as possible
    B. determine if the city operator's record is so bad that he should be fired
    C. get all the facts to establish the cause of the accident
    D. try to establish that the other driver was at least equally to blame

15. If witnesses to an automobile accident are interviewed separately, they are more likely to give different versions of the circumstances of the accident than if they are interviewed together.
    According to this statement, it is MOST probable that

    A. a truer picture of the circumstances of an accident can be gotten by interviewing the witnesses together rather than separately
    B. a witness's impression of what he saw is influenced by the statement of the other witnesses as to what they saw
    C. people who see an accident as a group will agree about the details of the accident more than people who are not together when they see the accident
    D. witnesses are less likely to tell the truth when interviewed privately than when interviewed as a group

16. A thorough investigation should always be made of an accident in which a city vehicle is involved.
    The MAIN value of such an investigation is to

    A. discover any factors that contributed to the accident which may be corrected
    B. keep compensation claims down
    C. provide good records from which statistics can be developed
    D. show the operators that accidents are taken seriously, no matter how small

17. An accident has been described as *an unplanned event caused by an unsafe act or condition.*
    An example of an unsafe act, rather than of an unsafe condition, in a garage is

    A. blocked fire exits
    B. defective tools or equipment
    C. horseplay or teasing
    D. oil and grease on floors

18. Of the following rules, the one that is LEAST directly concerned with the prevention of accidents is:

    A. Check brake fluid before leaving garage
    B. Do not use garage equipment if safety devices do not work
    C. No smoking in garage
    D. Reports of time lost due to accident must be submitted in 5 days

19. Which of the following entries on a Department Accident Report Form is MAINLY for the purpose of showing what is being done so that this type of accident will not happen again?

    A. Describe accident, including vehicle or vehicles involved
    B. What are you doing to prevent similar accidents?
    C. Why did the unsafe condition exist?
    D. Why was the unsafe act committed?

20. With respect to motor vehicle accidents, it is necessary to report in duplicate to the Bureau of Motor Vehicles on its printed forms

    A. all accidents
    B. only those accidents in which someone is killed or injured
    C. only those accidents in which someone is killed or injured or there is property damage of more than $50
    D. only those accidents in which someone is killed or injured or there is property damage of more than $100

21. A section of a garage used for parking vehicle measures 162 1/2' x 25 3/4'.
    If each vehicle to be parked in this section requires, on the average, 84 sq.ft. of parking space, the MAXIMUM number of vehicles that can be parked in this section is CLOSEST to

    A. 50   B. 45   C. 40   D. 35

22. Each of the 23 vehicles in a garage uses an average of 114 gallons of gas every 4 weeks.
    If the motor vehicle dispatcher is required to re-order gas when the gas tank in the garage shows no more than a one week supply, he MUST re-order when the gas tank shows _____ gallons.

    A. 655   B. 705   C. 830   D. 960

23. An employee's annual salary is $45,800. His total and annual deductions are 22% for withholding tax, 8 1/2% for pension and social security, and $1,820 for health insurance. The take-home pay that this employee would get on the check he receives every other week is MOST NEARLY

    A. $577.10   B. $845.00   C. $1,154.20   D. $1,220.40

24. A vehicle which averages 14 1/2 miles to a gallon of gas uses a quart of oil for every 21 1/2 gallons of gas.
    If the vehicle traveled 19,952 miles in a year, its oil consumption for the year would be _____ quarts.

    A. 52   B. 56   C. 60   D. 64

25. Thirteen percent of all the vehicles in a certain garage are trucks. 25.____
If there are 26 trucks, then the number of vehicles of other types in this garage is

   A. 174	B. 200	C. 260	D. 338

26. Of 12 employees in a garage, four earn $3,500 a year, two earn $3,150 a year, one earns 26.____
$4,550 a year, and the rest each earn $3,800 a year.
The average yearly salary of these employees is CLOSEST to

   A. $3,550	B. $3,650	C. $3,750	D. $3,850

27. A garage bin used for storing supplies and parts measures 1 yard x 2 yards x 7 feet. 27.____
The cubic volume of this bin is

   A. 5 1/3 cubic yards	B. 16 cubic feet
   C. 63 cubic feet	D. 126 cubic feet

28. A garage has a gas tank with a capacity of 1,300 gallons. If there are only 520 gallons of 28.____
gas in the tank, then the tank is _____ full.

   A. 40%	B. 33 1/3%	C. 25%	D. 16 3/4%

29. Of a specially selected group of vehicles, 1/5 are 6 months old, 2/5 are 12 months old, 29.____
and 2/5 are 15 months old.
The average age of this group of vehicles is _____ months.

   A. 9	B. 10	C. 11	D. 12

30. A suggestion has been made that every vehicle have its gas tank filled and oil and water 30.____
checked when it returns to the garage at the end of the day.
This suggestion is

   A. *good,* mainly because the gas pump can be kept locked the rest of the day
   B. *good,* mainly because vehicles will be ready to go out promptly the next day
   C. *poor,* mainly because it would take too long to fill each vehicle
   D. *poor,* mainly because not every vehicle will need gas, oil, and water

31. Brakes do not generally have to be adjusted until the clearance between the bottom of 31.____
the brake pedal and the floorboard goes below _____ inch(es).

   A. 2-2 1/2	B. 1 1/2-2	C. 1-1 1/2	D. 1/2-1

32. *Play* in the steering wheel is generally NOT considered to be excessive until it reaches 32.____
about _____ inch(es).

   A. 1/2	B. 1	C. 1 1/2	D. 2

33. If the oil pressure gauge in a sedan reads unduly high even after the engine is warmed 33.____
up, the MOST probable reason is

   A. a low oil level in the crankcase
   B. an internal leak in the oil system
   C. an obstruction in the oil line
   D. too light an oil being used

34. In order to keep tire pressure at the level recommended by the manufacturer, the air pressure in the tires should be

    A. checked at the end of the day's driving
    B. checked in the morning, before the vehicle is driven
    C. lower in summer than in winter
    D. reduced before a long trip to leave room for expansion

35. When inspecting one of your vehicles, you notice excessive wear on the center of the tread of both front tires.
    This unusual wear is MOST likely caused by

    A. excessive toe-in of the front wheels
    B. over-inflation of the front tires
    C. too much camber of the front wheels
    D. under-inflation of the front tires

36. The level of the fluid in the battery should be _____ the top of the plates.

    A. barely covering   B. exactly even with
    C. well below   D. well over

37. A heavy layer of oil on the water in the radiator would MOST probably indicate a

    A. cracked block   B. dirty air cleaner
    C. loose hose connection D. water pump leak

38. If a five gallon can of gasoline is spilled on the garage floor, the BEST action to take is to

    A. let the gasoline evaporate
    B. pour sand over the puddle of gasoline
    C. squirt a foam-producing fire extinguisher on the puddle
    D. use a hose to flush the gasoline away

39. Greasy rags and waste in a garage should be

    A. hung up on a line to air out
    B. put in boxes that will be emptied daily
    C. put in covered metal cans or barrels
    D. put in wire baskets outside the garage

40. Adjusting the carburetor to give a mixture that is richer in fuel is

    A. *good* practice in cold weather as it improves engine operation
    B. *good* practice in very hot weather as it prevents stalling
    C. *poor* practice as it increases the chance of vapor lock
    D. *poor* practice in stop-and-go city driving as it greatly increases gas consumption

KEY (CORRECT ANSWERS)

1. B	11. B	21. A	31. C
2. D	12. B	22. A	32. D
3. A	13. D	23. C	33. C
4. A	14. C	24. D	34. B
5. B	15. B	25. A	35. B
6. A	16. A	26. B	36. D
7. B	17. C	27. D	37. A
8. A	18. D	28. A	38. D
9. B	19. B	29. D	39. C
10. C	20. D	30. B	40. A

TEST 3

DIRECTIONS: Each question or incomplete statement is followed by several suggested answers or completions. Select the one that BEST answers the question or completes the statement. *PRINT THE LETTER OF THE CORRECT ANSWER IN THE SPACE AT THE RIGHT.*

Questions 1-10.

DIRECTIONS: Questions 1 through 10 are based on the information given in the map on page 2.

1. On pay day, you assign an operator to deliver paychecks by car to the four work crews assigned to street jobs in the area. He starts from the garage and is to return there when finished.
   The order of delivery that would take the operator over the shortest allowable route would be crew

   A. 1, 2, 3, 4
   B. 2, 1, 4, 3
   C. 3, 2, 1, 4
   D. 4, 3, 2, 1

   1.____

2. Work crew 4 will be finished with its job at 1 P.M. and has to be moved to a new work location at Fir Ave. and 5th St. Work crew 3 will be finished with its job at the same time and has to be moved to begin work on a new job at 6th St. and Elm Ave. The operator assigned to the truck is to start from and return to the garage.
   In order to get each of these crews to their new locations as soon as possible, the dispatcher should instruct the operator assigned to pick up crew

   A. 3 and drop them at their new location; then pick up crew 4 and drop them at their new location
   B. 4 and drop them at their new location; pick up crew 3 and drop them at their new location
   C. 3; pick up crew 4; drop off crew 3; drop off crew 4
   D. 4; pick up crew 3; drop off crew 3; drop off crew 4

   2.____

3. The shortest allowable route for driving from the repair shop to the garage is 2nd Street and

   A. Fir Ave.
   B. Gladiola Ave.
   C. Gladiola Ave., 3rd St., Fir Ave.
   D. Holly Ave., 1st St., Gladiola Ave.

   3.____

4. You have requests for the following pick-ups and deliveries: a record player and loudspeaker to be moved from the playground to the skating rink, a case of pictures to be taken from the museum to the high school, and a ticket box to be moved from the stadium to the skating rink.
   Using the shortest allowable route from the garage and back, the order in which these pick-ups and deliveries should be made with the LEAST number of stops is

   A. museum, high school, playground, skating rink, stadium
   B. museum, playground, high school, stadium, skating rink
   C. playground, skating rink, museum, high school, stadium
   D. stadium, skating rink, museum, high school, playground

   4.____

A ◯ indicates a street work crew.

A ✗ indicates a an entrance.

Arrows on streets indicate one-way and two-way streets.
No U turns are permitted.

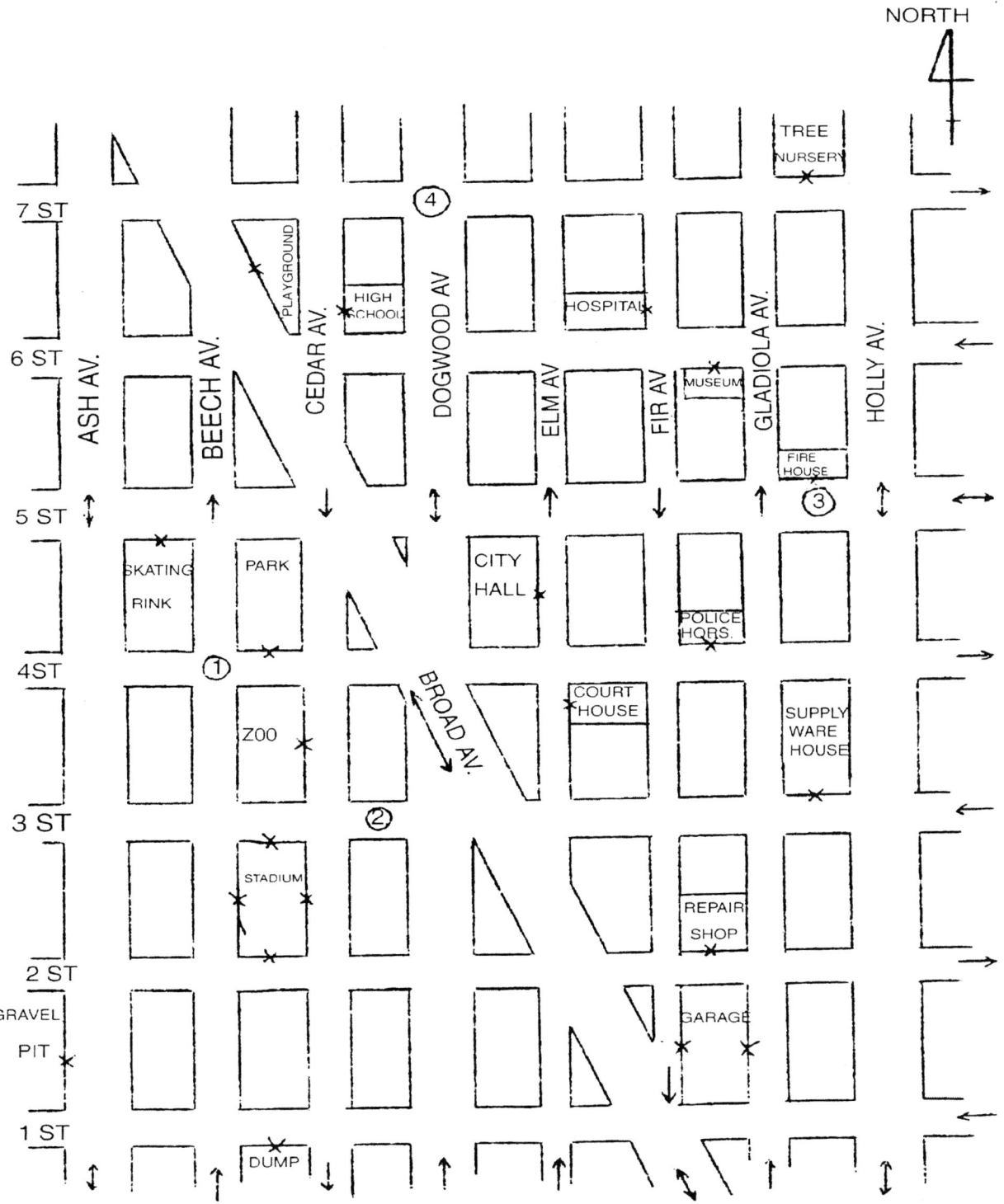

5. To help a newly assigned motor vehicle operator learn this area, you might ask him to study the direction of traffic patterns on the map.
   It would be MOST helpful if you pointed out to him that two-way traffic is permitted on

   A. all but one of the numbered streets
   B. all but three of the named avenues
   C. only one of the numbered streets
   D. only three of the named avenues

6. In routing motor equipment to the northwestern part of the mapped area, the dispatcher would be wise to use Broad Avenue MAINLY because it is

   A. a two-way street
   B. a wide street
   C. near the garage
   D. the most direct route

7. A disadvantage of the construction and location of the repair shop, according to the map, is that

   A. it has only one entrance on 2nd St.
   B. it is located too close to the garage as equipment breakdowns would happen in the field
   C. motor equipment leaving the garage must go around the block to enter the shop
   D. the shop is too small in comparison to the size of the garage

8. Two factors about the construction and location of the garage that are of special advantage to the dispatcher are that it

   A. has two entrances and is near the repair shop
   B. has two entrances and one-way streets on all sides
   C. is near the repair shop and occupies a whole block
   D. occupies a whole block and has one-way streets on all sides

9. When dispatching equipment from the garage to the hospital, the dispatcher should use the entrance on

   A. either Gladiola Ave. or Fir Ave.
   B. Fir Ave.
   C. Gladiola Ave.
   D. 2nd St.

10. You have requests to pick up some small trees at the tree nursery to be delivered to the park, to pick up gravel at the gravel pit and deliver the load to the zoo, to take some broken benches from the park to the repair shop, to pick up supplies at the warehouse for delivery to City Hall and the court house.
    The order in which a truck should do these jobs, starting from the garage and using the shortest allowable route is

    A. gravel pit, zoo; park, repair shop; warehouse, court house, City Hall; tree nursery, park, garage
    B. gravel pit, zoo; warehouse, court house, City Hall; tree nursery, park; park, repair shop; repair shop, garage
    C. tree nursery, park; park, repair shop; zoo, gravel pit; warehouse, court house, City Hall, garage
    D. warehouse, court house, City Hall; tree nursery, park; park, repair shop; gravel pit, zoo; zoo, garage

Questions 11-20.

DIRECTIONS: Answer Questions 11 through 20 ONLY on the basis of the information given below in the two charts and the Rules of the Department. You are to assume that you are the dispatcher in the garage where these charts are kept and where they are used in making daily assignments of operators and vehicles.

SECOND AVE. GARAGE MOTOR VEHICLE OPERATOR CONTROL SHEET Date: May 25, 19 __				SECOND AVE. GARAGE MOTOR VEHICLE OPERATOR CONTROL SHEET Date: May 25, 19 __			
Name of Operator	Cleared on	Hours of Overtime Credit as of May 25	On Vacation	Vehicle Number and Type	In Repair Shop as of May 25	Date Due in Shop for Preventive Maintenance Inspection	Date Last In Repair
Allen	P T	74		20-P		7/13	3/2
Boyd	P W	31	5/18-30	21-P		6/15	2/16
Cohen	P T	129		22-T		5/26	1/19
Diggs	P	15		23-P		6/1	5/8
Egan	P T	92	6/1-13	24-P		6/8	2/2
First	P T W	49		25-P		7/6	2/24
Gordon	P	57		26-W		6/1	1/21
Hanson	P T	143	6/15-27	27-T		7/20	4/6
				28-T	X	7/27	3/16
				29-P	X	5/18	1/12

Symbols: P - Passenger Car
T - Truck
W - Wrecker

Symbols: P - Passenger Car
T - Truck
W - Wrecker

RULES OF THE DEPARTMENT

1. A motor vehicle operator may be assigned to drive only those types of vehicles on which he has been cleared. No one but a motor vehicle operator may be assigned to drive a Department vehicle.

2. Private cars may not be used for Department business.

3. The motor vehicle dispatcher shall keep a daily record of overtime credits of all operators under his supervision to be sure that no operator acquires more than 150 hours of overtime credit. An assignment which involves overtime should be given, wherever possible, to the operator with the least overtime credit.

4. A vehicle due for preventive maintenance must be sent to the repair shop on the date it is due for preventive maintenance, except when a vehicle has been in the repair shop during the previous month.

5. All available vehicles are to be assigned to jobs as requested, with none held in reserve.

11. An official who is requesting a truck and operator for the three days beginning May 26th indicates to you that some overtime may be necessary for the operator, but he cannot predict how many hours of overtime will be needed. Under these circumstances, the MOST logical man for you to choose for this assignment would be operator

    A. Allen B. Boyd C. Diggs D. First

11.___

12. The vehicle which does NOT have to be sent to the shop for preventive maintenance on the date it is due is vehicle number

    A. 23 B. 25 C. 27 D. 29

12.___

13. As dispatcher, you receive a request on May 25th for a truck and motor vehicle operator for a job that will take three days, from May 26th through May 28th.
    The vehicle that it would be BEST for you to choose on May 25th for this assignment is vehicle number

    A. 28 B. 27 C. 22 D. 20

13.___

14. On May 25th, right after all the vehicles have left the garage on daily assignment, you receive a call from your Commissioner's secretary. She tells you that an emergency has come up and asks you for a car to be ready in fifteen minutes to take a messenger with important papers to be delivered to the Commissioner who is waiting for the papers at a court in another borough.
    Of the following, the BEST thing for you to do, after explaining to the secretary that you have no cars available, is to

    A. advise her she should give you advance notice the next time so that you can reserve a car for the messenger
    B. offer to drive the messenger yourself in your private car
    C. promise to get a car from another department
    D. suggest that the messenger use public transportation

14.___

15. To give you more leeway in assigning your operators to the available equipment, it would be MOST practical for you to

    A. ask your supervisor to assign two additional motor vehicle operators to the garage
    B. have additional operators cleared on the wrecker
    C. suggest to your supervisor that rule 3 be abolished
    D. suggest to your supervisor that rule 1 be abolished

15.___

16. Other things being equal, the operator who should probably be of MOST value to you, as the dispatcher, is

    A. Cohen B. Diggs C. First D. Hanson

16.___

17. The factor which indicates MOST strongly that there may not be enough operators assigned to this garage is the

    A. amount of overtime accumulated
    B. excess of number of vehicles over number of operators
    C. incomplete vacation schedule
    D. number of operators cleared on trucks

17.___

18. When dispatching men and equipment in the morning, it would be BEST for you to first dispatch men who 18._____

    A. are cleared on 1 vehicle
    B. are cleared on 2 vehicles
    C. are cleared on 3 vehicles
    D. have already had their vacations

19. The second week in June, you receive a call for an operator and wrecker. 19._____
    It is better to dispatch Boyd rather than First because

    A. he has already had his vacation
    B. he has less overtime
    C. he is not cleared on trucks
    D. unless there are special reasons, you might as well assign the men in alphabetical order for easier record keeping

20. You have requests for 6 passenger cars and 2 trucks for jobs on May 25th. All of these jobs will probably take the full day but none will require any overtime. 20._____
    How many of these requests for May 25th would you have to refuse?

    A. None B. One
    C. Two   D. More than two

KEY (CORRECT ANSWERS)

1.	B	11.	D
2.	A	12.	A
3.	D	13.	B
4.	B	14.	D
5.	C	15.	B
6.	D	16.	C
7.	C	17.	A
8.	A	18.	A
9.	C	19.	C
10.	B	20.	B

TEST 4

DIRECTIONS: Each question or incomplete statement is followed by several suggested answers or completions. Select the one that BEST answers the question or completes the statement. *PRINT THE LETTER OF THE CORRECT ANSWER IN THE SPACE AT THE RIGHT.*

1. In a program of switching tires on a vehicle at regular intervals to give longer tire life, the BEST system to follow is

    1.___

2. If an engine misfires when it is operated at low speed, the order in which the items below should be inspected, tested, and adjusted is

    2.___

    A. breaker contact points, distributor cap and rotor, high voltage wires, spark plugs
    B. distributor cap and rotor, breaker contact points, spark plugs, high voltage wires
    C. high voltage wires, spark plugs, breaker contact points, distributor can and rotor
    D. spark plugs, high voltage wires, distributor cap and rotor, breaker contact points

3. An operator complains that the headlights on his vehicle flare up and then dim as the speed of the vehicle changes.
   The MOST probable cause is

    3.___

    A. a burned out fuse or defective circuit breaker
    B. a defective dimmer switch
    C. a loose connection in the headlight wiring
    D. weak bulbs

4. A can of motor oil is marked *S.A.E. 20-20W.*
   This indicates that

    4.___

    A. a mistake was made, and the oil should not be used
    B. chemicals have been added to winterize the oil
    C. the oil may be used both in medium temperatures and in winter weather
    D. the oil should be used when the temperature is between 20 degrees below and 20 degrees above zero

5. A specific gravity reading of 1280 at 80° F means that a battery is

    5.___

    A. fully discharged   B. nearing a discharged condition
    C. about half charged   D. fully charged

6. If a generator constantly charges at a high rate, it is MOST probably due to a(n)

    6.___

    A. defective regulator   B. dirty commutator
    C. too tight fan belt adjustment   D. overcharged battery

7. In the servicing of spark plugs, it is IMPORTANT to

   A. bend the center electrode rather than the side electrode when adjusting the spark plug gap
   B. clean the spark plug recess in the cylinder head with a brush or compressed air after a spark plug has been removed
   C. make sure that each spark plug has only one gasket
   D. use an adjustable wrench to tighten a spark plug in its hole

8. If air gets into the lines of a hydraulic brake system, the MOST likely result will be

   A. a spongy pedal
   B. grabbing brakes
   C. locked brakes
   D. a hard pedal

9. In hooking test ammeters and voltmeters into a circuit, the ammeter

   A. should be connected in parallel and the voltmeter in series
   B. should be connected in series and the voltmeter in parallel
   C. and voltmeter should be connected in parallel
   D. and voltmeter should be connected in series

10. When brakes are correctly adjusted but one wheel takes hold before the others, it is MOST likely that the

    A. cup on the wheel cylinder has swelled
    B. relief port on the master cylinder isn't working
    C. push rod adjustment is faulty
    D. brake fluid has leaked into the lining

11. Racing an automobile engine on cold mornings to warm it up is

    A. *bad* practice, because there is poor lubrication of moving parts
    B. *good* practice, because the oil will reach moving parts faster
    C. *bad* practice, because it will form sludge in the engine
    D. *good* practice, because it will allow liquid gasoline to reach the crankcase

12. Using anti-freeze solution for more than a single season is

    A. *bad* practice, because it will cause excessive rust
    B. *good* practice, because it will be economical
    C. *bad* practice, because it will raise the boiling point
    D. *good* practice, because it will not clog the cooling system

13. The one of the following which is NOT usually a purpose of a preventive maintenance program for a fleet of automotive vehicles is

    A. a greater margin of safety in the operation of the vehicles
    B. easier and more comfortable driving
    C. improved mechanical ability of vehicle operators
    D. increased economy in vehicle operations

14. The one of the following which will NOT help improve gasoline mileage is

    A. driving at high speeds
    B. even acceleration
    C. keeping tires at recommended pressure
    D. using light oil in winter

15. An abnormally cool brake drum on one wheel after the vehicle has been in operation would MOST probably indicate a(n)

    A. dragging shoe
    B. improperly adjusted brake drum
    C. non-functioning brake
    D. underlubricated bearing

16. The pitman arm is part of the

    A. brake shoe assembly
    B. driving axle
    C. fan belt assembly
    D. steering mechanism

17. When he returns to the garage at the end of his shift, a motor vehicle operator complains to you that the engine *skips* on the car he is driving.
    When you prepare your requisition for a check-up of this vehicle, it is LEAST important for you to ask for a check of the

    A. battery
    B. carburetor
    C. condenser
    D. fuel line

18. In a garage where a vehicle preventive maintenance program is in operation, the one of the following which it is MOST important to do right away without waiting for next checkup is

    A. adjusting brakes that pull unevenly
    B. changing oil and lubrication to summer or winter grades
    C. checking spark plugs
    D. replacing an oil-soaked water hose

19. To test whether every cylinder has good compression, the instrument that should be used is a

    A. vacuum gauge
    B. gas analyzer
    C. creeper
    D. vent ball

20. It is generally recommended that the radiator of a passenger vehicle be flushed out

    A. every 1,000 miles
    B. every fall and spring
    C. every 2,000 miles
    D. once a year

KEY (CORRECT ANSWERS)

1.	A	11.	A
2.	D	12.	A
3.	C	13.	C
4.	C	14.	A
5.	D	15.	C
6.	A	16.	D
7.	C	17.	A
8.	A	18.	A
9.	B	19.	A
10.	D	20.	B

———

EXAMINATION SECTION
TEST 1

DIRECTIONS: Each question or incomplete statement is followed by several suggested answers or completions. Select the one that BEST answers the question or completes the statement. *PRINT THE LETTER OF THE CORRECT ANSWER IN THE SPACE AT THE RIGHT.*

1. Front stabilizer bars on automotive vehicles are set in such a manner that they

    A. apply force opposite to that of the springs when the springs are deflected equally
    B. normally connect to both lower control arms
    C. are adjustable in order to level the vehicle
    D. have one end attached to the lower control arm and the other end attached to the frame

2. Ignition point contact alignment is BEST adjusted by bending the

    A. movable point arm
    B. pivot post
    C. breaker plate
    D. stationary point bracket

3. When disc brake pads are retracted so as not to be touching the braking disc, the amount of retraction

    A. is affected by the piston return springs
    B. must be a minimum of 1/32 of an inch
    C. is affected by the piston seals
    D. is limited by the metering valve

4. A PROPERLY operating positive crankcase ventilation valve will

    A. control air flow as a direct function of engine speed
    B. increase air flow in direct proportion to the increase in manifold vacuum
    C. shut off air flow at high intake manifold vacuum
    D. reduce air flow at high intake manifold vacuum

5. The air-fuel ratio, by weight, in a properly functioning gasoline automotive engine is MOST NEARLY

    A. 15:1   B. 30:1   C. 600:1   D. 9000:1

6. Cam ground pistons are distinguished by

    A. being ground perfectly round
    B. having a larger diameter across the piston pin faces
    C. having a larger diameter parallel to the crankshaft centerline
    D. having a larger diameter perpendicular to the crankshaft centerline

7. In an automotive engine, the intake valves USUALLY open _____ TDC and close _____ BDC of the intake stroke.

    A. after; after
    B. after; before
    C. before; before
    D. before; after

8. In an automotive engine, the exhaust valves USUALLY open _____ BDC of the power stroke and _____ TDC of the intake stroke.

   A. after; before
   B. before; before
   C. before; after
   D. after; after

9. The PRIMARY function of a blower on a two-cycle diesel engine is to

   A. provide air for scavenging
   B. increase the compression ratio
   C. blow in the fuel-air mixture
   D. cool the oil after compression in the injector pump

10. Excessive free travel of the clutch pedal would be indicated if the

    A. transmission was hard to shift smoothly
    B. clutch slipped when fully engaged
    C. throwout bearing failed prematurely
    D. release levers were worn

11. Vacuum is usually referred to in inches of mercury.
    The number of pounds per square inch pressure above zero (absolute pressure) of a 20 inch vacuum is MOST NEARLY

    A. 4.9   B. 7.4   C. 9.6   D. 11.8

12. Only a portion of the heat energy released by the gasoline in an automotive engine is transmitted to the wheels for driving purposes.
    In an automobile in good condition and with an efficiently operating engine, this portion is MOST NEARLY

    A. 90%   B. 50%   C. 20%   D. 2%

13. An adjustment is made to the right front wheel of a vehicle equipped with shims at the junction of the upper suspension arm and the frame support by moving the upper suspension arm away from the frame a greater amount in the front than in the rear.
    This is done to

    A. increase the steering knuckle angle
    B. adjust the caster in a negative direction
    C. adjust the camber in a negative direction
    D. adjust the caster in a rotary direction

14. In an automotive rear axle in which the pinion gear engages the ring gear below the centerline of the axle, the cut of the pinion and ring gear is

    A. spiral bevel
    B. spur bevel
    C. double helical
    D. hypoid

15. Of the following statements concerning the operation in low gear of a fully synchronized (in forward gears) three-speed transmission, the one that is NOT correct is that

    A. both clutch sleeves must engage gears
    B. power is being transmitted through the countershaft gears
    C. one clutch sleeve must be engaged
    D. the reverse idler gear is being driven by a countershaft gear

Questions 16-17.

DIRECTIONS: Questions 16 and 17 are to be answered in accordance with the following paragraph.

Steam cleaners get their name from the fact that steam is used to generate pressure and is also a by-product of heating the cleaning solution. Steam itself has little cleaning power. It will melt some soils, but it does not dissolve them, break them up, or destroy their clinging power. Rather surprisingly, good machines generate as little steam as possible. Modern surface chemistry depends on a chemical solution to dissolve dirt, destroy its clinging power, and hold it in suspension. Steam actually hinders such a solution, but heat helps its physical and chemical action. Cleaning is most efficient when a hot solution reaches the work in heavy volume.

16. In accordance with the above paragraph, for MOST efficient cleaning,

    A. a heavy volume of steam is needed
    B. hot steam is needed to break up the soils
    C. steam is used to dissolve the surface dirt
    D. a hot chemical solution should always be used

17. With reference to the above paragraph, the steam in a steam cleaner is used to

    A. generate pressure
    B. create by-product chemicals
    C. slow down the chemical action of the cleaning solution
    D. dissolve accumulations of dirt

18. An electromechanical regulator for an automotive alternator differs from a DC generator in that the alternator regulator

    A. has a current regulator unit
    B. has a reverse current relay
    C. does not have a current regulator unit
    D. does not have a voltage regulator unit

19. Of the following statements concerning the charging of lead acid batteries, the one MOST NEARLY correct is that

    A. a fast charge (40-50 amp, 12V) can safely be used if the battery temperature does not exceed 185° F
    B. heavily sulphated batteries respond best to a slow charging rate
    C. a battery on trickle charge cannot be damaged by overcharging
    D. the higher the battery temperature, the smaller the charging current with constant applied voltage

20. The ignition points of a conventional ignition system are adjusted to increase the point gap.
    This adjustment will

    A. increase the dwell angle
    B. retard the ignition timing

C. advance the ignition timing
D. decrease the dwell angle with no change in ignition timing

21. A single diaphragm distributor vacuum advance unit

    A. advances the spark under part throttle operation
    B. is connected to the intake manifold
    C. advances the spark in proportion to engine speed
    D. advances the spark during acceleration or full throttle operation

21.___

22. The part of a conventional ignition system that could properly be considered part of BOTH the primary and secondary circuits would be the

    A. condenser   B. distributor rotor
    C. coil   D. ignition points

22.___

23. As compared to a conventional type of spark plug, a resistor type of spark plug will

    A. reduce the inductive portion of the spark
    B. lengthen the capacitive portion of the spark
    C. require a higher voltage to function properly
    D. have an auxiliary air gap

23.___

24. If the criterion that limits the yearly major repair expenses to 30% of the current value of equipment were reduced to 15% and the depreciation rate of 20% of original cost each year were increased to 25%, the expenses for major repairs in a shop handling a constant flow of equipment of the same type and age would

    A. decrease   B. remain the same
    C. increase slightly   D. increase markedly

24.___

Question 25.

DIRECTIONS: Question 25 is to be answered in accordance with the following paragraph.

The storage battery is a lead-acid, electrochemical device used for storing energy in its chemical form. The battery does not actually store electricity, but converts an electrical charge into chemical energy which is stored until the battery terminals are connected to a closed external circuit. When the circuit is closed, the chemical energy inside the battery is transformed back into electrical energy through a chemical action, and, as a result, current flows through the circuit.

25. According to the above paragraph, a lead-acid battery stores

    A. current   B. electricity
    C. electrical energy   D. chemical energy

25.___

26. A cam is to be fashioned from a circular disc with a hole drilled eccentrically on a diameter of the disc but perpendicularly to the surface of the disc. A keyed shaft is to be fitted into the hole so that the disc may be rotated in order to function as a cam.
    If the disc is 5 inches in diameter and 1/2 inch thick and the hole is to be 1 inch in diameter, the distance from the center of the disc to the center of the hole to be drilled in order for the disc to act as a cam with a 2 inch lift should be _____ inch(es).

    A. 2   B. 1 1/2   C. 1   D. 1/2

26.___

27. Sparks and open flames should be kept away from batteries that are being charged because of the danger of explosion or fire resulting from the ignition of the generated _____ gas.

   A. fluorine   B. nitrogen   C. hydrogen   D. argon

28. Safety standards indicate that the use of any motor vehicle equipment having an obstructed view to the rear

   A. requires a reverse signal alarm audible above the surrounding noise level
   B. requires the use of two back-up lights of at least 45 watt capacity each
   C. requires the use of a safety contact alarm rear bumper audible above the surrounding noise level
   D. is prohibited

29. In the performance of a compression test, it is found that the addition of a tablespoon of SAE 40 motor oil causes no significant increase in the low compression pressure. The low compression pressure is most probably NOT caused by

   A. a broken piston   B. a leaking head gasket
   C. sticking valves   D. worn piston rings

30. Automotive exhaust gas analyzers, as generally used in emission control maintenance, will NORMALLY indicate the percentage of

   A. NO   B. SO_2 C. CO_2 D. CO

Questions 31-33.

DIRECTIONS: Questions 31 through 33 are to be answered in accordance with the information given below.

For most efficient utilization of funds and facilities, the rule has been established that the repair cost of a part cannot exceed 50% of the vendor's price for a new part and that a part cannot be made in-house if the cost would be more than 70% of the vendor's price for a new one.

You have found that the average removed sprocket shaft, as shown below, requires both bearing sections to be built up and remachined and one sprocket section to be built up and remachined. The foreman of the machine shop has given you the following information relative to the manufacture or repair of the shafts:

	Time	Rate
Weld 1 bearing section	1.2 hours	$8/hr.
Weld 1 keyway and sprocket section	2.0 hours	$8/hr.
Turn 1 bearing section	0.6 hours	$8/hr.
Turn 1 sprocket section	0.7 hours	$8/hr.
Cut 1 keyway	0.5 hours	$8/hr.

Purchasing has quoted shaft material at $12/ft. and new shafts at $160 each.

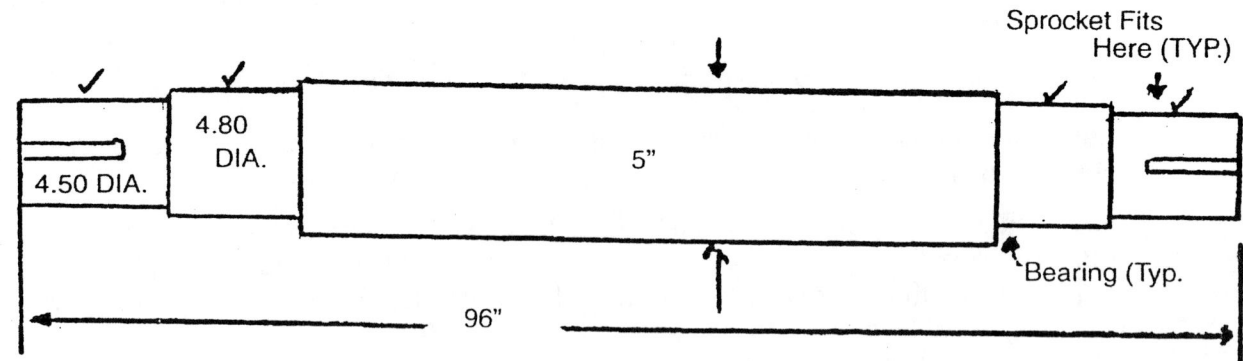

31. In accordance with the information given above, the cost for in-house manufacture of one shaft is

    A. $110.40   B. $112.00   C. $124.80   D. $132.60

32. In accordance with the information given above, the cost of in-house repair of one shaft is

    A. $68.40   B. $54.40   C. $30.40   D. $14.40

33. In accordance with the information given above, the PROPER procedure to follow, under the given rules, is to

    A. repair old shafts and buy new shafts
    B. repair old shafts and make new shafts
    C. make no repairs but make new shafts
    D. make no repairs but buy new shafts

34. The series of small vertical oscillations in the area of the center of a superimposed pattern on the screen of a properly adjusted oscilloscope showing the secondary circuit of a properly tuned automotive engine directly follows the instant at which the

    A. spark plugs fire   B. points open
    C. points close   D. coil starts to discharge

35. A rectangularly shaped repair facility for light trucks is 160 feet wide and 260 feet long. A 10 foot space is provided along each wall for benches and equipment. A 60 foot wide area in the middle of the floor is to remain clear for its entire 260 foot length. The entrance to the shop is at one end of this open area. Assuming that there are no columns to contend with, the MAXIMUM area available for parking of trucks is _____ square feet.

    A. 15,600   B. 19,200   C. 26,000   D. 41,600

36. A criterion is established that limits the yearly major repair expenses to 30% of the current value of the equipment. Equipment is depreciated at a rate of 20% of its original cost each year. A truck purchased on January 1, 2000 for $9,000 had a reconditioned engine installed in February 2003 at a total cost of $900.
    The amount of money available for additional major repairs on this truck in 2003 was

    A. none   B. $180   C. $360   D. $720

37. Twenty carburetors are ordered for your shop by the purchasing department. The terms are list, less 30% less 10%, less 5%.
If the list price of a carburetor is $70 and all terms are met upon delivery, the charges to your budget will be

   A. $1359.60   B. $1085.40   C. $837.90   D. $630.80

37.____

38. The cylinders of an 8 cylinder automotive engine have a bore of 4 inches and the pistons have a stroke of 4 inches. If the clearance volume in each cylinder is 6.0 cubic inches, the cubic inch displacement of the engine is MOST NEARLY

   A. 306   B. 354   C. 402   D. 450

38.____

39. An automotive engine cylinder has a bore of 4 inches and its pistons have a stroke of 4 inches.
If the clearance volume in the cylinder is 6.0 cubic inches, the compression ratio is MOST NEARLY

   A. 10.62:1   B. 9.37:1   C. 8.37:1   D. 7.62:1

39.____

40. Of the following deficiencies found during the inspection of passenger car brakes for issuance of a State Certificate of Inspection, the one that would be cause for REJECTION of the car brakes is that

   A. there is less than 3/64 in. of lining remaining above the drum brake shoe lining rivet heads
   B. the master cylinder brake fluid level is anything less than full
   C. the brake drums have been found to be more than .020 inches oversize
   D. the brake pedal reserve is less than one-half the total possible travel

40.____

41. When checking a fuel pump for proper operation, it is ALWAYS necessary to

   A. connect a vacuum gage to the fuel line between the pump and the carburetor
   B. make the vacuum test before the pressure test
   C. set the gages at floor level to maintain a consistent reference point
   D. make a vacuum test if the pressure or volume test results are not up to specification

41.____

42. On a single cylinder 4 stroke cycle internal combustion engine equipped with a flywheel magneto, the ignition points open at the end of the _____ strokes.

   A. intake and the compression
   B. compression and the exhaust
   C. power and the compression
   D. intake and the power

42.____

43. An impulse coupling is MOST usually found in

   A. an automatic transmission
   B. a limited slip differential
   C. the front axle of 4 wheel drive vehicles
   D. a magneto

43.____

8 (#1)

Questions 44-45.

DIRECTIONS: Questions 44 and 45 are to be answered in accordance with the following paragraph.

You have been instructed to expedite the fabrication of four special salt spreader trucks using chassis that are available in the shop. All four trucks must be delivered before the opening of business on December 1, 2005. Based on workload and available hours, the foreman of the body shop indicates that he could manufacture one complete salt spreader body in five weeks, with one additional week required for mounting and securing each body to the available chassis. No work could begin on the body until the engines and hydraulic components, which would have to be purchased, were available for use. The purchasing department has promised delivery of engines and hydraulic components three months after the order is placed. (Assume that all months have four weeks and the same crew is doing the assembling and manufacturing.)

44. With reference to the above paragraph, assuming that the purchasing department placed the order at the beginning of the first week in February 2005 and ultimate delivery of the engines and components was delayed by six weeks, the date of completion of the first salt spreader truck would be CLOSEST to the end of the _____ week in _____, 2005.

    A. fourth; July
    B. second; August
    C. fourth; August
    D. first; September

45. With reference to the above paragraph, the LATEST date that the engines and associated hydraulic components could be requisitioned in order to meet the specified deadline would be CLOSEST to the beginning of the _____ week in _____, 2005.

    A. first; February
    B. first; March
    C. third; March
    D. first; April

46. In an OHV internal combustion engine, excessive inlet valve guide clearance manifests itself initially by

    A. lowered cylinder compression pressure
    B. excessive oil consumption
    C. increased manifold vacuum
    D. fluffy black deposits on spark plugs

47. One of your mechanics has performed an automotive fuel system test and reports a fuel flow of 1/2 pint/minute at 500 rpm, a static fuel pump discharge pressure of 6 psi, and a 15 in.Hg vacuum at the pump inlet flex line.
These results should suggest to the mechanic that

    A. the system was operating properly
    B. he should check for a leaking pump inlet flex line
    C. he should replace the defective fuel pump
    D. check for a plugged inlet fuel line

9 (#1)

48. An electrician is wiring a light switch on a light truck. The light switch will operate the following lamp bulbs: 48.____

Quantity	No.	Description	Current (each)
2	194	Marker	.3
3	67	Clearance	.4
2	1157	Stop/tail	2.1/ .6
2	1141	Front park	1.5
2	6012	Headlamp	4.2/3.4

The parking lamps are to be on when the headlamps are on.
If the permissible current capacities of wire are

    16 gage   0 - 6 amp
    14 gage   6 - 15 amp
    12 gage   15 - 20 amp
    10 gage   20 - 25 amp

the smallest size wire that the electrician should use to supply power to the switch would be a _____ gage wire.

  A. 16   B. 14   C. 12   D. 10

49. In an automotive cooling system, the bypass passage or bypass valve 49.____

  A. permits a small amount of coolant to pass around the thermostat to maintain circulation
  B. permits the circulation of coolant through the engine block when the thermostat is closed
  C. directly connects the pump inlet to the pump discharge to prevent cavitation in the pump
  D. prevents the coolant in the system from developing excessive pressure

50. When adjusting a recirculating ball worm-and-nut steering gear, it is IMPROPER procedure to 50.____

  A. remove the pitman arm before making adjustments
  B. loosen the lash adjustment before checking bearing preload
  C. make the pitman shaft gear over center adjustment with the steering wheel in the center of travel position
  D. adjust the bearing preload with the steering wheel in the center of travel position

KEY (CORRECT ANSWERS)

1. B	11. A	21. A	31. C	41. D
2. D	12. C	22. C	32. B	42. B
3. C	13. B	23. A	33. A	43. D
4. D	14. D	24. A	34. C	44. A
5. A	15. A	25. D	35. B	45. B
6. D	16. D	26. C	36. B	46. B
7. D	17. A	27. C	37. C	47. D
8. C	18. C	28. A	38. C	48. B
9. A	19. B	29. D	39. B	49. B
10. A	20. C	30. D	40. B	50. D

EXAMINATION SECTION
TEST 1

DIRECTIONS: Each question or incomplete statement is followed by several suggested answers or completions. Select the one that BEST answers the question or completes the statement. *PRINT THE LETTER OF THE CORRECT ANSWER IN THE SPACE AT THE RIGHT.*

1. Excessive black exhaust smoke on a bus diesel engine is LEAST likely to be caused by

    A. a clogged air cleaner
    B. an air leak in the suction line between supply pump and tank
    C. improper timing of injectors
    D. leaking injection nozzles

2. Fuel tanks on a bus are vented in order to

    A. release fuel fumes
    B. reduce the temperature of the fuel
    C. prevent fuel leaks
    D. prevent a vacuum from forming in the tank

3. A tachometer is an instrument used for checking engine

    A. pressure   B. speed   C. timing   D. noise

4. Compared to a gasoline engine, the compression ratio of a bus diesel engine is GENERALLY

    A. one fourth as much   B. one half as much
    C. approximately the same   D. considerably higher

5. The presence of water in the fuel system of a bus diesel engine would MOST probably result in

    A. frequent engine stalling   B. sticking valves
    C. overspeeding of the engine   D. cylinder head hot spots

6. In the case of buses operating without anti-freeze, inhibitor should be placed in the engine cooling system when

    A. the engine runs hot
    B. the engine runs too cool
    C. the cooling system is refilled after a complete draining
    D. pressure builds up in the cooling system

7. Reverse flow flushing is a process which is used to clean out a(n)

    A. rear end housing   B. transmission housing
    C. engine cooling system   D. engine crankcase

8. In a diesel bus, if the starter cranks the engine at normal speed, but the engine fails to start, a POSSIBLE cause could be

    A. a plugged air cleaner   B. a weak battery
    C. a broken drive pinion gear   D. heavy engine oil

9. In engine maintenance, a compression gage is used to check

   A. engine vacuum
   B. oil pressure
   C. intake manifold pressure
   D. cylinder pressure

10. The normal voltage reading of each individual cell of a bus battery should be APPROXIMATELY _____ volts.

   A. 1   B. 2   C. 3   D. 6

11. For proper operation of a bus diesel engine, the coolant temperature should be APPROXIMATELY

   A. 100° F   B. 125° F   C. 165° F   D. 212° F

12. Levelling valves are used on buses in the

   A. torque converters
   B. air glide suspension system
   C. air brake system
   D. hydraulic control system

13. In a GM diesel engine, the air blower furnishes air under pressure for

   A. combustion in the engine
   B. cooling the cylinder walls
   C. increasing pressure of the fuel
   D. cooling the converter lubricant

14. In a GM diesel engine, the ports provided in the engine cylinder walls are MAINLY for

   A. the admission of intake air
   B. the admission of lubricating oil
   C. cooling the engine
   D. cleaning the cylinder

15. A LIKELY cause for excessive fuel consumption by a bus diesel engine would be

   A. faulty injectors
   B. high lubricating oil level
   C. emergency stop in full OFF position
   D. a completely plugged fuel tank cap

16. If a maintainer accidentally splashed a radiator cleaning solution on himself, the BEST immediate first aid procedure would be to

   A. apply vaseline
   B. blow the solution off the skin with an air hose
   C. rinse the solution off with large quantities of water
   D. wrap the affected area with a cloth without rinsing

17. With a standard measuring micrometer, starting with a zero reading, one complete revolution of the sleeve will give a reading of

   A. .250"   B. .100"   C. .050"   D. .025"

18. If the diameter of a shaft is required to be 2.125 inches plus or minus .006 inches, then the shaft will be satisfactory if it has a diameter of _____ inches.

    A. 1.525   B. 2.065   C. 2.118   D. 2.130

19. Gears which mesh together are ALWAYS designed to have

    A. one weak tooth to prevent shaft breakage if the gears jam
    B. a certain amount of backlash for proper running of the gears
    C. an idler in the gear assembly to distribute the gear load
    D. a definite amount of runout on the gear faces to prevent gear noise

20. Before checking toe-in and camber, it is good practice to

    A. place wheels in extreme left or right position
    B. place bus on a slight incline
    C. check tires for correct air pressure
    D. jack up the front end of the bus to reduce the wheel load

21. Of the following, the MOST likely cause of overheating in a bus diesel engine would be

    A. water thermostat opening at too low a temperature
    B. water thermostat removed
    C. improper timing
    D. holes in the exhaust muffler

22. In a bus air brake system, the quick release valve is for the purpose of speeding up the

    A. intake of air pressure into the brake chambers
    B. release of excess pressure from the main air reservoir
    C. exhaust of air pressure from the brake chambers
    D. filling up of the main air reservoir

23. Grease on a brake lining would PROBABLY result in

    A. smooth even braking   B. reducing brake lining failure
    C. wheel bearing failure   D. erratic braking

24. The lower the S.A.E. viscosity rating of a lubricating oil, the

    A. heavier it is
    B. fewer the impurities present
    C. easier it will flow at low temperatures
    D. harder it will be to start a bus engine

25. The MAIN reason for making a *stall test* on a bus is to

    A. obtain an overall performance check of engine and transmission under maximum load
    B. simply obtain the minimum speed at which the engine will idle without stalling
    C. obtain a check on the quality of fuel being used
    D. determine only if the valves are operating properly

26. Bad main bearings on a bus diesel engine would MOST likely be caused by

   A. engine idling
   B. excessive engine speed under load
   C. high crankcase oil level
   D. a leaking exhaust manifold

27. If a bus voltage regulator is set too low, the MOST likely result would be

   A. damage to the starter motor
   B. damage to the generator
   C. a run down battery
   D. damage to the regulator

28. Valve lash should be checked with a(n)

   A. feeler gauge
   B. micrometer
   C. machinist's scale
   D. inside caliper

29. Worn gears on a bus diesel engine fuel pump are LIKELY to cause

   A. high lubricating oil consumption
   B. lack of fuel supply to the engine
   C. blue exhaust smoke
   D. excessive crankcase pressure

30. The drag link is a part of the bus

   A. injector system
   B. brake system
   C. steering mechanism
   D. transmission

31. Squealing brakes on a bus could be caused by

   A. worn brake shoe lining
   B. excessive slack in the brake slack adjuster
   C. low pressure in the air tank
   D. dry brake lining

32. A DESIRABLE safety feature which is provided on buses is that the electrical circuit of the starter motor

   A. becomes inoperative when the passenger doors are opened
   B. becomes inoperative if the battery is not fully charged
   C. will operate only if the shift lever is in neutral
   D. will operate only if the bus engine is at normal operating temperature

33. If the intake screen on the lubricating oil pump on a bus diesel engine is clogged, the result would PROBABLY be

   A. low lubricating oil prezssure
   B. high lubricating oil pressure
   C. high lubricating consumption
   D. excessive crankcase pressure

34. In a GM diesel bus, if the engine is idling and the No. 1 injector follower is held down with a screwdriver and there is no noticeable difference in the sound and operation of the engine, then this is a DEFINITE indication that

    A. this cylinder is firing properly
    B. the remaining cylinders are not firing properly
    C. the idling speed is too high
    D. this cylinder is not firing properly

35. On a GM bus diesel engine a manometer is LEAST likely to be used to check _____ pressure.

    A. crankcase
    B. exhaust back
    C. air box
    D. lubricating oil

36. The BASIC difference between a gasoline engine and a diesel engine is in the method of

    A. filtering the fuel
    B. lubricating the engine
    C. cranking the engine
    D. igniting the fuel

37. The blower pressure in a GM diesel engine depends upon the

    A. air compressor speed
    B. engine speed
    C. setting of the air compressor governor
    D. setting of the air safety valve

38. The generators in the newer buses are self-rectifying a.c. generators. These generators

    A. have high output at low engine speeds
    B. feed a.c. to the bus batteries
    C. have commutators
    D. are lubricated with gear oil

39. On a GM diesel bus, the starting battery cable should be disconnected before working on the air blower rotors.
    The MAIN reason for doing this is to

    A. prevent excessive battery drain
    B. protect the starting motor
    C. prevent personal injury
    D. protect the air box

40. A hydrometer has a scale calibrated to read battery

    A. power
    B. current
    C. voltage
    D. specific gravity

KEY (CORRECT ANSWERS)

1. B	11. C	21. C	31. A
2. D	12. B	22. C	32. C
3. B	13. A	23. D	33. A
4. D	14. A	24. C	34. D
5. A	15. A	25. A	35. D
6. C	16. C	26. B	36. D
7. C	17. D	27. C	37. B
8. A	18. D	28. A	38. A
9. D	19. B	29. B	39. C
10. B	20. C	30. C	40. D

TEST 2

DIRECTIONS: Each question or incomplete statement is followed by several suggested answers or completions. Select the one that BEST answers the question or completes the statement. *PRINT THE LETTER OF THE CORRECT ANSWER IN THE SPACE AT THE RIGHT.*

1. A bearing removed from a bus is tagged R.R.O. for identification. This would indicate that the bearing is PROBABLY a _____ bearing.   1.____

   A. wheel B. converter
   C. fan D. compressor

2. In order to change front wheel toe-in, the adjustment is made on the   2.____

   A. stop screws B. tied rod
   C. steering knuckles D. king pins

3. When making a systematic engine tune-up on a GM bus diesel engine then, after adjusting valve lash, the very NEXT step should be to   3.____

   A. adjust the buffer screw
   B. time the fuel injectors
   C. adjust the injector control racks
   D. adjust the engine idling speed

4. On a GM hydraulic drive the fluid level should be checked once EVERY _____ miles.   4.____

   A. 3,000 B. 6,000
   C. 9,000 D. 12,000

5. A LIKELY cause for a bus diesel engine missing on one cylinder would be   5.____

   A. an obstruction in the muffler
   B. a warped engine valve
   C. water in the fuel tank
   D. clogging of the air cleaner

6. On a GM diesel engine, the emergency stop solenoid   6.____

   A. opens a valve which blows air into the engine
   B. moves the governor cam to the fuel position
   C. actuates the low oil pressure switch
   D. releases a choke valve to shut off air to the engine

7. If a bus battery constantly requires an excessive amount of distilled water, a check should be made of the   7.____

   A. battery ground connection
   B. vent holes in the battery plugs
   C. voltage reading of each cell
   D. voltage regulator

8. The MOST important reason for not testing the injection nozzle spray against the hands is that

   A. the pressure cannot be accurately judged
   B. it may puncture the skin and cause blood poisoning
   C. a true spray pattern would not be obtained
   D. the fuel would spatter widely

9. Of the following, the BEST measurement of a maintainer's ability to do his job properly is

   A. the opinion of his helper
   B. freedom from accidents
   C. performance of assigned work with little supervision
   D. speed in doing a job

10. Hard steering on a bus is LEAST likely to be caused by

    A. over-inflated front tires
    B. improper adjustment of steering gear worm bearing
    C. improper adjustment of sector shaft lash
    D. under-inflated tires

11. Inspection of engine pistons and rings through the cylinder wall ports CANNOT be made on _____ buses.

    A. GM 4510
    B. GM 5106
    C. GM 5301
    D. Mack C-49

12. If you have completed a certain bus maintenance job which you feel is O.K., but your foreman asks you to make certain changes in the job, it would be BEST for you to

    A. request the foreman to assign this work to another maintainer
    B. ask the foreman the reason for the changes
    C. have your helper verify that the job was done properly
    D. complain to the supervisor on this waste of time

13. Some timing gears have punch marks on their teeth to

    A. designate the idling gear
    B. assure proper installation
    C. indicate the gear is worn beyond use
    D. indicate the gear has been properly hardened

14. If a fellow maintainer brings you verbal instructions from the foreman on how to do a certain repair job, and you are unable to fully understand these instructions, then it would be BEST for you to

    A. check with another maintainer
    B. delay the job until the foreman comes to ask you about it
    C. see the foreman personally to clear the matter up
    D. read the manufacturer's maintenance manual on this job

15. When lifting the bus body of the Mack C-49 buses with a hoist or chain fall, special lifting blocks are used on the rebound rods.
    This precaution is NECESSARY in order to prevent damage to the

    A. axle   B. bus body   C. air bags   D. transmission

16. In a diesel engine, if fuel oil leaks into the engine cylinder head, then it is MOST likely that damage will result to the

    A. fuel pump
    B. governor
    C. engine bearings
    D. fuel injectors

17. On a GM coach with hydraulic V drive, a LIKELY cause for engine underspeeding would be

    A. a slipping hydraulic clutch
    B. that the accelerator linkage is preventing full rack positioning
    C. slipping of the everrunning clutch
    D. aerated and foaming hydraulic fluid

18. To check for variation in engine cylinder bore, the PROPER instrument to use is a(n)

    A. outside caliper
    B. dial indicator gauge
    C. No-Go gauge
    D. vernier caliper

19. In the Mack C-49 bus, the plungers of the injection pump are lubricated with

    A. fuel oil
    B. engine lubricating oil
    C. a mixture of fuel oil and lubricating oil
    D. oil from the injection pump sump

20. On GM 5301 buses, a regular pneumatic door engine is used

    A. only on the front doors
    B. only on the rear doors
    C. on both the front and rear doors
    D. on neither the front or rear doors

21. If a partly distorted bus front axle forging is to be straightened, it would be good practice to

    A. apply heat to the axle before straightening in order to make the job easier
    B. apply heat to the axle after straightening in order to make the axle stronger
    C. apply heat only during the straightening process because that is when it is the most useful
    D. straighten the axle without any heat in order to retain the original strength of the axle

22. One ADVANTAGE of an engine cooling system which is sealed and which utilizes a pressure release valve is that

    A. rust and corrosion are reduced
    B. the engine will reach operating temperatures more quickly
    C. the boiling point of the cooling liquid is raised
    D. leaks in the cooling system are prevented

23. A bus maintainer repeatedly performs an important maintenance procedure incorrectly. In this situation it would be MOST correct to conclude that the

    A. procedure is probably too difficult for the average maintainer
    B. written instructions for this job are incorrect
    C. foreman is exercising poor supervision
    D. maintainer is ill

24. In the GM 4510 bus engine, if one end of a rubber hose is connected to the fuel return manifold and the other end of the hose is placed into a container, with the engine running at about 1200 RPM, then foam appearing in the container would MOST probably indicate

    A. excessive fuel pump pressure
    B. insufficient fuel pump pressure
    C. that air is being pumped through the fuel system
    D. that the viscosity of the fuel is not correct

25. On buses having a water temperature indicator system consisting of a sending unit screwed into the engine water outlet and an electrical registering gauge, it is not advisable to use thread sealing compound on the sending unit MAINLY because the compound will

    A. cause clogging of the cooling system
    B. make it difficult to remove the sending unit
    C. short-circuit the sending unit
    D. increase the electrical resistance of the circuit

26. If you are a maintainer and a bus helper assigned to work under you turns out a normal day's output even though he spends considerable time during working hours talking to his co-workers, then it would be BEST for you to

    A. ignore his actions as long as his output is up to standard
    B. tell him that you will bring him up on charges
    C. instruct the other workers to steer clear of him
    D. give him more work so he has less time to talk

27. Assume you are instructed by your foreman on the procedure to use in performing a special rush job. Unforeseen difficulties arise which force you to change the procedure and not finding it possible to contact your foreman, you proceed on the new basis. When your foreman appears, he complains that you have not followed orders.
    In this case it would be BEST for you to

    A. say nothing and when he leaves, complete the job using your procedure
    B. make a formal complaint to the assistant supervisor
    C. tell the foreman he is to blame because he was not around
    D. explain the situation to the foreman

28. A good procedure to follow before applying artificial respiration to a fellow worker who has been overcome by carbon monoxide fumes and whose breathing has stopped is to

    A. check his mouth for the presence of any foreign objects
    B. give him a strong stimulant
    C. massage his legs
    D. use smelling salts

29. Vapor lock is MORE apt to occur on a gasoline engine than on a diesel engine because

   A. the gasoline engine has an electrical ignition system
   B. gasoline is more volatile than fuel oil
   C. the diesel engine uses injectors to spray the fuel into the cylinders
   D. the diesel engine operates at higher temperatures

30. The GM hydraulic drive employs a heat exchanger. The purpose of this heat exchanger is to

   A. warm the transmission oil
   B. cool the transmission oil
   C. warm the engine
   D. cool the engine

31. The newer GM buses have transistor type regulators. These regulators do NOT contain any

   A. relays   B. diodes   C. condensers   D. resistors

32. On a GM 4510 bus, if rear axle noise is experienced only when the bus is coasting, the trouble is MOST likely that

   A. there is a dragging brake
   B. the tires are unevenly inflated
   C. excess lubricant is present in the differential
   D. the differential pinion and ring gear are out of adjustment

33. When fitting a cylinder head to a cylinder block, it is NECESSARY to

   A. remove material only from the cylinder block
   B. tighten all head bolts as much as possible
   C. always use a double gasket to compensate for unevenness
   D. keep the amount of material removed from the cylinder head and the cylinder block within certain limits

34. When inspecting the main bearings of a GM diesel engine, if the backs of the bearing shells have bright spots, it will indicate that the

   A. bearings have overheated
   B. shells must be reground undersize
   C. shells are in good condition
   D. bearing shells have shifted in their supports

35. On a bus, a speed control valve is used on the

   A. door engines   B. transmission
   C. fuel pump   D. brake system

36. In the GM 5301 bus, the electrical circuit having the highest voltage is the one feeding the _____ lights.

   A. fluorescent   B. head
   C. tell-tale   D. directional

37. On a bus with hydraulic drive, the upshift speed can be changed by adjusting the
    A. engine governor
    B. transmission governor
    C. throttle air cylinder
    D. clutch air cylinder

38. In a GM fuel injector, the plunger is rotated by the motion of the
    A. injector rack
    B. rocker arm
    C. filter spring
    D. follower stop pin

39. On a bus diesel engine, combustion leakage into the cooling system could be caused by
    A. leakage in the water pump
    B. a defective cylinder head gasket
    C. a leak in the cooling system suction hose
    D. low level of coolant

40. The LEAST likely cause for loss of compression in a bus diesel engine would be
    A. worn cylinders
    B. broken piston rings
    C. an inoperative fuel pump
    D. defective exhaust valves

KEY (CORRECT ANSWERS)

1. A	11. D	21. D	31. A
2. B	12. B	22. C	32. D
3. B	13. B	23. C	33. D
4. A	14. C	24. C	34. D
5. B	15. C	25. D	35. A
6. D	16. C	26. D	36. A
7. D	17. B	27. D	37. B
8. B	18. B	28. A	38. A
9. C	19. A	29. B	39. B
10. A	20. A	30. B	40. C

EXAMINATION SECTION
TEST 1

DIRECTIONS: Each question or incomplete statement is followed by several suggested answers or completions. Select the one that BEST answers the question or completes the statement. *PRINT THE LETTER OF THE CORRECT ANSWER IN THE SPACE AT THE RIGHT.*

1. The MAIN function of the breather tube which is commonly located on the top of an automobile gasoline engine is to

    A. limit the amount of unburned hydrocarbon exhaust emission
    B. filter impurities from the engine oil
    C. prevent a buildup of gas pressure in the crankcase
    D. indicate the level of oil remaining in the crankcase

    1.____

2. In a typical bus air conditioning system, heat is removed from the recirculated air as it passes over an evaporator located underneath the floor.
   The MOST heat is removed while the refrigerant is changing from a _____ to a _____.

    A. liquid; solid
    B. liquid; vapor
    C. vapor; liquid
    D. vapor; solid

    2.____

3. Assume that a maintainer is to replace a worn ring gear on a bus rear axle differential unit.
   Of the following, a procedure which he SHOULD follow is to

    A. heat the bearings with a torch when removing the ring gear
    B. file all chipped teeth on the drive pinion and reinstall the ring gear
    C. adjust for increased backlash after replacing the ring gear
    D. replace the ring gear and drive pinion with a matched set

    3.____

4. A 0.001 inch feeler gauge fits snugly between a cylinder wall and piston when the piston is making contact with the other side of the cylinder wall.
   If the cylinder bore is 4.250 inches, then the diameter of the piston is MOST NEARLY

    A. 4.245" B. 4.249" C. 4.252" D. 4.260"

    4.____

5. A maintainer finds that the toe-in measures 3/8 inch on a certain bus.
   If the specification for the bus calls for a toe-in of 3/16", then the maintainer should make the necessary adjustment to _____ the toe-in by _____.

    A. *decrease*; 3/32"
    B. *increase*; 3/32"
    C. *decrease*; 3/16"
    D. *increase*; 3/16"

    5.____

6. A MAJOR difference between primary and secondary wiring in an automobile ignition system is that the

    A. primary wiring has a heavier layer of insulation than the secondary wiring
    B. secondary wiring has a heavier layer of insulation than the primary winding
    C. primary wiring is better for carrying spark plug voltages than the secondary wiring
    D. secondary wiring is better for carrying battery voltage than the primary wiring

    6.____

2 (#1)

7. Assume that a maintainer has pushed his finger through the matching holes in two different plates which must be aligned and clamped.
   This practice of using his finger to align the two metal plates is a

   A. *good* practice, mainly because he has the most control when his finger is in the holes
   B. *good* practice, mainly because a finger is the best tool for aligning mating parts
   C. *poor* practice, mainly because this could easily lead to injury to his finger
   D. *poor* practice, mainly because he will need both hands free to hold the pieces for clamping

8. While performing routine inspection and maintenance of an automotive vehicle, it would be PROPER for a maintainer to add ethylene glycol to the

   A. battery in order to increase the electrical charge
   B. cooling system in order to prevent freezing
   C. fuel tank in order to remove water condensate
   D. lubricating oil in order to reduce air pollution

9. While repairing an automobile engine, a maintainer has occasion to inspect certain journals for wear.
   A journal is that part of a

   A. bearing which presses onto a shaft
   B. gear which presses onto a shaft
   C. shaft which rides in a bearing
   D. housing which accepts a retaining ring

10. The SAE number of an engine oil indicates its

    A. cetane number B. octane number
    C. vapor pressure D. viscosity

11. If a maintainer inspects a hydraulic brake master cylinder and finds that the cylinder walls are scored, he may recondition the cylinder by

    A. honing the cylinder walls
    B. etching the cylinder walls with acid
    C. wire brushing the cylinder walls to remove the marks
    D. relining the cylinder walls with babbitt

12. A maintainer should wear safety goggles while he

    A. aligns the front end of a bus
    B. adjusts the valve backlash on a diesel engine
    C. changes the air filters on a bus air conditioning system
    D. charges a bus air conditioning system with a freon type refrigerant

13. The wear between a bus differential ring gear and drive pinion will be least when they are properly adjusted. One method used by maintainers to determine whether the ring gear and pinion are *properly* adjusted is to check for proper

    A. torque with a dynamometer
    B. bearing lubrication
    C. tooth contact

D. runout of the ring gear

14. Of the following, the condition which would MOST likely result in pre-ignition in an automobile gasoline engine is that

    A. the engine is cold
    B. the engine is overheated
    C. there is a coating of oil on the breaker points
    D. the condenser across the breaker points is defective

15. Of the following, the condition which would MOST likely result in an excessive rate of charge from an alternator is that the

    A. field is grounded
    B. brushes are worn
    C. slip rings are burned
    D. charging circuit is open

16. While making a compression test on a gasoline engine, a maintainer should mount the compression gage into

    A. the intake manifold
    B. a spark plug hole
    C. the tailpipe
    D. the fuel line

17. Assume that while running a vacuum check on a certain engine, a maintainer finds that the vacuum drops from 20 inches to 5 inches at regular intervals.
    Of the following, the MOST likely cause for a regular drop of this magnitude is that the

    A. carburetor mounting flange gasket is leaking
    B. carburetor idle mixture is adjusted incorrectly
    C. ignition timing is retarded
    D. head gasket is blown

18. Automobile gasoline engines sometimes stall because of *vapor lock.*
    One way to prevent *vapor lock* stalls is to

    A. adjust the carburetor for a rich fuel mixture
    B. maintain the proper level of oil in the engine crank-case
    C. preheat the oil in the engine crankcase
    D. shield the fuel line from excessive engine heat

19. If the valve in an automobile positive crankcase ventilation system becomes plugged, the MOST likely result is that the engine will

    A. idle roughly
    B. increase rpm at idle
    C. increase blowby at idle
    D. backfire into the intake manifold

20. Of the following, the MOST likely cause of frequent stalling of an automobile gasoline engine is that the

    A. clutch is slipping
    B. carburetor is dirty
    C. piston rings are worn
    D. battery cable connections are loose

21. Of the following, the instrument which a maintainer should use for checking concentricity of the valve guide and valve seat on an automobile engine is a

    A. dial indicator
    B. feeler gage
    C. radius gage
    D. tapered plug gage

22. In order to bleed air from a hydraulic brake system, a maintainer should depress the brake pedal slowly *after*

    A. disconnecting the master cylinder
    B. removing the master cylinder end plug
    C. removing the rubber boots from one wheel cylinder
    D. unscrewing a valve at each wheel

23. If a vehicle equipped with hydraulic brakes and a dual master cylinder (double piston) should develop a leak in the rear right wheel cylinder, the result is likely to be that the brake action is *defective* on

    A. all four wheels
    B. the two wheels on the right side
    C. the two wheels in the rear
    D. the rear right wheel only

24. If a maintainer observes a pool of reddish fluid under an automobile that has been parked for a long time, which of the following components is MOST likely at fault?

    A. Rear main bearing
    B. Crankcase
    C. Shock absorber
    D. Automatic transmission

Questions 25-30.

DIRECTIONS: Questions 25 through 30, inclusive, are based on the sketch of a relay circuit shown on the next page. Consult this sketch when answering these questions.

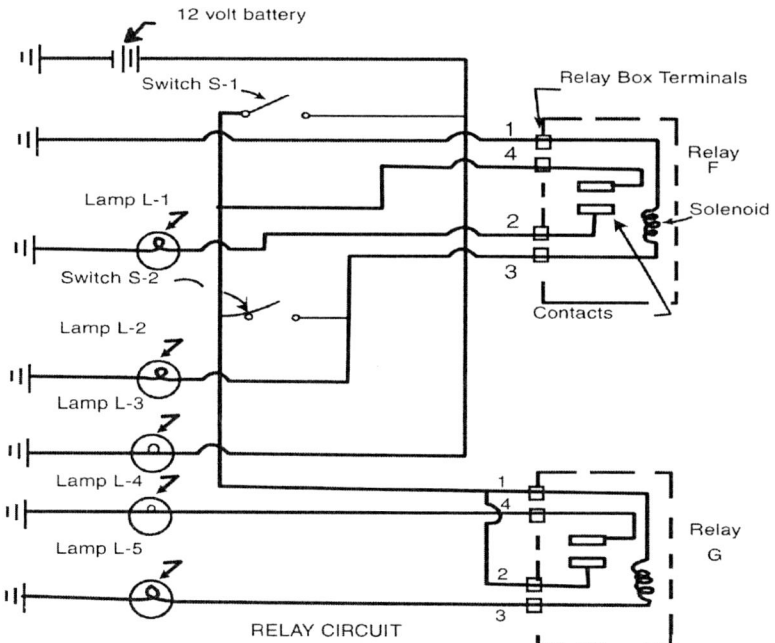

RELAY CIRCUIT

25. If Switch S-1 and Switch S-2 are both *open*, the condition of the lamps will be such that _____ is lit.

    A. only Lamp L-2
    B. only Lamp L-3
    C. only Lamp L-5
    D. none of the lamps

26. If Switch S-1 is *open* and Switch S-2 is *closed*, the condition of the contacts of both relays is such that the contacts of Relay

    A. F are *closed* while those of Relay G are *open*
    B. G are *closed* while those of Relay F are *open*
    C. F and Relay G are both *closed*
    D. F and Relay G are both *open*

27. If Switch S-2 is *open* and Switch S-1 is *closed*, the condition of the lamps will be such that ONLY Lamp

    A. L-1 is lit
    B. L-3 is lit
    C. L-1, Lamp L-2, and Lamp L-3 are lit
    D. L-3, Lamp L-4, and Lamp L-5 are lit

28. If Switch S-1 and Switch S-2 are both *closed*, the condition of the contacts of both relays is such that the contacts of Relay

    A. F are *closed*, while those of Relay G are *open*
    B. G are *closed*, while those of Relay F are *open*
    C. F and Relay G are both *closed*
    D. F and Relay G are both *open*

29. If Lamp L-5 is burned out, then with both Switches S-1 and S-2 *closed*, the condition of the lamps will be such that ONLY Lamp

    A. L-1 is lit
    B. L-3 is lit
    C. L-1, Lamp L-2, and Lamp L-3 are lit
    D. L-3 and Lamp L-4 are lit

30. A maintainer can use a meter to check the proper performance of Relay G if he closes Switch S-1 and connects a(n) _____ across Terminals _____.

    A. ohmmeter; 1 and 2
    B. ohmmeter; 2 and 3
    C. voltmeter; 1 and 3
    D. voltmeter; 2 and 4

KEY (CORRECT ANSWERS)

1.	C	16.	B
2.	B	17.	D
3.	D	18.	D
4.	B	19.	A
5.	C	20.	B
6.	B	21.	A
7.	C	22.	D
8.	B	23.	C
9.	C	24.	D
10.	D	25.	B
11.	A	26.	D
12.	D	27.	D
13.	C	28.	C
14.	B	29.	C
15.	A	30.	D

TEST 2

DIRECTIONS: Each question or incomplete statement is followed by several suggested answers or completions. Select the one that BEST answers the question or completes the statement. *PRINT THE LETTER OF THE CORRECT ANSWER IN THE SPACE AT THE RIGHT.*

1. On an automobile gasoline engine ignition system which is equipped with a vacuum advance mechanism, when the engine manifold vacuum is suddenly decreased, the result SHOULD be that the _____ of the spark is _____.   1._____

    A. timing; advanced
    B. timing; decreased
    C. intensity; increased
    D. intensity; decreased

2. While tuning an engine having a conventional ignition system, a maintainer should use a timing light in order to   2._____

    A. adjust the ballast resistor to the proper setting
    B. check the ignition coil for proper polarity
    C. set the proper spark plug gap
    D. position the distributor cam at the proper setting

3. A full floating-type rear axle is an axle which serves   3._____

    A. only to drive the wheels
    B. only to support the wheels
    C. both to support and drive the wheels
    D. to support the wheels, to retain the wheels, and also to drive the wheels

4. A manifold heat control valve on an automobile gasoline engine is a valve which   4._____

    A. provides a temperature signal to the dashboard indicator
    B. increases the amount of fuel to the engine at higher speeds
    C. warms up the fuel mixture in the manifold while the engine is cold
    D. reduces the amount of fresh air supplied to the intake manifold while engine is cold

5. Intake and exhaust valves in an automobile gasoline engine are held closed by   5._____

    A. hydraulic lifters
    B. mechanical lifters
    C. compression springs
    D. tension springs

6. After completing a road test on a vehicle, a maintainer observed that the brake drum on one wheel was abnormally cool.
From this observation, the maintainer should suspect that the trouble is   6._____

    A. an inoperative brake
    B. an out-of-round drum
    C. a worn brake lining
    D. the presence of grease or brake fluid on the lining

7. A piece of equipment that is commonly used on automobiles and is composed of such parts as yokes, struts, release levers, pressure springs, and pilot bearings is a   7._____

    A. clutch assembly
    B. differential unit
    C. torque converter
    D. power steering unit

8. Of the following, the condition which would MOST likely cause an automobile starter to crank too slowly is that the

   A. breaker points are welded together
   B. main engine bearings are seized
   C. water pump impeller is loose
   D. battery cable connections are loose

Questions 9-14.

DIRECTIONS: Questions 9 through 14, inclusive, are matching questions based on Columns I and II below. For each type of automotive mechanical problem listed in Column I, select the condition described in Column II which is the MOST likely cause of this type of problem.

COLUMN I	COLUMN II
9. Steering is erratic	A. Toe-in is incorrect
10. Tires are scuffed on one edge only	B. Tire pressure is too high
11. Car rides hard	C. Tire pressure is too low
12. Tires are worn in the center of the treads	D. Wheel bearings are worn
13. Tires squeal on turning corners	
14. Wheels are noisy	

15. A maintainer is to tighten the cylinder head stud nuts on the head of a six-cylinder V-type diesel engine as shown in the sketch at the right.
Of the following, the sequence which the maintainer should follow in drawing the nuts and bolts down to proper torque is

    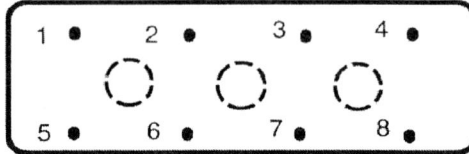

    A. 1, 2, 3, 4, 5, 6, 7, 8
    B. 1, 5, 4, 8, 2, 6, 3, 7
    C. 7, 2, 6, 3, 8, 1, 5, 4
    D. 7, 4, 1, 8, 5, 2, 6, 3

16. While conducting a road test of a certain vehicle, a maintainer finds that the hydraulic brakes fail to slow the vehicle when the foot pedal is depressed.
If he finds that the pedal feels soft and spongy when depressed, he should inspect the vehicle for

    A. a loose wheel bearing
    B. a frozen master cylinder
    C. grease on the brake lining
    D. air in the hydraulic lines

17. Of the following, the condition which would MOST likely result in the overcharging of a battery in an automobile electrical system is that

    A. the voltage regulator coil is open
    B. the starter motor draws too much current

C. the water level in the battery cells is too low
D. there is excessive resistance in the charging circuit

18. Of the following, the condition which would MOST likely result in grabbing of hydraulic brakes is that

    A. there is air in the hydraulic lines
    B. there is a leak in the hydraulic lines
    C. the wheel bearings are too loose
    D. a wheel cylinder piston is frozen

18.____

19. Assume that while servicing an automobile storage battery a maintainer has spilled battery acid on his hand.
    Of the following, the BEST first-aid practice is for the maintainer to

    A. remove the acid by wiping his hand with a dry towel
    B. flush the acid off his hand with a large quantity of water
    C. wash the acid off his hand with a large quantity of gasoline
    D. spread ointment over the acid and cover it with a clean dressing

19.____

20. A maintainer can perform an engine compression test on a diesel engine in order to determine

    A. the no-load speed of the engine
    B. the condition of the valves and piston rings
    C. the torque of the engine at maximum load
    D. how closely the injectors have been calibrated and matched

20.____

21. Of the following, the condition which would MOST likely cause excessive pressure in the crankcase of a diesel engine is that the

    A. piston rings are severely worn
    B. gears in the fuel pump are severely worn
    C. exhaust back pressure is excessively low
    D. pressure in the engine cooling system is excessively high

21.____

22. The compressor of a bus air conditioning system is equipped with unloader mechanism on two cylinders.
    Of the following, the MOST important function of these unloaders is to

    A. regulate the compressor lubricating oil pressure
    B. reduce the pressure in these cylinders at start-up
    C. regulate the pressure of the air supplied to the bus coach interior
    D. empty the refrigerant receiver if the system pressure becomes excessive

22.____

23. In the operation of a diesel engine, fuel is introduced into the cylinder _____ stroke.

    A. at the beginning of the air intake
    B. just before the end of the compression
    C. after the beginning of the power
    D. just before the end of the exhaust

23.____

24. A driver reports that his bus's diesel engine is exhausting smoke and lacks power. Of the following, the MOST likely cause of the reported smoke condition is that the

    A. exhaust pipe is partially blocked
    B. fuel mixture is too lean
    C. governor speed setting is too high
    D. blower is supplying too much intake air

25. If a bus diesel engine is cranked at normal speed and still will not start, the one of the following conditions which is MOST likely the cause is that

    A. the compression ratio is too low
    B. the injector timing is incorrect
    C. the injection pump pressure is too high
    D. an exhaust valve is leaking

KEY (CORRECT ANSWERS)

1.	B	11.	B
2.	D	12.	B
3.	A	13.	C
4.	C	14.	D
5.	C	15.	C
6.	A	16.	D
7.	A	17.	A
8.	D	18.	C
9.	A	19.	B
10.	A	20.	B

21.	A
22.	B
23.	B
24.	A
25.	B

TEST 3

DIRECTIONS: Each question or incomplete statement is followed by several suggested answers or completions. Select the one that BEST answers the question or completes the statement. *PRINT THE LETTER OF THE CORRECT ANSWER IN THE SPACE AT THE RIGHT.*

1. Of the following, the MOST likely cause for high *pop pressure* in diesel injector is that   1.____

    A. the fuel tank cap is plugged
    B. the fuel has a low cetane rating
    C. a valve spring is broken
    D. there is carbon in the spray tip holes

2. Of the following, the BEST method for cooling the injectors on a bus diesel engine is to   2.____

    A. spray the injectors with engine cooling water
    B. spray the injectors with engine lubricating oil
    C. pump fuel oil through the injectors
    D. pump intake air over the injectors

3. The BASIC difference between a gasoline engine and a diesel engine is in the method of   3.____

    A. igniting the fuel
    B. driving the crankshaft
    C. sealing the combustion chamber
    D. exhausting the combustion products

4.   4.____

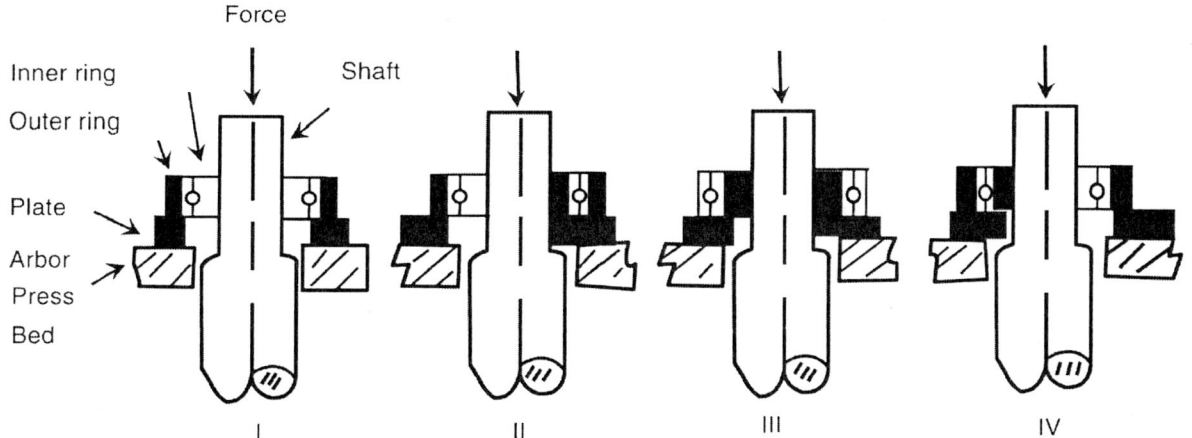

When a ball bearing is to be removed from a shaft, the CORRECT shop setup is the one shown in

    A. I   B. II   C. III   D. IV

5. The one of the following jobs for which a maintainer should wear safety goggles is   5.____

    A. pulling wheel bearings
    B. inspecting brake drums
    C. inspecting wheel bearings
    D. adjusting brake shoes

6. Of the following, the BEST method of locating a misfiring cylinder in a bus diesel engine is to

   A. crank the engine slowly by hand
   B. remove the cylinder head and observe the pistons
   C. loosen all the cylinder head nuts while running the engine
   D. loosen each injector nozzle while running the engine

7. A maintainer is to check a bus diesel engine for a possible piston slap condition.
   Of the following, the BEST time to check for piston slap is

   A. while the engine is still cold
   B. after the engine oil has been changed
   C. after new rings have been installed
   D. while adjusting the exhaust valve backlash

8. Assume that a maintainer has taken from the storage battery a specific sample of electrolyte which reads 1.125 at 105 degrees F.
   If 0.001 must be added to the hydrometer readings for each degrees above 80 degrees F in order to correct for temperature conditions, the corrected hydrometer reading should be MOST NEARLY

   A. 1.115   B. 1.125   C. 1.135   D. 1.425

9. The one of the following jobs which is BEST suited to the use of compressed air from a shop air supply is

   A. blowing the dust from brake drums
   B. blowing the dust from a maintainer's uniform
   C. speeding up the drying of newly painted surfaces
   D. putting out trash fires

10. Of the following operations to be performed on a newly overhauled engine, the one a maintainer should do FIRST is to

    A. crank the engine
    B. pressurize the lubrication system
    C. break in the engine on an engine dynamometer stand
    D. operate the engine at fast idle until the normal operating temperature is reached

11. Before a liquid fuel can burn efficiently in an internal combustion engine, it should be

    A. cooled   B. dehydrated
    C. filtered   D. atomized

12. A maintainer has requisitioned a repair kit which contains check valves, diaphragm, a diaphragm oil seal, and a gasket.
    Of the following, the equipment he will repair using this kit is MOST likely a(n)

    A. hydraulic brake master cylinder
    B. carburetor
    C. ignition distributor
    D. mechanical fuel pump

13. A fluid coupling, hydraulic servos, oil pumps, planetary gear sets, brake bands, and multiple disc clutches are ALL parts relating to an automotive   13.____

    A. engine
    B. hydraulic brake system
    C. power steering system
    D. automatic transmission

14. An internal gear, sun gear, and pinion carriers are ALL parts relating to an automobile   14.____

    A. rear end
    B. overdrive unit
    C. steering mechanism
    D. transmission synchronizer unit

15. Of the following, the automotive equipment which would MOST likely include needle bearings is a(n)   15.____

    A. air brake compressor
    B. engine camshaft
    C. drive train slip joint
    D. transmission universal joint

16. A maintainer should straighten a bent connecting rod by   16.____

    A. turning it between centers on an engine lathe
    B. applying force to it with a hydraulic press
    C. heating it with an oxyacetylene torch
    D. pressing it between the jaws of a machinist's vise

17. A typical valve-in-head engine is classified as a(n) _____ engine.   17.____

    A. *F-head*   B. *I-head*   C. *L-head*   D. *T-head*

18. An overdrive unit attached to the rear of an automobile transmission will change the engine speed while maintaining the same road speed.   18.____
    If a car is shifted from third gear to overdrive at 50 miles per hour, the engine speed in overdrive will be MOST NEARLY _____ than the engine speed in third gear.

    A. 30% less
    B. 30% greater
    C. 60% greater
    D. 90% greater

19. Of the following, the condition which would MOST likely result in flooding of the carburetor is that   19.____

    A. the fuel filter is clogged
    B. the float level is too high
    C. there is no longer a vacuum in the fuel line
    D. the fuel pump linkage is worn

20. Assume that an automobile engine fails to warm up to normal operating temperature after 1/2 hour of operation. Of the following, the condition which would MOST likely result in below-normal engine temperature is that the   20.____

    A. fan drive belt is loose
    B. engine oil level is low
    C. thermostat is inoperative
    D. water pump impeller is slipping

21. Of the following, the condition which would MOST likely result in piston slap is that the

    A. cylinders are worn
    B. flywheel is loose
    C. rocker arms are sticking
    D. tappet clearance is incorrect

22. Of the following, the condition which would MOST likely result in wheel shimmy is that the

    A. shock absorbers are defective
    B. brake linings are glazed
    C. propeller shaft is bent
    D. rear seal is leaking

23. The four *principal* parts of a tapered roller bearing are the _____, and rollers.

    A. addendum, dedendum, face
    B. cage, cone, cup
    C. journal, separator, sleeve
    D. plate, spacer, spider

24. The air brake system on a bus should be balanced so that all brakes are applied concurrently.
    The component which provides for the rapid application of the rear brakes is the rear brake

    A. relay valve
    B. exhaust valve
    C. low-air-pressure switch
    D. pressure-protection switch

25. Of the following, the sequence which represents the CORRECT firing order for a six-cylinder engine is

    A. 1, 2, 3, 4, 5, 6
    B. 1, 3, 5, 2, 4, 6
    C. 1, 4, 2, 5, 3, 6
    D. 1, 5, 3, 6, 2, 4

KEY (CORRECT ANSWERS)

1. D
2. C
3. A
4. C
5. A

6. D
7. A
8. C
9. A
10. B

11. D
12. D
13. D
14. B
15. D

16. B
17. B
18. A
19. B
20. C

21. A
22. A
23. B
24. A
25. D

WORK SCHEDULING
EXAMINATION SECTION
TEST 1

DIRECTIONS: Each question or incomplete statement is followed by several suggested answers or completions. Select the one that BEST answers the question or completes the statement. *PRINT THE LETTER OF THE CORRECT ANSWER IN THE SPACE AT THE RIGHT.*

Questions 1-7.

DIRECTIONS: Questions 1 through 7 are to be answered SOLELY on the basis of the instructions and chart given below.

The following WORK ASSIGNMENT CHART is used by Mary B. Steiner, a supervisor, to keep track of the work performed by the five data entry operators under her supervision. When Ms. Steiner receives work for processing, she enters the Work Batch number, date and time in the appropriate columns. She then assigns the work for entry and enters the name of the operator in the *Entered* column. After the work is punched, Ms. Steiner assigns an operator to verify the work and enters that operator's name in the *Verified* column. When the work has been verified, which completes the processing, Ms. Steiner indicates the completion date and time in the appropriate columns and places her initials in the *Completed* column. The five operators whom Ms. Steiner supervises are L. Hopkins, M. Thomas, A. Smith, T. Day, and B. Hanes, and their workday is from 9:00 A.M. to 5:00 P.M.

Work Batch Number	Date In	Time In	Data Entered	Verified	Date Out	Time Out	Completed
L-7103	12/1	9:05 AM	L. Hopkins	T. Day	12/1	3:45 PM	S.K.J.
L-7104	12/1	9:15 AM	M. Thomas	B. Hanes	12/1	4:30 PM	S.K.J.
L-7105	12/1	10:30 AM	A. Smith	T. Day	12/2	3:30 PM	S.K.J.
L-7106	12/1	3:30 PM	T. Day	L. Hopkins	12/2	10:35 AM	S.K.J.
L-7107	12/1	4:30 PM	B. Hanes	M. Thomas	12/2	3:45 PM	S.K.J.
M-7108	12/2	10:30 AM	L. Hopkins	B. Hanes	12/2	2:10 PM	S.K.J.
M-7109	12/2	10:45 AM	A. Smith	L. Hopkins	12/2	4:15 PM	S.K.J.
M-7110	12/2	2:30 PM	B. Hanes	A. Smith			
M-7111	12/2	3:45 PM	T. Day	M. Thomas			
M-7112	12/2	3:30 PM	M. Thomas	T. Day	12/3	5:00 PM	S.K.J.

1. According to the above chart, which of the following Work Batches has NOT yet been verified?

   A. L-7103   B. M-7108   C. M-7110   D. M-7112

2. Based on the above chart, the Work Batch which was completed LAST on 12/2 is Batch

   A. M-7112   B. M-7109   C. M-7107   D. M-7104

2 (#1)

3. Of the Work Batches which were received on 12/1, the one which took the SHORTEST period of time to process is Batch

   A. L-7103   B. L-7104   C. L-7106   D. L-7107

3.____

4. Based on the information contained in the above chart, which of the following is a CORRECT statement?
   Operators _____ did the data entry or verifying of Batch _____.

   A. Day and Smith; M-7111
   B. Hopkins and Hanes; M-7109
   C. Hopkins and Thomas; L-7107
   D. Smith and Day; L-7105

4.____

5. Of the Work Batches received on 12/2, the one which has been completed and took the LONGEST period of time to process is Batch

   A. M-7112   B. M-7111   C. M-7109   D. L-7107

5.____

6. According to the above chart, Work Batch M-7109 was verified by Operator _____ and entered by Operator _____.

   A. Hanes; Hopkins   B. Smith; Hanes
   C. Hopkins; Smith   D. Smith; Hopkins

6.____

7. Based on the information contained in the above chart, which of the following is a CORRECT statement?
   Only Operators _____ did the data entry or verifying of
   Batches _____.

   A. Hopkins and Day; L-7103 and M-7108
   B. Day and Thomas; M-7111 and M-7112
   C. Hopkins and Hanes; M-7108 and M-7110
   D. Hanes and Thomas; M-7107 and M-7112

7.____

KEY (CORRECT ANSWERS)

1. C
2. B
3. C
4. D
5. A
6. C
7. B

TEST 2

Questions 1-10.

DIRECTIONS: Questions 1 through 10 are to be answered SOLELY on the basis of the information given below and the two tables which follow. Some of the questions require taking into consideration the information in one or both of the two tables and in the following paragraphs. No question relates to a previous question.

As a General Park Foreman, R. Carson has been newly assigned to Undulant Memorial Park, District 841. The schedules have been made up by the previous General Park Foreman for the week of June 30 to July 6. The park has 500 acres of grass, a wooded picnic area of 200 acres, 4 comfort stations, a surfaced playground area for children, *10 tennis courts, 2 baseball diamonds, 4 softball diamonds, 6 basketball courts, and 100 acres of additional wooded area which are being converted to picnic grounds. The conversion of the wooded area is to be completed by July 4th.*

The roster of personnel assigned to District 841 includes 1 General Park Foreman, 2 Park Foremen, 9 Laborers, 4 Attendants (whose activities are restricted to the tennis courts and locker rooms), and 12 Seasonal Park Helpers. The equipment assigned to District 841 includes 1 pickup truck, 1 dump truck, 1 tractor and grass cutting attachment, 2 Toro mowers, and 2 hand mowers.

The operating requirements (weekly scheduled operations which must be met) for District 841 include a daily morning garbage pickup for the picnic area, a twice weekly pickup Monday and Friday for the rest of the District, and a weekly walking pickup of the entire area on Thursday (see Table II). A garbage pickup of the picnic area takes 4 hours and requires the use of 3 men and a dump truck. The garbage pickup for the rest of the district requires the use of that crew for an additional 3 hours. The walking pickup takes 8 hours and requires the use of 6 men and a pickup truck.

The hours of operation for all facilities in District 841 are 8 A.M. to 9 P.M. Seasonal Park Helpers are scheduled to work 6 days per week, and employees in all other titles are scheduled to work 5 days per week. One hour is given for lunch or supper.

TABLE I
TIME SCHEDULE

Dept. of Parks
District: 841
Periods: From June 23 to June 29
Park: Undulant Memorial Park

Title	Sat. 6/23	Sun. 6/24	Mon. 6/25	Tues. 6/26	Wed. 6/27	Thurs 6/28	Fri. 6/29
General Park Foreman	8-5	8-5	8-5	8-5	8-5		
Park Foreman		8-5	8-5	8-5		8-5	8-5
Park Foreman	1-9		1-9		1-9	1-9	1-9
Laborers 3*	8-5			8-5	8-5	8-5	8-5
Laborers 3		8-5	8-5	8-5	8-5	8-5	
Laborers 3	1-9		1-9		1-9	1-9	1-9
Seasonal Park Helper 3	8-5		8-5	8-5	8-5	8-5	8-5
Seasonal Park Helper 3		8-5	8-5	8-5	8-5	8-5	8-5
Seasonal Park Helper 3	1-9		1-9	1-9	1-9	1-9	1-9
Seasonal Park Helper 3		1-9	1-9	1-9	1-9	1-9	1-9
Attendant 2	10-6	10-6	10-6	10-6	10-6		
Attendant 2	10-6	10-6			10-6	10-6	10-6

LEGEND
*Number of employees in that title on that time schedule
8-5 Tour of duty from 8 A.M. to 5 P.M. (8-hour shift)
1-9 Tour of duty from 1 P.M. to 9 P.M. (7-hour shift)
10-6 Tour of duty from 10 A.M. to 6 P.M. (7-hour shift)

TABLE II
OPERATING REQUIREMENTS
MEN

Equipment	Sat. 6/23	Sun. 6/24	Mon. 6/25	Tues. 6/26	Wed. 6/27	Thurs. 2/68	Fri. 6/29
Pickup Truck						6 / 8	
Dump Truck	3 / 4	3 / 4	3 / 7	3 / 4	3 / 4	3 / 4	3 / 7

LEGEND

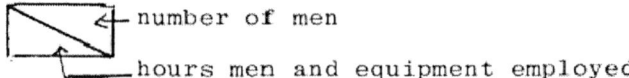

– number of men
– hours men and equipment employed

1. A man using the tractor with grass-cutting attachment can cut an average of ten acres of grass per hour; with a Toro mower, 4 acres per hour; and with a hand mower, 1 acre per hour. Only 250 of the 400 acres of grass can be cut with the tractor.
The total number of <u>man-hours</u> (one man-hour is defined as one hour of work for one man) it will take to cut all 500 acres of grass using all the available machinery simultaneously is MOST NEARLY

    A. 50   B. 100   C. 125   D. 200

2. The conversion of the wooded area to picnic grounds is complete except for the installation of 100 additional picnic tables. It is estimated that this project requires the use of a pickup truck and 2 men for 40 hours. Because this is a priority item, it will be worked on during all the hours the park is open.
   If the project must be completed by Friday noon for the 4th of July holiday, considering that the operating requirements listed in Table II must be met, we would expect the project to begin

   A. Saturday afternoon
   B. Sunday morning
   C. Monday afternoon
   D. Tuesday afternoon

3. Assuming that all the operating requirements must be met, of the following the day on which there will NOT be a sufficient number of men available to install baseball and softball backstops, a project requiring the simultaneous use of 8 men for 7 hours, is

   A. Saturday
   B. Monday
   C. Thursday
   D. Friday

4. It has become obvious that the dump truck is in need of repairs. These repairs will take two days, during which time the truck cannot be used. However, the pickup truck can be substituted for the dump truck in picking up the garbage, but requires twice the time to perform this operation.
   Of the following, the day on which the dump truck should be entered for repairs, if the operating requirements are to be met, is

   A. Monday
   B. Tuesday
   C. Wednesday
   D. Thursday

5. Excluding the General Park Foreman and the Park Foremen, Attendants, and those scheduled for a garbage pickup, the number of man-hours available for assignment on Monday is

   A. 79
   B. 105
   C. 114
   D. 135

6. The number of man-hours expended in meeting the operating requirements during the one-week period ending June 29 is

   A. 130
   B. 150
   C. 200
   D. 250

7. In making out the schedule for this week, the previous General Park Foreman neglected to assign enough men for Sunday, June 24, to set up benches for a concert to be given the following Monday. It is estimated that this project requires 85 man-hours and must be completed by closing hours Sunday evening.
   To complete this project and fulfill the operating requirements, the number of ADDITIONAL men for an 8-5 (8 hr.) shift that must be reassigned to work on Sunday is

   A. 1
   B. 2
   C. 3
   D. 4

8. There is a 120-acre section of grass which requires earlier than usual cutting because of its low-lying, well-watered location. This section can only be cut by the Toro power mowers, which cut four acres per hour, and the hand mowers, which cut one acre per hour. Assume that one of the Toro power mowers is in the repair shop.
   The number of ADDITIONAL hours it will take to cut this 120-acre section of grass using the remaining grass-cutting machinery (in comparison with using all of the Toro power mowers and hand mowers) is

   A. 8
   B. 10
   C. 12
   D. 20

9. Of those Laborers and Seasonal Park Helpers scheduled to work on Friday, the percent- 9.___
age that is employed in fulfilling the operating requirements is MOST NEARLY

   A. 8.2   B. 16.6   C. 23.8   D. 37.5

10. For scheduling purposes, the General Park Foreman must 10.___
know how long it will take to complete the garbage collection on Monday, June 25, if both the dump truck and the pickup truck are used.
If the pickup truck takes twice as long as the dump truck in collecting garbage, the number of hours it takes to collect the garbage using both trucks is MOST NEARLY

   A. 2.1   B. 3.2   C. 4.7   D. 6.3

KEY (CORRECT ANSWERS)

1. C
2. C
3. A
4. B
5. C
6. B
7. D
8. A
9. B
10. C

TEST 3

Questions 1-10.

DIRECTIONS: Questions 1 through 10 are to be answered SOLELY on the basis of the information given below in the two charts and the RULES OF THE DEPARTMENT. You are to assume that you are the dispatcher in the garage where these charts are kept and where they are used in making daily assignments of operators and vehicles.

SECOND AVE. GARAGE MOTOR VEHICLE OPERATOR CONTROL SHEET
Date: May 25

Name of Operator	Cleared On	Hours of Overtime Credit as of May 25	On Vacation
Allen	P T	74	....
Boyd	P W	31	5/18-30
Cohen	P T	129	....
Diggs	P	15	....
Egan	P T	92	6/1-13
First	P T W	49	....
Gordon	P	57	....
Hanson	P T	143	6/15-27

Symbols: P - Passenger Car
T - Truck
W - Wrecker

SECOND AVE. GARAGE MOTOR VEHICLE OPERATOR CONTROL SHEET
Date: May 25

Vehicle Number and Type	In Repair Shop as of May 25	Date Due in Shop for Preventive Maintenance Inspection	Date Last In Repair
20-P		7/13	3/2
21-P		6/15	2/16
22-T		5/26	1/19
23-P		6/1	5/8
24-P		6/8	2/2
25-P		7/6	2/24
26-W		6/1	1/21
27-T		7/20	4/6
28-T	X	7/27	3/16
29-P	X	5/18	1/12

RULES OF THE DEPARTMENT

1. A motor vehicle operator may be assigned to drive only those types of vehicles on which he has been cleared. No one but a motor vehicle operator may be assigned to drive a Department vehicle.

2. Private cars may not be used for Department business.

3. The motor vehicle dispatcher shall keep a daily record of overtime credits of all operators under his supervision to be sure that no operator acquires more than 150 hours of overtime credit. An assignment which involves overtime should be given, wherever possible, to the operator with the least overtime credit.

4. A vehicle due for preventive maintenance must be sent to the repair shop on the date it is due for preventive maintenance, except when a vehicle has been in the repair shop during the previous month.

5. All available vehicles are to be assigned to jobs as requested, with none held in reserve.

1. An official who is requesting a truck and operator for the three days beginning May 26th indicates to you that some overtime may be necessary for the operator, but he cannot predict how many hours of overtime will be needed.
   Under these circumstances, the MOST logical man for you to choose for this assignment would be operator
   A. Allen   B. Boyd   C. Diggs   D. First

2. The vehicle which does NOT have to be sent to the shop for preventive maintenance on the date it is due is vehicle number
   A. 23   B. 25   C. 27   D. 29

3. As dispatcher, you receive a request on May 25th for a truck and motor vehicle operator for a job that will take three days, from May 26th through May 28th.
   The vehicle that it would be BEST for you to choose on May 25th for this assignment is vehicle number
   A. 28   B. 27   C. 22   D. 20

4. On May 25th, right after all the vehicles have left the garage on daily assignment, you receive a call from your Commissioner's secretary. She tells you that an emergency has come up and asks you for a car to be ready in fifteen minutes to take a messenger with important papers to be delivered to the Commissioner who is waiting for the papers at a court in another borough.
   Of the following, the BEST thing for you to do, after explaining to the secretary that you have no cars available, is to
   A. advise her she should give you advance notice the next time so that you can reserve a car for the messenger
   B. offer to drive the messenger yourself in your private car
   C. promise to get a car from another department
   D. suggest that the messenger use public transportation

5. To give you more leeway in assigning your operators to the available equipment, it would be MOST practical for you to
   A. ask your supervisor to assign two additional motor vehicle operators to the garage
   B. have additional operators cleared on the wrecker
   C. suggest to your supervisor that Rule 3 be abolished
   D. suggest to your supervisor that Rule 1 be abolished

6. Other things being equal, the operator who should probably be of MOST value to you, as the dispatcher, is
   A. Cohen   B. Diggs   C. First   D. Hanson

7. The factor which indicates MOST strongly that there may not be enough operators assigned to this garage is the
   A. amount of overtime accumulated
   B. excess of number of vehicles over number of operators
   C. incomplete vacation schedule
   D. number of operators cleared on trucks

8. When dispatching men and equipment in the morning, it would be BEST for you to first dispatch men who

    A. are cleared on 1 vehicle
    B. are cleared on 2 vehicles
    C. are cleared on 3 vehicles
    D. have already had their vacations

9. The second week in June, you receive a call for an operator and wrecker. It is better to dispatch Boyd rather than First because

    A. he has already had his vacation
    B. he has less overtime
    C. he is not cleared on trucks
    D. unless there are special reasons, you might as well assign the men in alphab order for easier record keeping

10. You have requests for 6 passenger cars and 2 trucks for jobs on May 25th. All of these jobs will probably take the full day but none will require any overtime. How many of these requests for May 25th would you have to refuse?

    A. None
    B. One
    C. Two
    D. More than two

KEY (CORRECT ANSWERS)

1. D
2. A
3. B
4. D
5. B
6. C
7. A
8. A
9. C
10. B

TEST 4

Questions 1-9.

DIRECTIONS: Questions 1 through 9 are to be answered SOLELY on the basis of the information given below and the schedule given on the following page.

This schedule is an incomplete and incorrect draft of the February work schedule for round-the-clock coverage in the telephone room. Your answers to the questions are based on the schedule as it is shown in its incomplete and incorrect form. The schedule is supposed to be based on the following guidelines.

1. There is one Senior Telephone Operator assigned to supervise each shift. There is an asterisk (*) preceding this person's name.

2. The telephone operator with the most seniority assumes the role of the Senior Telephone Operator when he(she) is not scheduled. There is a dash (-) preceding the person's name so designated for each shift.

3. For each shift, there must be either the Senior Telephone Operator or the designated substitute scheduled to work.

4. Each operator should have two consecutive days off weekly and work a maximum of two weekends per month.

5. There must be at least two operators assigned each day to the 8-4 and 4-12 shifts and at least one person to the 12-8 shift.

6. There must be one operator from both the 8-4 and 4-12 shifts scheduled to begin work 15 minutes prior to the regular shift starting time. When more than one operator is scheduled to work on the 12-8 shift, one of them should be assigned to begin work 15 minutes prior to the regular shift starting time.

7. The workload does not vary with the day of the week. It does vary according to the hour of the day, with the greatest load during the 8-4 shift.

8. The work week for the telephone room begins on Monday and ends on Sunday.

KEY TO LETTERS AND SYMBOLS ON SCHEDULE

V	= Vacation Day	M	= Monday
D	= Day Off	T	= Tuesday
#	= Report 15 minutes early	W	= Wednesday
*	= Senior Telephone Operator	Th	= Thursday
-	= Designated Alternate	F	= Friday
		Sa	= Saturday
		Su	= Sunday

1. D. Saturday and Sunday

2. The operator who is scheduled to work only one weekend during the month of February is

   A. Steven Epps
   B. Marjorie Esposito
   C. Michael Figueroa
   D. Michelle Li

3. According to the schedule in its present incomplete form, the days on which ALL operators on every shift are scheduled to be at work are February

   A. 2-3   B. 13-27   C. 22-23   D. 24-27

4. Which of the following is the MOST advisable way to schedule Rose Tucker on Thursday, February 11?

   A. 4   B. 4#   C. Vacation Day   D. Day Off

5. Which of the following choices lists ALL the operators on the 12-8 shift who are scheduled to work for more than five consecutive days during the month of February?

   A. Barbara Donovan and Steven Epps
   B. Steven Epps and Esther Porto
   C. Barbara Donovan and Esther Porto
   D. Anita Skinner and Steven Epps

6. According to the schedule in its present incomplete form, on which Wednesday in February is the GREATEST number of operators on the 8-4 shift scheduled to work? February

   A. 3   B. 10   C. 17   D. 24

7. An error has been made in the schedule in its present incomplete form. On a certain date, neither the Senior Telephone Operator nor the designated alternate, on the 8-4 shift, has been scheduled to work.
   The date on which this occurs is February

   A. 9   B. 12   C. 20   D. 26

8. According to the schedule in its present incomplete form, how many days in February are there in which the total number of operators, on all shifts, scheduled for either a vacation day or a day off is six or more?

   A. 2   B. 4   C. 5   D. 7

9. Which one of the following statements regarding the starting time of the Senior Telephone Operator assigned to the 8-4 shift is CORRECT?

   A. When the Senior Telephone Operator is scheduled to work, she is always scheduled to begin work early.
   B. The Senior Telephone Operator and her designated alternate rotate the early starting time between them with the Senior Telephone Operator scheduled for the early starting time more than half of her assigned work days.
   C. The Senior Telephone Operator and her designated alternate rotate the early starting time between them with her alternate scheduled for the early starting time more than half of her assigned work days.

D. The Senior Telephone Operator and her designated alternate rotate the early starting time, and each one is scheduled for the early starting time immediately following her two consecutive days off each week in February.

KEY (CORRECT ANSWERS)

1. D
2. B
3. C
4. B
5. B
6. A
7. D
8. C
9. B

TEST 5

Questions 1-7.

DIRECTIONS: Questions 1 through 7 are to be answered SOLELY on the basis of the schedule and information given below. Note that there is a blank column in the schedule which you may use in order to answer these questions.

DIRECTIONS FOR SCHEDULING

The schedule below has been filled in for three weeks of a four-week rotation schedule of the workers in a flatwork ironing department. The primary purpose of this schedule is to rotate employees at the feeding end of the flatwork ironer machine so that they spend no more than one week at a time at the feeding end because of the tiring nature of this work. There are five flatwork ironing machines, identified by letters as Machines A, B, C, D, and E. Each machine requires that two workers be located at the feeding end and one worker at the receiving end. There are twenty employees in the department. Those not operating the flatwork ironer machines during a particular week sort the linen before it is given to the employees at the flatwork ironing machines.

An additional purpose of this rotation is to acquaint employees in this flatwork department with the various tasks performed in the department. Therefore, ALL employees should be scheduled to sort linen, to work at the feeding end of the flatwork ironer, and to work at the receiving end of the flatwork ironer during the four-week schedule. Employees may be assigned to work at different machines from one week to another. However, it is essential that no employee is to be scheduled to work at the feeding end of the ironer for more than one week at a time.

SCHEDULE

	First Week	Second Week	Third Week	Fourth Week
MACHINE A Feeder #1 Feeder #2 Receiver	Jean Bracken Doris McCane Francis Luther	Francis Luther Carol Hayes Jean Bracken	Susan Rubel Estelle Hines Karen Sachs	
MACHINE B Feeder #1 Feeder #2 Receiver	Anita Keller Claire Mayo Carol Hayes	JoAnne Graham Mary Patton Doris McCane	Elaine Killman Barbara Lucas Rose Pulver	
MACHINE C Feeder #1 Feeder #2 Receiver	Linda Fontaine Anne Campbell JoAnne Graham	Pearl Miller Karen Sachs Anita Keller	Linda Fontaine Anne Campbell Louise Rogers	
MACHINE D Feeder #1 Feeder #2 Receiver	Elaine Killman Barbara Lucas Mary Patton	Louise Rogers Margaret Hays Claire Mayo	Doris McCane Claire Mayo Margaret Hays	
MACHINE E Feeder #1 Feeder #2 Receiver	Estelle Hines Susan Rubel Pearl Miller	Pat Turner Rose Pulver Linda Fontaine	Anita Keller Jean Bracken Pat Turner	
SORTERS	Karen Sachs Louise Rogers Margaret Hays Pat Turner Rose Pulver	Anne Campbell Elaine Killman Barbara Lucas Estelle Hines Susan Rubel	Francis Luther Carol Hayes JoAnne Graham Mary Patton Pearl Miller	

1. According to the chart, the one of the following who has worked at the feeding end of the machine for two out of the three weeks, but who has not yet worked at the receiving end, is

   A. Elaine Killman
   B. Pearl Miller
   C. Carol Hayes
   D. Rose Pulver

2. Which one of the following worked at the same flatwork ironing machine during the first and third weeks of the schedule?

   A. Anne Campbell
   B. Mary Patton
   C. Carol Hayes
   D. Pat Turner

3. According to the chart, which of the following employees are scheduled to work the feeding end of the flatwork ironing machine during the first and third weeks?

   A. Carol Hayes and Claire Mayo
   B. Louise Rogers and Karen Sachs
   C. Anne Campbell and Susan Rubel
   D. Francis Luther and Anita Keller

4. Which of the following employees should be scheduled to work the feeding end of the flatwork ironing machine during the fourth week?

    A. Barbara Lucas
    B. Estelle Hines
    C. Anita Keller
    D. Pearl Miller

5. In order to give each of the twenty employees an opportunity during the four weeks to do all of the three different tasks (work the feeding end of the machine, work the receiving end of the machine, and sort linen), which of the following employees MUST be scheduled to sort linen during the fourth week of the schedule?

    A. Doris McCane and Louise Rogers
    B. Jean Bracken and Estelle Hines
    C. Anita Keller and Margaret Hays
    D. Jean Bracken and Linda Fontaine

6. According to the chart, during the first three weeks, which one of the following employees has NOT yet sorted linen?

    A. Margaret Hays
    B. Susan Rubel
    C. Claire Mayo
    D. Carol Hayes

7. According to the above chart, during the first three weeks, which one of the following employees has NOT yet worked at the receiving end of the flatwork ironer?

    A. Mary Patton
    B. Linda Fontaine
    C. Pat Turner
    D. Barbara Lucas

KEY (CORRECT ANSWERS)

1. A
2. A
3. C
4. D
5. D
6. C
7. D

TEST 6

Questions 1-8.

DIRECTIONS: Questions 1 through 8 are to be answered SOLELY on the basis of the following scheduling problems, worksheet, and table.

To set up his work schedule for the coming year at a certain Ferry Terminal, the supervisor asked each man to give him a first and second choice for preferred days off during the week, and for his preferred shift. The supervisor made it clearly understood that the decisions as to days off would be made first and would be final, and that assignments to shift would be made afterward. He told them that all assignments would be made on the basis of their requests and that conflicts in requests would be resolved on the basis of seniority. No requests for change in either kinds of assignments would be considered after this submission of requests. The supervisor received from his men the information shown in the table below, REQUESTS FOR DAYS OFF AND SHIFTS. He then proceeded to make up his SCHEDULE OF ASSIGNMENTS on the basis of the requests made. A worksheet for the schedule of assignments follows.

SHIFT ARRANGEMENTS AND CONDITIONS OF WORK AT THE FERRY TERMINAL

1. A total of 8 men worked under the Ferry Terminal Supervisor.

2. Each man worked 40 hours a week, 8 hours a day for 5 days and had 2 days off per week.

3. There were three 8-hour shifts per day (8 AM to 4 PM, 4 PM to 12 Midnight, and 12 Midnight to 8 AM) to cover 320 man-hours per week (8 men multiplied by 40 hours).

4. Every shift had full coverage of 2 men at all times except for the 12-to-8 shift on Saturdays and Sundays, which had only one man.

5. Two men were off each weekday, and 3 men were off each Saturday and Sunday.

HOW THE WORKSHEET WAS USED AND THE SCHEDULE DRAWN UP

First, the supervisor decided what days off each man had, regardless of shift. Since requests were granted in order of seniority, he started by writing the name of the man with the highest seniority at the bottom of the two columns for the two days that that man wanted (see the worksheet). Michaels had the highest seniority, so his name was written at the bottom of the two columns for Saturday and Sunday. After this, the supervisor simply proceeded to assign the names at the bottom of the "day" columns, according to seniority two men off a day, except for Saturday and Sunday, when there were three men off. If a man could not get his choice of the first pair of days, he was given his second pair of days. If he could not get any choice because of low seniority, he was given what was left over. After filling in his schedule of days off by writing the names at the bottom of each "day" column, the supervisor made his assignments to shifts. He did this by writing in the column under SHIFT ASSIGNMENT the name of the person with the greatest seniority on the line of the shift requested by that man who, of course, was Michaels (as shown on the worksheet). The supervisor proceeded to fill in, as far as possible, all shift assignments, according to seniority. If the shift requested by a man was filled and could not be given to him, then his second choice was given to him, if (still) possible, under the seniority guidelines. Irregular shifts (different shifts each day) went to the men with the lowest seniority. The supervisor then used the worksheet to determine the schedule of days off, days on, and shift assignments. Michaels, the man with greatest seniority, as shown in the worksheet, had Saturday and Sunday off and worked in the 12-8 shift.

WORKSHEET

SHIFT	Monday	Tuesday	Wednesday	Thursday	Friday	Saturday	Sunday	Shift Assignment
8 AM to 4 PM								
4 PM to 12 Midnight								
12 Midnight to 8 AM	Michaels on	Michaels on	Michaels on	Michaels on	Michaels on	Michaels off / No Assignment	Michaels off / No Assignment	Michaels
Days Off →						Michaels	Michaels	

REQUESTS FOR DAYS OFF AND SHIFTS

Name	Appointment Date	1st Choice	2nd Choice	Requests For Shifts 1st Choice	2nd Choice
Anderson	1/7	Thurs. & Fri.	Wed. & Thurs.	8-4	4-12
Carlson	4/19	Wed. & Thurs.	Sun. & Mon.	12-8	8-4
Jackson	9/21	Sat. & Sun.	Fri. & Sun.	4-12	8-4
Davis	12/17	Fri. & Sat.	Sat. & Sun.	12-8	4-12
Michaels	3/10	Sat. & Sun.	Fri. & Sat.	12-8	8-4
Diaz	8/4	Sat. & Sun.	Thurs. & Fri.	12-8	8-4
Sullivan	10/11	Sun. & Mon.	Thurs. & Fri.	8-4	4-12
Marinello	6/13	Thurs. & Sat.	Mon. & Tues.	12-8	8-4

1. Of the following, the man who received the days off he requested in his first choice is

   A. Jackson   B. Davis   C. Anderson   D. Sullivan

1.___

2. Of the following, it would be MOST correct to state that, based on his requests for days off and shifts, Anderson was assigned his _____ choice of days off and his _____ choice of shift.

    A. first; first
    B. first; second
    C. second; first
    D. second; second

3. Of the following groups of men, the one in which all of the men work Sundays is

    A. Anderson, Davis, Marinello
    B. Sullivan, Diaz, Anderson
    C. Carlson, Jackson, Anderson
    D. Carlson, Anderson, Michaels

4. Which one of the following men received his second choice of work shift?

    A. Anderson   B. Sullivan   C. Diaz   D. Davis

5. One man who works a rotating shift is

    A. Sullivan   B. Davis   C. Jackson   D. Carlson

6. Two men who always work together on the same days and shift are

    A. Michaels and Diaz
    B. Sullivan and Marinello
    C. Jackson and Davis
    D. Carlson and Jackson

7. Which of the following men did NOT receive either his first or second choice of days off?

    A. Marinello   B. Sullivan   C. Davis   D. Anderson

8. Which one of the following men works the 4-12 Midnight shift on Saturday?

    A. Anderson   B. Davis   C. Jackson   D. Carlson

KEY (CORRECT ANSWERS)

1. B
2. C
3. A
4. D
5. A
6. A
7. B
8. C

EXAMINATION SECTION
TEST 1

DIRECTIONS: Each question or incomplete statement is followed by several suggested answers or completions. Select the one that BEST answers the question or completes the statement. *PRINT THE LETTER OF THE CORRECT ANSWER IN THE SPACE AT THE RIGHT.*

1. Which of the following is the MOST likely action a supervisor should take to help establish an effective working relationship with his departmental superiors?

    A. Delay the implementation of new procedures received from superiors in order to evaluate their appropriateness.
    B. Skip the chain of command whenever he feels that it is to his advantage.
    C. Keep supervisors informed of problems in his area and the steps taken to correct them.
    D. Don't take up superiors' time by discussing anticipated problems but wait until the difficulties occur.

2. Of the following, the action a supervisor could take which would *generally* be MOST conducive to the establishment of an effective working relationship with employees includes

    A. maintaining impersonal relationships to prevent development of biased actions
    B. treating all employees equally without adjusting for individual differences
    C. continuous observation of employees on the job with insistence on constant improvement
    D. careful planning and scheduling of work for your employees

3. Which of the following procedures is the LEAST likely to establish effective working relationships between employees and supervisors?

    A. Encouraging *two-way* communication with employees
    B. Periodic discussion with employees regarding their job performance
    C. Ignoring employees' gripes concerning job difficulties
    D. Avoiding personal prejudices in dealing with employees

4. Criticism can be used as a tool to point out the weak areas of a subordinate's work performance.
   Of the following, the BEST action for a supervisor to take so that his criticism will be accepted is to

    A. focus his criticism on the act instead of on the person
    B. exaggerate the errors in order to motivate the employee to do better
    C. pass judgment quickly and privately without investigating the circumstances of the error
    D. generalize the criticism and not specifically point out the errors in performance

5. In trying to improve the motivation of his subordinates, a supervisor can achieve the BEST results by taking action based upon the assumption that most employees

    A. have an inherent dislike of work
    B. wish to be closely directed
    C. are more interested in security than in assuming responsibility
    D. will exercise self-direction without coercion

6. When there are conflicts or tensions between top management and lower-level employees in any department, the supervisor should FIRST attempt to

    A. represent and enforce the management point of view
    B. act as the representative of the workers to get their ideas across to management
    C. serve as a two-way spokesman, trying to interpret each side to the other
    D. remain neutral, but keep informed of changes in the situation

7. A probationary period for new employees is usually provided in many agencies.
   The MAJOR purpose of such a period is *usually* to

    A. allow a determination of employee's suitability for the position
    B. obtain evidence as to employee's ability to perform in a higher position
    C. conform to requirements that ethnic hiring goals be met for all positions
    D. train the new employee in the duties of the position

8. An effective program of orientation for new employees usually includes all of the following EXCEPT

    A. having the supervisor introduce the new employee to his job, outlining his responsibilities and how to carry them out
    B. permitting the new worker to tour the facility or department so he can observe all parts of it in action
    C. scheduling meetings for new employees, at which the job requirements are explained to them and they are given personnel manuals
    D. testing the new worker on his skills and sending him to a centralized in-service workshop

9. In-service training is an important responsibility of many supervisors.
   The MAJOR reason for such training is to

    A. avoid future grievance procedures because employees might say they were not prepared to carry out their jobs
    B. maximize the effectiveness of the department by helping each employee perform at his full potential
    C. satisfy inspection teams from central headquarters of the department
    D. help prevent disagreements with members of the community

10. There are many forms of useful in-service training. Of the following, the training method which is NOT an appropriate technique for leadership development is to

    A. provide special workshops or clinics in activity skills
    B. conduct institutes to familiarize new workers with the program of the department and with their roles
    C. schedule team meetings for problem-solving, including both supervisors and leaders
    D. have the leader rate himself on an evaluation form periodically

11. Of the following techniques of evaluating work training programs, the one that is BEST is to 11._____

    A. pass out a carefully designed questionnaire to the trainees at the completion of the program
    B. test the knowledge that trainees have both at the beginning of training and at its completion
    C. interview the trainees at the completion of the program
    D. evaluate performance before and after training for both a control group and an experimental group

12. Assume that a new supervisor is having difficulty making his instructions to subordinates clearly understood. 12._____
    The one of the following which is the FIRST step he should take in dealing with this problem is to

    A. set up a training workshop in communication skills
    B. determine the extent and nature of the communications gap
    C. repeat both verbal and written instructions several times
    D. simplify his written and spoken vocabulary

13. A director has not properly carried out the orders of his assistant supervisor on several occasions to the point where he has been successively warned, reprimanded, and severely reprimanded. 13._____
    When the director once again does not carry out orders, the PROPER action for the assistant supervisor to take is to

    A. bring the director up on charges of failing to perform his duties properly
    B. have a serious discussion with the director, explaining the need for the orders and the necessity for carrying them out
    C. recommend that the director be transferred to another district
    D. severely reprimand the director again, making clear that no further deviation will be countenanced

14. A supervisor with several subordinates becomes aware that two of these subordinates are neither friendly nor congenial. 14._____
    In making assignments, it would be BEST for the supervisor to

    A. disregard the situation
    B. disregard the situation in making a choice of assignment but emphasize the need for teamwork
    C. investigate the situation to find out who is at fault and give that individual the less desirable assignments until such time as he corrects his attitude
    D. place the unfriendly subordinates in positions where they have as little contact with one another as possible

15. A DESIRABLE characteristic of a good supervisor is that he should 15._____

    A. identify himself with his subordinates rather than with higher management
    B. inform subordinates of forthcoming changes in policies and programs only when they directly affect the subordinates' activities
    C. make advancement of the subordinates contingent on personal loyalty to the supervisor
    D. make promises to subordinates only when sure of the ability to keep them

16. The supervisor who is MOST likely to be successful is the one who

    A. refrains from exercising the special privileges of his position
    B. maintains a formal attitude toward his subordinates
    C. maintains an informal attitude toward his subordinates
    D. represents the desires of his subordinates to his superiors

17. Application of sound principles of human relations by a supervisor may be expected to _____ the need for formal discipline.

    A. decrease   B. have no effect on
    C. increase   D. obviate

18. The MOST important generally approved way to maintain or develop high morale in one's subordinates is to

    A. give warnings and reprimands in a jocular manner
    B. excuse from staff conferences those employees who are busy
    C. keep them informed of new developments and policies of higher management
    D. refrain from criticizing their faults directly

19. In training subordinates, an IMPORTANT principle for the supervisor to recognize is that

    A. a particular method of instruction will be of substantially equal value for all employees in a given title
    B. it is difficult to train people over 50 years of age because they have little capacity for learning
    C. persons undergoing the same course of training will learn at different rates of speed
    D. training can seldom achieve its purpose unless individual instruction is the chief method used

20. Over an extended period of time, a subordinate is MOST likely to become and remain most productive is the supervisor

    A. accords praise to the subordinate whenever his work is satisfactory, withholding criticism except in the case of very inferior work
    B. avoids both praise and criticism except for outstandingly good or bad work performed by the subordinate
    C. informs the subordinate of his shortcomings, as viewed by management, while according praise only when highly deserved
    D. keeps the subordinate informed of the degree of satisfaction with which his performance of the job is viewed by management

KEY (CORRECT ANSWERS)

1.	C	11.	D
2.	D	12.	B
3.	C	13.	A
4.	A	14.	D
5.	D	15.	D
6.	C	16.	D
7.	A	17.	A
8.	D	18.	C
9.	B	19.	C
10.	D	20.	D

TEST 2

DIRECTIONS: Each question or incomplete statement is followed by several suggested answers or completions. Select the one that BEST answers the question or completes the statement. *PRINT THE LETTER OF THE CORRECT ANSWER IN THE SPACE AT THE RIGHT.*

1. A supervisor has just been told by a subordinate, Mr. Jones, that another employee, Mr. Smith, deliberately disobeyed an important rule of the department by taking home some confidential departmental material.
   Of the following courses of action, it would be MOST advisable for the supervisor first to

   A. discuss the matter privately with both Mr. Jones and Mr. Smith at the same time
   B. call a meeting of the entire staff and discuss the matter generally without mentioning any employee by name
   C. arrange to supervise Mr. Smith's activities more closely
   D. discuss the matter privately with Mr. Smith

2. The one of the following actions which would be MOST efficient and economical for a supervisor to take to minimize the effect of periodic fluctuations in the work load of his unit is to

   A. increase his permanent staff until it is large enough to handle the work of the busy loads
   B. request the purchase of time and labor saving equipment to be used primarily during the busy loads
   C. lower, temporarily, the standards for quality of work performance during peak loads
   D. schedule for the slow periods work that is not essential to perform during the busy periods

3. Discipline of employees is usually a supervisor's responsibility. There may be several useful forms of disciplinary action.
   Of the following, the form that is LEAST appropriate is the

   A. written reprimand or warning
   B. involuntary transfer to another work setting
   C. demotion or suspension
   D. assignment of added hours of work each week

4. Of the following, the MOST effective means of dealing with employee disciplinary problems is to

   A. give personality tests to individuals to identify their psychological problems
   B. distribute and discuss a policy manual containing exact rules governing employee behavior
   C. establish a single, clear penalty to be imposed for all wrongdoing irrespective of degree
   D. have supervisors get to know employees well through social mingling

5. A recently developed technique for appraising work performance is to have the supervisor record on a continual basis all significant incidents in each subordinate's behavior that indicate unsuccessful action and those that indicate poor behavior.
Of the following, a MAJOR disadvantage of this method of performance appraisal is that it

    A. often leads to overly close supervision
    B. results in competition among those subordinates being evaluated
    C. tends to result in superficial judgments
    D. lacks objectivity for evaluating performance

6. Assume that you are a supervisor and have observed the performance of an employee during a period of time. You have concluded that his performance needs improvement.
In order to improve his performance, it would, therefore, be BEST for you to

    A. note your findings in the employee's personnel folder so that his behavior is a matter of record
    B. report the findings to the personnel officer so he can take prompt action
    C. schedule a problem-solving conference with the employee
    D. recommend his transfer to simpler duties

7. When an employee's absences or latenesses seem to be nearing excessiveness, the supervisor should speak with him to find out what the problem is.
Of the following, if such a discussion produces no reasonable explanation, the discussion usually BEST serves to

    A. affirm clearly the supervisor's adherence to proper policy
    B. alert other employees that such behavior is unacceptable
    C. demonstrate that the supervisor truly represents higher management
    D. notify the employee that his behavior is being observed and evaluated

8. Assume that an employee willfully and recklessly violates an important agency regulation. The nature of the violation is of such magnitude that it demands immediate action, but the facts of the case are not entirely clear. Further, assume that the supervisor is free to make any of the following recommendations.
The MOST appropriate action for the supervisor to take is to recommend that the employee be

    A. discharged   B. suspended
    C. forced to resign   D. transferred

9. Although employees' titles may be identical, each position in that title may be considerably different.
Of the following, a supervisor should carefully assign each employee to a specific position based PRIMARILY on the employee's

    A. capability   B. experience
    C. education   D. seniority

10. The one of the following situations where it is MOST appropriate to transfer an employee to a similar assignment is one in which the employee

    A. lacks motivation and interest
    B. experiences a personality conflict with his supervisor

C. is negligent in the performance of his duties
D. lacks capacity or ability to perform assigned tasks

11. The one of the following which is LEAST likely to be affected by improvements in the morale of personnel is employee

    A. skill
    B. absenteeism
    C. turnover
    D. job satisfaction

12. The one of the following situations in which it is LEAST appropriate for a supervisor to delegate authority to subordinates is where the supervisor

    A. lacks confidence in his own abilities to perform certain work
    B. is overburdened and cannot handle all his responsibilities
    C. refers all disciplinary problems to his subordinate
    D. has to deal with an emergency or crisis

13. Assume that it has come to your attention that two of your subordinates have shouted at each other and have almost engaged in a fist fight. Luckily, they were separated by some of the other employees.
    Of the following, your BEST immediate course of action would *generally* be to

    A. reprimand the senior of the two subordinates since he should have known better
    B. hear the story from both employees and any witnesses and then take needed disciplinary action
    C. ignore the matter since nobody was physically hurt
    D. immediately suspend and fine both employees pending a departmental hearing

14. You have been delegating some of your authority to one of your subordinates because of his leadership potential. Which of the following actions is LEAST conducive to the growth and development of this individual for a supervisory position?

    A. Use praise only when it will be effective
    B. Give very detailed instructions and supervise the employee closely to be sure that the instructions are followed precisely
    C. Let the subordinate proceed with his planned course of action even if mistakes, within a permissible range, are made
    D. Intervene on behalf of the subordinate whenever an assignment becomes difficult for him

15. A rumor has been spreading in your department concerning the possibility of layoffs due to decreased revenues.
    As a supervisor, you should GENERALLY

    A. deny the rumor, whether it is true or false, in order to keep morale from declining
    B. inform the men to the best of your knowledge about this situation and keep them advised of any new information
    C. tell the men to forget about the rumor and concentrate on increasing their productivity
    D. ignore the rumor since it is not authorized information

16. Within an organization, every supervisor should know to whom he reports and who reports to him.
The one of the following which is achieved by use of such structured relationships is

    A. unity of command
    B. confidentiality
    C. esprit de corps
    D. promotion opportunities

16.____

17. Almost every afternoon, one of your employees comes back from his break ten minutes late without giving you any explanation.
Which of the following actions should you take FIRST in this situation?

    A. Assign the employee to a different type of work and observe whether his behavior changes
    B. Give the employee extra work to do so that he will have to return on time
    C. Ask the employee for an explanation for his lateness
    D. Tell the employee he is jeopardizing the break for everyone

17.____

18. When giving instructions to your employees in a group, which one of the following should you make certain to do?

    A. Speak in a casual, offhand manner
    B. Assume that your employees fully understand the instructions
    C. Write out your instructions beforehand and read them to the employees
    D. Tell exactly who is to do what

18.____

19. A fist fight develops between two men under your supervision.
The MOST advisable course of action for you to take FIRST is to

    A. call the police
    B. have the other workers pull them apart
    C. order them to stop
    D. step between the two men

19.____

20. You have assigned some difficult and unusual work to one of your most experienced and competent subordinates.
If you notice that he is doing the work incorrectly, you should

    A. assign the work to another employee
    B. reprimand him in private
    C. show him immediately how the work should be done
    D. wait until the job is completed and then correct his errors

20.____

KEY (CORRECT ANSWERS)

1.	D	11.	A
2.	D	12.	C
3.	D	13.	B
4.	B	14.	B
5.	A	15.	B
6.	C	16.	A
7.	D	17.	C
8.	B	18.	D
9.	A	19.	C
10.	B	20.	C

EXAMINATION SECTION
TEST 1

DIRECTIONS: Each question or incomplete statement is followed by several suggested answers or completions. Select the one that BEST answers the question or completes the statement. *PRINT THE LETTER OF THE CORRECT ANSWER IN THE SPACE AT THE RIGHT.*

1. Assume that a supervisor finds that his employees have become fatigued from doing a very long and repetitious job.
   The one of the following which would be the BEST way to relieve this fatigue is to

   A. assign other work so that the employees can switch to different assignments in the middle of the day
   B. let the employees listen to a radio while they work
   C. break the job down into very small parts so that each employee can concentrate on one simple task
   D. allow the employees to take frequent rest periods

   1.____

2. Assume that one of your subordinates is injured and will be out for at least six weeks.
   Of the following, the BEST way to handle the work normally assigned to this person is to

   A. allow the work to remain uncompleted until the injured person returns, since he is the one who can best do this work
   B. divide this work equally among the persons under your supervision who can do this work
   C. do all the work yourself
   D. give the injured person's work to the most efficient member of your staff

   2.____

3. Suppose that another supervisor tells you about a new way to organize some of your unit's work. The idea sounds good to you. However, before you were in this unit, a similar plan was tried and it failed.
   The MOST important thing for you to do FIRST is to

   A. find out why the previous attempt failed
   B. suggest that the other supervisor tell his idea to top management
   C. try the plan to see whether it works
   D. find proof that the plan has worked elsewhere

   3.____

4. One of your subordinates comes to you with a grievance. You discuss it with him so that you may fully understand the problem as he sees it.
   However, since you are uncertain as to the proper answer, you should

   A. tell him that you cannot help him with this problem
   B. tell him that you will have to check further and make an appointment to see him again
   C. send him to see your immediate superior for a solution to the problem
   D. ask him to find out from his co-workers whether this problem has come up before

   4.____

5. A supervisor reprimanded one of his subordinates severely for making a serious error in judgment while performing an assignment for which he had volunteered.
   The supervisor's action was

   5.____

A. *incorrect,* chiefly because in the future the worker will probably try to avoid taking on responsibility
B. *correct,* chiefly because this will insure that the worker will not make the same mistake in the future
C. *correct,* chiefly because the worker should be discouraged from using his own judgment on the job
D. *incorrect,* chiefly because the reprimand came too late to correct the error that had already been made

6. Of the following, the BEST way for a supervisor to inform all his subordinates of a change in lunch rules is, in MOST cases, to

   A. call a staff meeting
   B. tell each one individually
   C. issue a memorandum
   D. tell one or two employees to pass the word around

7. For a supervisor to assign work giving only general instructions to his subordinate would be advisable when

   A. the supervisor is confident that the worker knows how to do the job
   B. the assignment is a simple one
   C. the subordinate is himself a supervisory employee
   D. errors in the work will not cause serious delay

8. One of the DISADVANTAGES of setting minimum standards of performance for custodial employees is that

   A. such standards eliminate the basis for evaluating employees
   B. the custodial employees may keep their performance at the minimum level
   C. standards are always subject to change
   D. the supervisor may feel that his initiative is being restricted

9. One of your subordinates has been functioning below his usual level. You feel that something of a personal nature may be affecting his work. When you ask him casually whether anything is wrong, he says everything is fine.
   As a next step, it would be BEST for you to

   A. make frequent casual and humorous comments about the poor quality of his work but refrain, at this time, from any serious discussion
   B. warn him that failure to maintain his customary level of performance might result in disciplinary action
   C. express your concern privately and reveal your interest in the reason for his change in work performance
   D. discuss with him the work of another employee, suggesting that the other employee would be a good example to follow

10. Assume you are teaching a new job to one of your subordinates.
    After you have demonstrated the job, you can BEST maintain the worker's interest by

    A. showing him training films about the job
    B. giving him printed material that explains why the job is important

C. having him observe other workers do the job
D. letting him attempt to do the job by himself under supervision

11. *Insubordination is sometimes a protest against inferior or arbitrary leadership.*
    For the supervisor, the MOST basic implication of this statement is:

    A. Accusations of insubordination are easy to make, but usually difficult to prove
    B. Insubordination cannot be permitted if an organization wishes to remain effective
    C. When an employee discusses an order instead of carrying it out, he has not understood it
    D. When an employee questions an order, review it to make sure it is reasonable

12. In appraising a subordinate's mistakes, a supervisor should ALWAYS consider the

    A. absolute number of mistakes, without regard to severity
    B. number of mistakes in proportion to the number of decisions made
    C. total number of mistakes made by others, regardless of assignment
    D. number of mistakes which were discovered upon higher review

13. If you are the supervisor of an office in which the work frequently involves lifting heavy boxes, you should instruct your staff in the proper method of lifting to avoid injury.
    In giving these instructions, you should stress that a person lifting heavy objects MUST

    A. keep his feet close together
    B. bend at the waist
    C. keep his back as straight as possible
    D. use his back muscles to straighten up

14. Of the following, the BEST qualified supervisor is one who

    A. knows the basic principles and procedures of all the jobs which he supervises
    B. has detailed working knowledge of all aspects of the job he supervises but knows little about principles of supervision
    C. is able to do exceptionally well at least one of the jobs which he supervises and has some knowledge of the others
    D. knows little or nothing about most of the jobs which he supervises but knows the principles of supervision

15. The rate at which an employee will learn will vary according to a number of considerations.
    Of the following, which is LEAST likely to be controllable by the supervisor or the trainer?
    The

    A. manner in which the material is presented
    B. state of readiness of the learner
    C. scheduling of practice sessions
    D. nature of the material

16. When considering whether to use written material rather than oral instructions as a means of giving instructions to employees, the one of the following which should be given GREATEST consideration is the employees'

    A. personal preferences
    B. attitude toward supervision
    C. general educational level
    D. salary level

17. Assume that one of your subordinates has been assigned to attend job training classes. The one of the following which would probably be the BEST evidence of the success of the course is that the employee

    A. feels that he has learned something
    B. continues to study after the course is over
    C. has had a good class record
    D. improves in his work performance

18. Of the following, the situation LEAST likely to result if a supervisor shows favoritism toward particular employees is

    A. laxity in the work of the favored employees
    B. resentment from the other, less-favored employees
    C. increased ability among the favored employees
    D. lowering of morale among employees

19. The one of the following reasons for evaluating employees' performance, whether done formally or informally, which is NOT considered to be POSITIVE in nature is to

    A. give individual counsel to employees
    B. motivate employees toward improvement
    C. provide recognition of superior service
    D. set penalties for substandard performance

20. Assume that, because there has been an unexpected and temporary increase in the short-term work of your unit, you have had temporarily assigned to you several staff members from another agency.
    Of the following, in dealing with these employees, it would be LEAST advisable to

    A. assign them to long-term projects
    B. organize tasks so that they can begin work immediately
    C. set standards, making allowances to give them time to learn your ways
    D. direct them in the same way, in general, as you do your regular staff

21. It has been suggested that one way to increase employee productivity would be to require employees dealing with the public to have proficiency in a relevant foreign language.
    Of the following, the MAJOR reason for implementing such a proposal, from the viewpoint of effective public administration, would be to

    A. encourage the foreign-born to learn English
    B. exchange information more rapidly and accurately
    C. increase the public prestige of the agency
    D. stimulate ethnic pride among all groups

22. Assume that the clerk who normally keeps your unit's records will be on vacation for four weeks.
If other clerks are equally qualified to keep these records, your BEST choice to replace the clerk would be the person who

    A. has skills which are needed least for other duties during this period
    B. volunteers for this work
    C. is next in turn for a special assignment
    D. has handled this task before

23. Assume that you have under your supervision several young clerical employees who have the bad habit of fooling around when they should be working.
Of the following, the BEST disciplinary action to take would be to

    A. ignore it; these young people will outgrow it
    B. join in the fun briefly in order to bring it to a quicker end each time it occurs
    C. bring to their attention the fact that this behavior is not acceptable and if it continues shift the make-up of the group to keep these young persons apart
    D. warn them that this type of behavior is reason for dismissal and be quick to make an example of the first one who starts it again

24. Seeking the advice of community leaders has human relations value for a public agency in planning or executing its programs CHIEFLY because it

    A. allows for the keeping of careful records concerning individual suggestions
    B. lets community leaders know that the agency has regard for their opinions
    C. permits the agency to state in writing which programs seem most appropriate
    D. unifies community leaders against the programs of competing private agencies

25. Good community relations is often action-oriented. Which of the following activities of a public agency is LEAST likely to be considered as action-oriented by the people of a local community?

    A. Conducting a survey to gather information about the local community
    B. Extending the use of a facility to those previously excluded
    C. Providing a service that was formerly non-existent
    D. Removing something considered objectionable by the local community

KEY (CORRECT ANSWERS)

1. A
2. B
3. A
4. B
5. A

6. C
7. A
8. B
9. C
10. D

11. D
12. B
13. C
14. A
15. B

16. C
17. D
18. D
19. D
20. A

21. B
22. A
23. C
24. B
25. A

TEST 2

DIRECTIONS: Each question or incomplete statement is followed by several suggested answers or completions. Select the one that BEST answers the question or completes the statement. *PRINT THE LETTER OF THE CORRECT ANSWER IN THE SPACE AT THE RIGHT.*

1. Methods of communication with employees are of three types: oral, written, and visual. A MAJOR advantage of the written word is that it

   A. insures that content will remain unchanged no matter how many persons may be involved in its transmission
   B. facilitates two-way communication in delicate or confidential situations
   C. strengthens chain-of-command procedures in transmission of information and instruction by requiring the use of prescribed channels
   D. encourages the active participation of employees in the solution of complicated problems

   1.____

2. The use of the conference technique in training often requires more preparatory work on the part of the trainer than does a good lecture PRIMARILY because

   A. a conference would cover material of a more technical nature
   B. the trainer will be required to supply more printed material to the participants
   C. a conference usually involves a greater number of trainees
   D. the trainer must be prepared for a wide variety of possible occurrences

   2.____

3. The one of the following which is NOT an advantage of the lecture over most other methods of training is that it can be given

   A. over the radio or on record
   B. to large numbers of trainees
   C. without interruptions
   D. with little preparation

   3.____

4. Of the following, the one which is LEAST appropriate as a purpose for using an employee attitude survey is to

   A. develop a supervisory training program
   B. learn the identity of dissatisfied employees
   C. re-evaluate employee relations policies
   D. re-orient publications designed for employees

   4.____

5. The competent trainer seeks to become knowledgeable both in the work of the agency and in the duties of the positions for which he is to conduct training.
   Of the following, the GREATEST practical value that results when the trainer gains such knowledge is that

   A. he will be more likely to instruct employees to perform their work in a manner consistent with actual practice
   B. all levels of staff will be favorably impressed by a display of interest in the agency and its work

   5.____

C. employees will become familiar with the trainer and will not consider him an outsider
D. the trainer will gain an accurate picture of the capacity of each employee for training

6. Assume that you, the supervisor of a small office, are involved in planning the reorganization of your bureau's work. Management has decided not to inform your staff of the reorganization until the plans are completed.
If one of your subordinates tells you that he has heard a rumor about reorganization of the department, you should reply that

   A. the reorganization involves the bureau, not the department
   B. you haven't heard anything about departmental reorganization and that he should stop spreading rumors
   C. you will inform your staff at the appropriate time if any definite plans are made involving a reorganization
   D. you do not know what is being planned but you will ask your superior for details

7. Of the following training methods, the one in which the trainee's role is usually LEAST active is the _____ method.

   A. case-study   B. conference
   C. group discussion   D. lecture

8. Differences in morale between two work groups can sometimes be attributed to differences in the supervision they receive.
Of the following, the behavior MOST characteristic of a supervisor of a group with high morale is that he

   A. assigns the least difficult tasks to employees with the most seniority
   B. is concerned primarily with his ultimate responsibility, production
   C. delegates authority and responsibility to his staff
   D. is lenient with his workers when they violate rules

9. Informal performance evaluations of individual employees, prepared systematically and regularly over a period of several years, are considered to be useful to a supervisor PRIMARILY because

   A. He will be able to assign tasks based only on these records
   B. Unlike formal records, since they are fitted to the characteristics of individual employees, they provide for quick comparisons
   C. He need not discuss them with employees, since they are informal
   D. Whatever personnel action he recommends can be substantiated by cumulative records

10. When instructing first-line supervisors in the proper method of evaluating the performance of probationary employees, it is LEAST important for a higher-level supervisor to

    A. explain in detail the standards to be used
    B. inform them of the possibility of higher management review
    C. caution them concerning common errors of evaluation
    D. mention the purposes of probationary employee evaluation

11. Assume that your agency is considering abolishing its official performance rating system but that you, a supervisor of a fairly large office, would like to devise a system for your own use.
    The FIRST step in setting up a system would be to

    A. decide what factors and personal characteristics are important and should be rated
    B. compare several rating methods to see which would be easiest to use
    C. have a private conference with each employee to discuss his performance
    D. set specific standards of employee performance, allowing your workers to make suggestions

12. The basic organizational structure of a municipal agency may have come about for several reasons.
    Of the following, the MOST important influence on the nature of its structure is the agency's

    A. professional attitude   B. public reputation
    C. overall goal   D. staff morale

13. The term *formal organization* refers to that organization structure agreed upon by top management whereas the term *informal organization* refers to the more spontaneous and flexible organizational ties developed by subordinates. The one of the following which BEST describes the usual *informal organization* is that it represents a(n)

    A. destructive system of relationships which should be eliminated
    B. concealed system of relationships whose goals are the same as management's
    C. actual system of relationships which should be recognized
    D. dysfunctional system of relationships which should be ignored

14. The reluctance of supervisors to delegate work to subordinates when they should is GENERALLY due to the supervisor's

    A. feelings of insecurity in work situations
    B. need to acquire additional experience
    C. inability to exercise control over his subordinates
    D. lack of technical knowledge

15. Assume that you have just been made the supervisor of a group of people you did not know before.
    For you to talk casually with each of your new subordinates with the purpose of getting to know them personally would be

    A. *advisable,* chiefly because subordinates have more confidence in a supervisor who shows personal interest in them
    B. *inadvisable,* chiefly because subordinates resent having their supervisor ask about their outside interests
    C. *advisable,* chiefly because one of the supervisor's main concerns should be to help his subordinates with their personal problems
    D. *inadvisable,* chiefly because a supervisor should not allow his relations with his subordinates to be influenced by their personalities

16. It has been found that high-producing subdivisions of organizations usually have supervisors whose behavior is employee-centered, whereas low-producing units usually have supervisors whose behavior is work-centered. Therefore, it could be concluded from these findings that

    A. a high-producing unit may cause a supervisor to be authoritarian
    B. a low-producing unit may cause a supervisor to be work-centered
    C. close supervision usually increases production
    D. employee-centered leadership may reduce production

17. A recent study in managerial science showed that, as the amount of praise increased and amount of criticism decreased, the supervisor was more likely to be perceived by his subordinates as being

    A. concerned with their career advancement
    B. production oriented, through subtle intimidation
    C. seeking personal satisfaction, irrespective of production
    D. uncertain of the subordinates' reliability

18. The power to issue directives or instructions to employees is derived from employees as much as from management. It follows MOST logically from this statement that

    A. attitudes toward management can be changed
    B. emphasis on discipline is needed
    C. authority is dependent upon acceptance
    D. employees should be properly supervised for work to be done

19. "In the decision-making process, it is a rare problem that has only one possible solution. Such a solution should be suspected of being nothing but a plausible argument for a preconceived idea."
    The author of the foregoing quotation apparently does NOT believe that

    A. there is usually only one possible solution to a problem
    B. the risks involved in any solution should be weighed against expected gains
    C. each alternative should be evaluated to determine the effort needed
    D. actions should be based on the urgency of problems

20. The supervisor who relies on punitive discipline to enforce his authority is putting limits on the potential of his leadership. Fear of punishment may secure obedience, but it destroys initiative. Such a supervisor's autocratic methods have cut off upward communications. Of the following, the major DISADVANTAGE of such autocratic behavior is that

    A. difficulties in the supervision of his subordinates will arise if limits are placed on the supervisor's responsibility
    B. policies that affect the public will be changed too frequently
    C. the supervisor will apply punishment subjectively rather than objectively
    D. instructions will be obeyed to the letter, regardless of changing circumstances

21. The need for a supervisor to carefully coordinate and direct the work of his unit increases as the work becomes

    A. more routine   B. more specialized
    C. less complex   D. less technical

22. The MAIN goal of discipline as used by a supervisor should be to

    A. keep the employees' respect
    B. influence behavior, so that work will be completed properly
    C. encourage the employees to work faster
    D. set an example for others

23. One of your subordinates has exhibited discourtesy and non-cooperation on several occasions.
    Of the following, the MOST appropriate attitude for you to adopt in dealing with this problem is that

    A. disciplinary measures for such an individual generally creates additional problems
    B. failure to correct such behavior may lead to worse offenses
    C. it is a mistake to make an issue out of minor infractions
    D. the harsher the medicine, the faster the cure

24. Assume that an employee has complained to you, his supervisor, that he cannot concentrate on his work because two of his co-workers make too much noise. You pay particular attention to these employees for several days and do not find them making excessive noise.
    The NEXT step you should take in handling this grievance is to

    A. have a talk with all three employees, urging them to cooperate and be considerate of one another
    B. arrange for the complainant to change his work location to a place away from the two co-workers
    C. talk to the complainant to find out if the complaint he made to you is the real cause of his dissatisfaction
    D. tell the complainant that you have found his grievance to be unfounded ?

25. In planning the application of an existing agency program to a local community, it is generally necessary to discover relevant problems and possibilities for service.
    Of the following, the BEST way to learn about such problems and possibilities for service would usually be to

    A. begin the program on a full-scale basis and await reactions
    B. seek opinions and advice from community residents and leaders
    C. hold staff meetings with agency employees who have worked in similar communities
    D. study official Federal reports about already completed programs of the same kind

KEY (CORRECT ANSWERS)

1. A
2. D
3. D
4. B
5. A

6. C
7. D
8. C
9. D
10. B

11. A
12. C
13. C
14. A
15. A

16. B
17. A
18. C
19. A
20. D

21. B
22. B
23. B
24. C
25. B

TEST 3

DIRECTIONS: Each question or incomplete statement is followed by several suggested answers or completions. Select the one that BEST answers the question or completes the statement. *PRINT THE LETTER OF THE CORRECT ANSWER IN THE SPACE AT THE RIGHT.*

1. Which of the following characteristics would be LEAST detrimental to a supervisor in his efforts to set up and maintain good relations with other supervisors with whom he must deal in the course of his duties?

    A. Not getting involved in consultation on any supervisory problems they might have
    B. Indicating that they should improve their supervising methods and offering suggestions on how to do so
    C. Emphasizing his own role as a member of management
    D. Sharing information which has proved useful in his unit

2. Both trainers and supervisors might agree that there is usually a best way to do a particular job. Yet a supervisor or instructor sometimes does not teach a new employee the best way, the most efficient way, to do a complex job. Sometimes, in such cases, the supervisor temporarily changes the sequence of operations, increases the number of steps needed to do a job, or makes other changes in the method, which then deviates from the one considered most efficient.
   When is such a difference in approach MOST justified when teaching a new employee a complex job?

    A. When the changes in approach correspond to the learning ability of the new employee
    B. When the new employee's performance on the job is closely supervised to compensate for a change in approach
    C. Where the steps in performing the task have not been defined in a manual of procedures
    D. When the instructor has ideas of improving upon the methods for doing the job

3. Considerable thought in the field of management is directed toward the advantages and disadvantages of authoritarian methods of influencing behavior, and, in the so-called authoritarian model, a nucleus of rather consistent ideas prevail.
   Which of the following is LEAST characteristic of an administrative system based on the authoritarian model?

    A. A conviction of a need for order and efficiency in a world consisting mainly of people who lack direction and incentive
    B. Rules and contracts are the basis for action, and decisions are made on an impersonal basis
    C. The right to give orders and instructions is inherent in the hierarchial arrangement of an organizational structure
    D. Realization that subordinates' needs for affiliation and recognition can contribute to management's objectives

4. Of the following, the FIRST step in planning an operation is to

    A. obtain relevant information
    B. identify the goal to be achieved
    C. consider possible alternatives
    D. make necessary assignments

5. A supervisor who is extremely busy performing routine tasks is MOST likely making incorrect use of what basic principle of supervision?

   A. Homogeneous Assignment
   B. Span of Control
   C. Work Distribution
   D. Delegation of Authority

6. Controls help supervisors to obtain information from which they can determine whether their staffs are achieving planned goals.
   Which one of the following would be LEAST useful as a control device?

   A. Employee diaries
   B. Organization charts
   C. Periodic inspections
   D. Progress charts

7. A certain employee has difficulty in effectively performing a particular portion of his routine assignments, but his overall productivity is average.
   As a direct supervisor of this individual, your BEST course of action would be to

   A. attempt to develop the investigator's capacity to execute the problematical facets of his assignments
   B. diversify the investigator's work assignments in order to build up his confidence
   C. reassign the investigator to less difficult tasks
   D. request in a private conversation that the investigator improve his work output

8. A supervisor who uses persuasion as a means of supervising a unit would GENERALLY also use which of the following practices to supervise his unit?

   A. Supervise and control the staff with an authoritative attitude to indicate that he is a *take-charge* individual
   B. Make significant changes in the organizational operations so as to improve job efficiency
   C. Remove major communication barriers between himself, subordinates, and management
   D. Supervise everyday operations while being mindful of the problems of his subordinates

9. Whenever a supervisor in charge of a unit delegates a routine task to a capable subordinate, he tells him exactly how to do it.
   This practice is GENERALLY

   A. *desirable,* chiefly because good supervisors should be aware of the traits of their subordinates and delegate responsibilities to them accordingly
   B. *undesirable,* chiefly because only non-routine tasks should be delegated
   C. *desirable,* chiefly because a supervisor should frequently test the willingness of his subordinates to perform ordinary tasks
   D. *undesirable,* chiefly because a capable subordinate should usually be allowed to exercise his own discretion in doing a routine job

10. The one of the following activities through which a supervisor BEST demonstrates leadership ability is by

A. arranging periodic staff meetings in order to keep his subordinates informed about professional developments in the field of investigation
B. frequently issuing definite orders and directives which will lessen the need for subordinates to make decisions in handling any investigations assigned to them
C. devoting the major part of his time to supervising subordinates so as to stimulate continous improvement
D. setting aside time for self-development and research so as to improve the investigative techniques and procedures of his unit

11. The following three statements relate to supervision of employees:
    I. The assignment of difficult tasks that offer a challenge is more conducive to good morale than the assignment of easy tasks
    II. The same general principles of supervision that apply to men are equally applicable to women
    III. The best retraining program should cover all phases of an employee's work in a general manner

    Which of the following choices lists ALL of the above statements that are generally CORRECT?

    A. II and III
    B. I
    C. I and II
    D. I, II, and III

12. Which of the following examples BEST illustrates the application of the *exception principle* as a supervisory technique?
    A(n)

    A. complex job is divided among several employees who work simultaneously to complete the whole job in a shorter time
    B. employee is required to complete any task delegated to him to such an extent that nothing is left for the superior who delegated the task except to approve it
    C. superior delegates responsibility to a subordinate but retains authority to make the final decisions
    D. superior delegates all work possible to his subordinates and retains that which requires his personal attention or performance

13. Assume that you are a supervisor. Your immediate superior frequently gives orders to your subordinates without your knowledge.
    Of the following, the MOST direct and effective way for you to handle this problem is to

    A. tell your subordinates to take orders only from you
    B. submit a report to higher authority in which you cite specific instances
    C. discuss it with your immediate superior
    D. find out to what extent your authority and prestige as a supervisor have been affected

14. In an agency which has as its primary purpose the protection of the public against fraudulent business practices, which of the following would GENERALLY be considered an auxiliary or staff rather than a line function?

    A. Interviewing victims of frauds and advising them about their legal remedies
    B. Daily activities directed toward prevention of fraudulent business practices
    C. Keeping records and statistics about business violations reported and corrected
    D. Follow-up inspections by investigators after corrective action has been taken

15. A supervisor can MOST effectively reduce the spread of false rumors through the *grape-vine* by

    A. identifying and disciplining any subordinate responsible for initiating such rumors
    B. keeping his subordinates informed as much as possible about matters affecting them
    C. denying false rumors which might tend to lower staff morale and productivity
    D. making sure confidential matters are kept secure from access by unauthorized employees

16. A supervisor has tried to learn about the background, education, and family relationships of his subordinates through observation, personal contact, and inspection of their personnel records.
    These supervisory actions are GENERALLY

    A. *inadvisable,* chiefly because they may lead to charges of favoritism
    B. *advisable,* chiefly because they may make him more popular with his subordinates
    C. *inadvisable,* chiefly because his efforts may be regarded as an invasion of privacy
    D. *advisable,* chiefly because the information may enable him to develop better understanding of each of his subordinates

17. In an emergency situation, when action must be taken immediately, it is BEST for the supervisor to give orders in the form of

    A. direct commands, which are brief and precise
    B. requests, so that his subordinates will not become alarmed
    C. suggestions, which offer alternative courses of action
    D. implied directives, so that his subordinates may use their judgment in carrying them out

18. When demonstrating a new and complex procedure to a group of subordinates, it is ESSENTIAL that a supervisor

    A. go slowly and repeat the steps involved at least once
    B. show the employees common errors and the consequences of such errors
    C. go through the process at the usual speed so that the employees can see the rate at which they should work
    D. distribute summaries of the procedure during the demonstration and instruct his subordinates to refer to them afterwards

19. The PRIMARY value of office reports and procedures is to

    A. assist top management in controlling key agency functions
    B. measure job performance
    C. save time and labor
    D. control the activities and use of time of all staff members

20. Of the following, which is considered to be the GREATEST advantage of the oral report? It

    A. allows for accurate transmission of information from one individual to another
    B. presents an opportunity to discuss or clarify any immediate questions raised by the receiver of the report

C. requires less office work to maintain records on actions taken when an oral report is involved
D. takes only a short amount of time to plan and prepare material for an oral report

21. A supervisor who is to make a report about a job he has done can make an oral report of a written report.
Of the following, which is the BEST time to make an oral report?
When

    A. the work covers an emergency situation
    B. a record is needed for the files
    C. the report is channeled to other departments
    D. the report covers additional work he will do

21._____

22. Suppose that a new employee has been assigned to you. It is your responsibility to see to it that he understands how to fill out properly the forms he is required to use. What would be the BEST way to do this?

    A. Explain the use of each form to the new technician and show him how to fill them out
    B. Give the new employee a copy of each form he must use so that he can learn by studying them
    C. Ask an experienced worker to explain clearly to him how the forms should be filled out
    D. Tell the new employee that filling out forms is simple and he should follow the instructions on each form

22._____

23. As a supervisor, you want to have your staff take part in improving work methods.
Of the following, the BEST way to do this is to

    A. make critical appraisals of their work frequently
    B. encourage them to make suggestions
    C. make no changes without their approval
    D. hold regular staff meetings

23._____

24. A good relationship with other supervisors is important to a senior supervisor.
Close cooperation among supervisory personnel is MOST likely to result in

    A. increasing the probability for support of supervisory actions and decisions
    B. stimulating supervisors to achieve higher status in the organization
    C. helping to control the flow of work within a unit
    D. a clearer definition of the responsibilities of individual supervisors

24._____

25. Which of the following is MOST likely to gain a supervisor the respect and cooperation of his staff?

    A. Assigning the most difficult jobs to the experienced staff members
    B. Giving each staff member the same number of assignments
    C. Assigning jobs according to each staff member's ability
    D. Giving each staff member the same types of assignments

25._____

KEY (CORRECT ANSWERS)

1.	D	11.	C
2.	A	12.	D
3.	D	13.	C
4.	B	14.	C
5.	D	15.	B
6.	B	16.	D
7.	A	17.	A
8.	D	18.	A
9.	D	19.	A
10.	C	20.	B

21. A
22. A
23. B
24. A
25. C

PREPARING WRITTEN MATERIALS

EXAMINATION SECTION
TEST 1

DIRECTIONS: Each question or incomplete statement is followed by several suggested answers or completions. Select the one that BEST answers the question or completes the statement. *PRINT THE LETTER OF THE CORRECT ANSWER IN THE SPACE AT THE RIGHT.*

Questions 1-25.

DIRECTIONS: Questions 1 through 25 consist of sentences which may or may not be examples of good English usage. Consider grammar, punctuation, spelling, capitalization, awkwardness, etc. Examine each sentence, and then choose the correct statement about it from the four choices below it. If the English usage in the sentence given is better than it would be with any of the changes suggested in options B, C, and D, choose option A. Do not choose an option that will change the meaning of the sentence.

1. According to Judge Frank, the grocer's sons found guilty of assault and sentenced last Thursday.

    A. This is an example of acceptable writing.
    B. A comma should be placed after the word *sentenced*.
    C. The word *were* should be placed after *sons*.
    D. The apostrophe in grocer's should be placed after the *s*.

    1.____

2. The department heads assistant said that the stenographers should type duplicate copies of all contracts, leases, and bills.

    A. This is an example of acceptable writing.
    B. A comma should be placed before the word *contracts*.
    C. An apostrophe should be placed before the *s* in *heads*.
    D. Quotation marks should be placed before *the stenographers* and after *bills*.

    2.____

3. The lawyers questioned the men to determine who was the true property owner?

    A. This is an example of acceptable writing.
    B. The phrase *questioned the men* should be changed to *asked the men questions*.
    C. The word *was* should be changed to *were*.
    D. The question mark should be changed to a period.

    3.____

4. The terms stated in the present contract are more specific than those stated in the previous contract.

    A. This is an example of acceptable writing.
    B. The word *are* should be changed to *is*.
    C. The word *than* should be changed to *then*.
    D. The word *specific* should be changed to *specified*.

    4.____

5. Of the few lawyers considered, the one who argued more skillful was chosen for the job. 5.____

    A. This is an example of acceptable writing.
    B. The word *more* should be replaced by the word *most*.
    C. The word *skillful* should be replaced by the word *skillfully*.
    D. The word *chosen* should be replaced by the word *selected*.

6. Each of the states has a court of appeals; some states have circuit courts. 6.____

    A. This is an example of acceptable writing.
    B. The semi-colon should be changed to a comma.
    C. The word *has* should be changed to *have*.
    D. The word *some* should be capitalized.

7. The court trial has greatly effected the child's mental condition. 7.____

    A. This is an example of acceptable writing.
    B. The word *effected* should be changed to *affected*.
    C. The word *greatly* should be placed after *effected*.
    D. The apostrophe in *child's* should be placed after the *s*.

8. Last week, the petition signed by all the officers was sent to the Better Business Bureau. 8.____

    A. This is an example of acceptable writing.
    B. The phrase *last week* should be placed after *officers*.
    C. A comma should be placed after *petition*.
    D. The word *was* should be changed to *were*.

9. Mr. Farrell claims that he requested form A-12, and three booklets describing court procedures. 9.____

    A. This is an example of acceptable writing.
    B. The word *that* should be eliminated.
    C. A colon should be placed after *requested*.
    D. The comma after *A-12* should be eliminated.

10. We attended a staff conference on Wednesday the new safety and fire rules were discussed. 10.____

    A. This is an example of acceptable writing.
    B. The words *safety, fire,* and *rules* should begin with capital letters.
    C. There should be a comma after the word *Wednesday*.
    D. There should be a period after the word *Wednesday,* and the word *the* should begin with a capital letter.

11. Neither the dictionary or the telephone directory could be found in the office library. 11.____

    A. This is an example of acceptable writing.
    B. The word *or* should be changed to *nor*.
    C. The word *library* should be spelled *libery*.
    D. The word *neither* should be changed to *either*.

12. The report would have been typed correctly if the typist could read the draft. 12.____

    A. This is an example of acceptable writing.
    B. The word *would* should be removed.
    C. The word *have* should be inserted after the word *could*.
    D. The word *correctly* should be changed to *correct*.

13. The supervisor brought the reports and forms to an employees desk. 13.____

    A. This is an example of acceptable writing.
    B. The word *brought* should be changed to *took*.
    C. There should be a comma after the word *reports* and a comma after the word *forms*.
    D. The word *employees* should be spelled *employee's*.

14. It's important for all the office personnel to submit their vacation schedules on time. 14.____

    A. This is an example of acceptable writing.
    B. The word *It's* should be spelled *Its*.
    C. The word *their* should be spelled *they're*.
    D. The word *personnel* should be spelled *personal*.

15. The supervisor wants that all staff members report to the office at 9:00 A.M. 15.____

    A. This is an example of acceptable writing.
    B. The word *that* should be removed and the word *to* should be inserted after the word *members*.
    C. There should be a comma after the word *wants* and a comma after the word *office*.
    D. The word *wants* should be changed to *want*, and the word *shall* should be inserted after the word *members*.

16. Every morning the clerk opens the office mail and distributes it. 16.____

    A. This is an example of acceptable writing.
    B. The word *opens* should be changed to *open*.
    C. The word *mail* should be changed to *letters*.
    D. The word *it* should be changed to *them*.

17. The secretary typed more fast on a desktop computer than on a tablet. 17.____

    A. This is an example of acceptable writing.
    B. The words *more fast* should be changed to *faster*.
    C. There should be a comma after the words *desktop computer*.
    D. The word *than* should be changed to *then*.

18. The typist used an extention cord in order to connect her typewriter to the outlet nearest to her desk. 18.____

    A. This is an example of acceptable writing.
    B. A period should be placed after the word *cord*, and the word *in* should have a capital *I*.
    C. A comma should be placed after the word *typewriter*.
    D. The word *extention* should be spelled *extension*.

19. He would have went to the conference if he had received an invitation.   19.____
    A. This is an example of acceptable writing.
    B. The word *went* should be replaced by the word *gone*.
    C. The word *had* should be replaced by *would have*.
    D. The word *conference* should be spelled *conferance*.

20. In order to make the report neater, he spent many hours rewriting it.   20.____
    A. This is an example of acceptable writing.
    B. The word *more* should be inserted before the word *neater*.
    C. There should be a colon after the word *neater*.
    D. The word *spent* should be changed to *have spent*.

21. His supervisor told him that he should of read the memorandum more carefully.   21.____
    A. This is an example of acceptable writing.
    B. The word *memorandum* should be spelled *memorandom*.
    C. The word *of* should be replaced by the word *have*.
    D. The word *carefully* should be replaced by the word *careful*.

22. It was decided that two separate reports should be written.   22.____
    A. This is an example of acceptable writing.
    B. A comma should be inserted after the word *decided*.
    C. The word *be* should be replaced by the word *been*.
    D. A colon should be inserted after the word *that*.

23. She don't seem to understand that the work must be done as soon as possible.   23.____
    A. This is an example of acceptable writing.
    B. The word *doesn't* should replace the word *don't*.
    C. The word *why* should replace the word *that*.
    D. The word *as* before the word *soon* should be eliminated.

24. He excepted praise from his supervisor for a job well done.   24.____
    A. This is an example of acceptable writing.
    B. The word *excepted* should be spelled *accepted*.
    C. The order of the words *well done* should be changed to *done well*.
    D. There should be a comma after the word *supervisor*.

25. What appears to be intentional errors in grammar occur several times in the passage.   25.____
    A. This is an example of acceptable writing.
    B. The word *occur* should be spelled *occurr*.
    C. The word *appears* should be changed to *appear*.
    D. The phrase *several times* should be changed to *from time to time*.

KEY (CORRECT ANSWERS)

1. C
2. C
3. D
4. A
5. C

6. A
7. B
8. A
9. D
10. D

11. B
12. C
13. D
14. A
15. B

16. A
17. B
18. D
19. B
20. A

21. C
22. A
23. B
24. B
25. C

TEST 2

DIRECTIONS: Each question consists of a sentence which may or may not be an example of good formal English usage. Examine each sentence, considering grammar, punctuation, spelling, capitalization, and awkwardness. Then choose the CORRECT statement about it from the four options below it. If the English usage in the sentence given is better than any of the changes suggested in options B, C, or D, pick option A. Do not pick an option that will change the meaning of the sentence. *PRINT THE LETTER OF THE CORRECT ANSWER IN THE SPACE AT THE RIGHT.*

1. I don't know who could possibly of broken it. 1.____
   - A. This is an example of acceptable writing.
   - B. The word *who* should be replaced by the word *whom*.
   - C. The word *of* should be replaced by the word *have*.
   - D. The word *broken* should be replaced by the word *broke*.

2. Telephoning is easier than to write. 2.____
   - A. This is an example of acceptable writing.
   - B. The word *telephoning* should be spelled *telephoneing*.
   - C. The word *than* should be replaced by the word *then*.
   - D. The words *to write* should be replaced by the word *writing*.

3. The two operators who have been assigned to these consoles are on vacation. 3.____
   - A. This is an example of acceptable writing.
   - B. A comma should be placed after the word *operators*.
   - C. The word *who* should be replaced by the word *whom*
   - D. The word *are* should be replaced by the word *is*.

4. You were suppose to teach me how to operate a plugboard. 4.____
   - A. This is an example of acceptable writing.
   - B. The word *were* should be replaced by the word *was*.
   - C. The word *suppose* should be replaced by the word *supposed*.
   - D. The word *teach* should be replaced by the word *learn*.

5. If you had taken my advice; you would have spoken with him. 5.____
   - A. This is an example of acceptable writing.
   - B. The word *advice* should be spelled *advise*.
   - C. The words *had taken* should be replaced by the word *take*.
   - D. The semicolon should be changed to a comma.

6. The clerk could have completed the assignment on time if he knows where these materials were located. 6.____
   - A. This is an example of acceptable writing.
   - B. The word *knows* should be replaced by *had known*.
   - C. The word *were* should be replaced by *had been*.
   - D. The words *where these materials were located* should be replaced by *the location of these materials*.

7. All employees should be given safety training. Not just those who have accidents.   7.____
   A. This is an example of acceptable writing.
   B. The period after the word *training* should be changed to a colon.
   C. The period after the word *training* should be changed to a semicolon, and the first letter of the word *Not* should be changed to a small *n*.
   D. The period after the word *training* should be changed to a comma, and the first letter of the word *Not* should be changed to a small *n*.

8. This proposal is designed to promote employee awareness of the suggestion program, to encourage employee participation in the program, and to increase the number of suggestions submitted.   8.____
   A. This is an example of acceptable writing.
   B. The word *proposal* should be spelled *preposal*.
   C. The words *to increase the number of suggestions submitted* should be changed to *an increase in the number of suggestions is expected*.
   D. The word *promote* should be changed to *enhance*, and the word *increase* should be changed to *add to*.

9. The introduction of inovative managerial techniques should be preceded by careful analysis of the specific circumstances and conditions in each department.   9.____
   A. This is an example of acceptable writing.
   B. The word *techniques* should be spelled *techneques*.
   C. The word *inovative* should be spelled *innovative*.
   D. A comma should be placed after the word *circumstances* and after the word *conditions*.

10. This occurrence indicates that such criticism embarrasses him.   10.____
    A. This is an example of acceptable writing.
    B. The word *occurrence* should be spelled *occurence*.
    C. The word *criticism* should be spelled *criticism*.
    D. The word *embarrasses* should be spelled *embarasses*.

11. He can recommend a mechanic whose work is reliable.   11.____
    A. This is an example of acceptable writing.
    B. The word *reliable* should be spelled *relyable*.
    C. The word *whose* should be spelled *who's*.
    D. The word *mechanic* should be spelled *mecanic*.

12. She typed quickly; like someone who had not a moment to lose.   12.____
    A. This is an example of acceptable writing.
    B. The word *not* should be removed.
    C. The semicolon should be changed to a comma.
    D. The word *quickly* should be placed before instead of after the word *typed*.

13. She insisted that she had to much work to do.   13.____
    A. This is an example of acceptable writing.
    B. The word *insisted* should be spelled *insisted*.

C. The word *to* used in front of *much* should be spelled *too*.
D. The word *do* should be changed to *be done*.

14. The report, along with the accompanying documents, were submitted for review. 14.___
    A. This is an example of acceptable writing.
    B. The words *were submitted* should be changed to *was submitted*.
    C. The word *accompanying* should be spelled *accompaning*.
    D. The comma after the word *report* should be taken out.

15. If others must use your files, be certain that they understand how the system works, but insist that you do all the filing and refiling. 15.___
    A. This is an example of acceptable writing.
    B. There should be a period after the word *works*, and the word *but* should start a new sentence.
    C. The words *filing* and *refiling* should be spelled *fileing* and *refileing*.
    D. There should be a comma after the word *but*.

16. The appeal was not considered because of its late arrival. 16.___
    A. This is an example of acceptable writing.
    B. The word *its* should be changed to *it's*.
    C. The word *its* should be changed to *the*.
    D. The words *late arrival* should be changed to *arrival late*.

17. The letter must be read carefuly to determine under which subject it should be filed. 17.___
    A. This is an example of acceptable writing.
    B. The word *under* should be changed to *at*.
    C. The word *determine* should be spelled *determin*.
    D. The word *carefuly* should be spelled *carefully*.

18. He showed potential as an office manager, but he lacked skill in delegating work. 18.___
    A. This is an example of acceptable writing.
    B. The word *delegating* should be spelled *delagating*.
    C. The word *potential* should be spelled *potencial*.
    D. The words *he lacked* should be changed to *was lacking*.

19. His supervisor told him that it would be all right to receive personal mail at the office. 19.___
    A. This is an example of acceptable writing.
    B. The words *all right* should be changed to *alright*.
    C. The word *personal* should be spelled *personel*.
    D. The word *mail* should be changed to *letters*.

20. The report, along with the accompanying documents, were submitted for review. 20.___
    A. This is an example of acceptable writing.
    B. The words *were submitted* should be changed to *was submitted*.
    C. The word *accompanying* should be spelled *accompaning*.
    D. The comma after the word *report* should be taken out.

KEY (CORRECT ANSWERS)

1.	C	11.	A
2.	D	12.	C
3.	A	13.	C
4.	C	14.	B
5.	D	15.	A
6.	B	16.	A
7.	D	17.	D
8.	A	18.	A
9.	C	19.	A
10.	A	20.	B

PREPARING WRITTEN MATERIAL

PARAGRAPH REARRANGEMENT
COMMENTARY

The sentences which follow are in scrambled order. You are to rearrange them in proper order and indicate the letter choice containing the correct answer at the space at the right.

Each group of sentences in this section is actually a paragraph presented in scrambled order. Each sentence in the group has a place in that paragraph; no sentence is to be left out. You are to read each group of sentences and decide upon the best order in which to put the sentences so as to form as well-organized paragraph.

The questions in this section measure the ability to solve a problem when all the facts relevant to its solution are not given.

More specifically, certain positions of responsibility and authority require the employee to discover connections between events sometimes, apparently, unrelated. In order to do this, the employee will find it necessary to correctly infer that unspecified events have probably occurred or are likely to occur. This ability becomes especially important when action must be taken on incomplete information.

Accordingly, these questions require competitors to choose among several suggested alternatives, each of which presents a different sequential arrangement of the events. Competitors must choose the MOST logical of the suggested sequences.

In order to do so, they may be required to draw on general knowledge to infer missing concepts or events that are essential to sequencing the given events. Competitors should be careful to infer only what is essential to the sequence. The plausibility of the wrong alternatives will always require the inclusion of unlikely events or of additional chains of events which are NOT essential to sequencing the given events.

It's very important to remember that you are looking for the best of the four possible choices, and that the best choice of all may not even be one of the answers you're given to choose from.

There is no one right way to these problems. Many people have found it helpful to first write out the order of the sentences, as they would have arranged them, on their scrap paper before looking at the possible answers. If their optimum answer is there, this can save them some time. If it isn't, this method can still give insight into solving the problem. Others find it most helpful to just go through each of the possible choices, contrasting each as they go along. You should use whatever method feels comfortable, and works, for you.

While most of these types of questions are not that difficult, we've added a higher percentage of the difficult type, just to give you more practice. Usually there are only one or two questions on this section that contain such subtle distinctions that you're unable to answer confidently, and you then may find yourself stuck deciding between two possible choices, neither of which you're sure about.

EXAMINATION SECTION
TEST 1

DIRECTIONS: Each question consists of several sentences which can be arranged in a logical sequence. For each question, select the choice which places the numbered sentences in the MOST logical sequence. *PRINT THE LETTER OF THE CORRECT ANSWER IN THE SPACE AT THE RIGHT.*

1. I. A body was found in the woods.
   II. A man proclaimed innocence.
   III. The owner of a gun was located.
   IV. A gun was traced.
   V. The owner of a gun was questioned.
   The CORRECT answer is:

   A. IV, III, V, II, I
   B. II, I, IV, III, V
   C. I, IV, III, V, II
   D. I, III, V, II, IV
   E. I, II, IV, III, V

1.____

2. I. A man was in a hunting accident.
   II. A man fell down a flight of steps.
   III. A man lost his vision in one eye.
   IV. A man broke his leg.
   V. A man had to walk with a cane.
   The CORRECT answer is:

   A. II, IV, V, I, III
   B. IV, V, I, III, II
   C. III, I, IV, V, II
   D. I, III, V, II, IV
   E. I, III, II, IV, V

2.____

3. I. A man is offered a new job.
   II. A woman is offered a new job.
   III. A man works as a waiter.
   IV. A woman works as a waitress.
   V. A woman gives notice.
   The CORRECT answer is:

   A. IV, II, V, III, I
   B. IV, II, V, I, III
   C. II, IV, V, III, I
   D. III, I, IV, II, V
   E. IV, III, II, V, I

3.____

4. I. A train left the station late.
   II. A man was late for work.
   III. A man lost his job.
   IV. Many people complained because the train was late.
   V. There was a traffic jam.
   The CORRECT answer is:

   A. V, II, I, IV, III
   B. V, I, IV, II, III
   C. V, I, II, IV, III
   D. I, V, IV, II, III
   E. II, I, IV, V, III

4.____

5.
   I. The burden of proof as to each issue is determined before trial and remains upon the same party throughout the trial.
   II. The jury is at liberty to believe one witness' testimony as against a number of contradictory witnesses.
   III. In a civil case, the party bearing the burden of proof is required to prove his contention by a fair preponderance of the evidence.
   IV. However, it must be noted that a fair preponderance of evidence does not necessarily mean a greater number of witnesses.
   V. The burden of proof is the burden which rests upon one of the parties to an action to persuade the trier of the facts, generally the jury, that a proposition he asserts is true.
   VI. If the evidence is equally balanced, or if it leaves the jury in such doubt as to be unable to decide the controversy either way, judgment must be given against the party upon whom the burden of proof rests.

   The CORRECT answer is:

   A. III, II, V, IV, I, VI
   B. I, II, VI, V, III, IV
   C. III, IV, V, I, II, VI
   D. V, I, III, VI, IV, II
   E. I, V, III, VI, IV, II

6.
   I. If a parent is without assets and is unemployed, he cannot be convicted of the crime of non-support of a child.
   II. The term *sufficient ability* has been held to mean sufficient financial ability.
   III. It does not matter if his unemployment is by choice or unavoidable circumstances.
   IV. If he fails to take any steps at all, he may be liable to prosecution for endangering the welfare of a child.
   V. Under the penal law, a parent is responsible for the support of his minor child only if the parent is *of* sufficient ability.
   VI. An indigent parent may meet his obligation by borrowing money or by seeking aid under the provisions of the Social Welfare Law.

   The CORRECT answer is:

   A. VI, I, V, III, II, IV
   B. I, III, V, II, IV, VI
   C. V, II, I, III, VI, IV
   D. I, VI, IV, V, II, III
   E. II, V, I, III, VI, IV

7.
   I. Consider, for example, the case of a rabble rouser who urges a group of twenty people to go out and break the windows of a nearby factory.
   II. Therefore, the law fills the indicated gap with the crime of *inciting to riot*.
   III. A person is considered guilty of inciting to riot when he urges ten or more persons to engage in tumultuous and violent conduct of a kind likely to create public alarm.
   IV. However, if he has not obtained the cooperation of at least four people, he cannot be charged with unlawful assembly.
   V. The charge of inciting to riot was added to the law to cover types of conduct which cannot be classified as either the crime of *riot* or the crime of *unlawful assembly*.
   VI. If he acquires the acquiescence of at least four of them, he is guilty of unlawful assembly even if the project does not materialize.

   The CORRECT answer is:

A. III, V, I, VI, IV, II	B. V, I, IV, VI, II, III
C. III, IV, I, V, II, VI	D. V, I, IV, VI, III, II
E. V, III, I, VI, IV, II	

8. I. If, however, the rebuttal evidence presents an issue of credibility, it is for the jury to determine whether the presumption has, in fact, been destroyed.
    II. Once sufficient evidence to the contrary is introduced, the presumption disappears from the trial.
    III. The effect of a presumption is to place the burden upon the adversary to come forward with evidence to rebut the presumption.
    IV. When a presumption is overcome and ceases to exist in the case, the fact or facts which gave rise to the presumption still remain.
    V. Whether a presumption has been overcome is ordinarily a question for the court.
    VI. Such information may furnish a basis for a logical inference.
    The CORRECT answer is:

8._____

A. IV, VI, II, V, I, III	B. III, II, V, I, IV, VI
C. V, III, VI, IV, II, I	D. V, IV, I, II, VI, III
E. II, III, V, I, IV, VI	

9. I. An executive may answer a letter by writing his reply on the face of the letter itself instead of having a return letter typed.
    II. This procedure is efficient because it saves the executive's time, the typist's time, and saves office file space.
    III. Copying machines are used in small offices as well as large offices to save time and money in making brief replies to business letters.
    IV. A copy is made on a copying machine to go into the company files, while the original is mailed back to the sender.
    The CORRECT answer is:

9._____

A. I, II, IV, III	B. I, IV, II, III
C. III, I, IV, II	D. III, IV, II, I

10. I. Most organizations favor one of the types but always include the others to a lesser degree.
     II. However, we can detect a definite trend toward greater use of symbolic control.
     III. We suggest that our local police agencies are today primarily utilizing material control.
     IV. Control can be classified into three types: physical, material, and symbolic.
     The CORRECT answer is:

10._____

A. IV, II, III, I	B. II, I, IV, III
C. III, IV, II, I	D. IV, I, III, II

11. I. Project residents had first claim to this use, followed by surrounding neighborhood children.
     II. By contrast, recreation space within the project's interior was found to be used more often by both groups.
     III. Studies of the use of project grounds in many cities showed grounds left open for public use were neglected and unused, both by residents and by members of the surrounding community.

11._____

IV. Project residents had clearly laid claim to the play spaces, setting up and enforcing unwritten rules for use.
V. Each group, by experience, found their activities easily disrupted by other groups, and their claim to the use of space for recreation difficult to enforce.
The CORRECT answer is:

A. IV, V, I, II, III
B. V, II, IV, III, I
C. I, IV, III, II, V
D. III, V, II, IV, I

12. I. They do not consider the problems correctable within the existing subsidy formula and social policy of accepting all eligible applicants regardless of social behavior and lifestyle.
II. A recent survey, however, indicated that tenants believe these problems correctable by local housing authorities and management within the existing financial formula.
III. Many of the problems and complaints concerning public housing management and design have created resentment between the tenant and the landlord.
IV. This same survey indicated that administrators and managers do not agree with the tenants.
The CORRECT answer is:

A. II, I, III, IV
B. I, III, IV, II
C. III, II, IV, I
D. IV, II, I, III

13. I. In single-family residences, there is usually enough distance between tenants to prevent occupants from annoying one another.
II. For example, a certain small percentage of tenant families has one or more members addicted to alcohol.
III. While managers believe in the right of individuals to live as they choose, the manager becomes concerned when the pattern of living jeopardizes others' rights.
IV. Still others turn night into day, staging lusty entertainments which carry on into the hours when most tenants are trying to sleep.
V. In apartment buildings, however, tenants live so closely together that any misbehavior can result in unpleasant living conditions.
VI. Other families engage in violent argument.
The CORRECT answer is:

A. III, II, V, IV, VI, I
B. I, V, II, VI, IV, III
C. II, V, IV, I, III, VI
D. IV, II, V, VI, III, I

14. I. Congress made the commitment explicit in the Housing Act of 1949, establishing as a national goal the realization of *a decent home and suitable environment for every American family.*
II. The result has been that the goal of decent home and suitable environment is still as far distant as ever for the disadvantaged urban family.
III. In spite of this action by Congress, federal housing programs have continued to be fragmented and grossly underfunded.
IV. The passage of the National Housing Act signalled a new federal commitment to provide housing for the nation's citizens.
The CORRECT answer is:

A. I, IV, III, II
B. IV, I, III, II
C. IV, I, II, III
D. II, IV, I, III

15. I. The greater expense does not necessarily involve *exploitation,* but it is often perceived as exploitative and unfair by those who are aware of the price differences involved, but unaware of operating costs.
   II. Ghetto residents believe they are *exploited* by local merchants, and evidence substantiates some of these beliefs.
   III. However, stores in low-income areas were more likely to be small independents, which could not achieve the economies available to supermarket chains and were, therefore, more likely to charge higher prices, and the customers were more likely to buy smaller-sized packages which are more expensive per unit of measure.
   IV. A study conducted in one city showed that distinctly higher prices were charged for goods sold in ghetto stores than in other areas.

The CORRECT answer is:

A. IV, II, I, III
B. IV, I, III, II
C. II, IV, III, I
D. II, III, IV, I

15.____

KEY (CORRECT ANSWERS)

1. C
2. E
3. B
4. D
5. D

6. C
7. A
8. B
9. C
10. D

11. D
12. C
13. B
14. B
15. C

PHILOSOPHY, PRINCIPLES, PRACTICES AND TECHNICS
OF
SUPERVISION, ADMINISTRATION, MANAGEMENT AND ORGANIZATION

TABLE OF CONTENTS

		Page
I.	MEANING OF SUPERVISION	1
II.	THE OLD AND THE NEW SUPERVISION	1
III.	THE EIGHT (8) BASIC PRINCIPLES OF THE NEW SUPERVISION	1
	1. Principle of Responsibility	1
	2. Principle of Authority	2
	3. Principle of Self-Growth	2
	4. Principle of Individual Worth	2
	5. Principle of Creative Leadership	2
	6. Principle of Success and Failure	2
	7. Principle of Science	3
	8. Principle of Cooperation	3
IV.	WHAT IS ADMINISTRATION?	3
	1. Practices commonly classed as "Supervisory"	3
	2. Practices commonly classed as "Administrative"	3
	3. Practices classified as both "Supervisory" and "Administrative"	4
V.	RESPONSIBILITIES OF THE SUPERVISOR	4
VI.	COMPETENCIES OF THE SUPERVISOR	4
VII.	THE PROFESSIONAL SUPERVISOR—EMPLOYEE RELATIONSHIP	4
VIII.	MINI-TEXT IN SUPERVISION, ADMINISTRATION, MANAGEMENT AND ORGANIZATION	5
	A. Brief Highlights	5
	1. Levels of Management	5
	2. What the Supervisor Must Learn	6
	3. A Definition of Supervision	6
	4. Elements of the Team Concept	6
	5. Principles of Organization	6
	6. The Four Important Parts of Every Job	6
	7. Principles of Delegation	6
	8. Principles of Effective Communications	7
	9. Principles of Work Improvement	7

TABLE OF CONTENTS (CONTINUED)

10. Areas of Job Improvement		7
11. Seven Key Points in Making Improvements		7
12. Corrective Techniques for Job Improvement		7
13. A Planning Checklist		8
14. Five Characteristics of Good Directions		8
15. Types of Directions		8
16. Controls		8
17. Orienting the New Employee		8
18. Checklist for Orienting New Employees		8
19. Principles of Learning		9
20. Causes of Poor Performance		9
21. Four Major Steps in On-The-Job Instructions		9
22. Employees Want Five Things		9
23. Some Don'ts in Regard to Praise		9
24. How to Gain Your Workers' Confidence		9
25. Sources of Employee Problems		9
26. The Supervisor's Key to Discipline		10
27. Five Important Processes of Management		10
28. When the Supervisor Fails to Plan		10
29. Fourteen General Principles of Management		10
30. Change		10

B. Brief Topical Summaries — 11
    I.   Who/What is the Supervisor? — 11
    II.   The Sociology of Work — 11
    III.   Principles and Practices of Supervision — 12
    IV.   Dynamic Leadership — 12
    V.   Processes for Solving Problems — 12
    VI.   Training for Results — 13
    VII.   Health, Safety and Accident Prevention — 13
    VIII.   Equal Employment Opportunity — 13
    IX.   Improving Communications — 14
    X.   Self-Development — 14
    XI.   Teaching and Training — 14
        A. The Teaching Process — 14
            1. Preparation — 14
            2. Presentation — 15
            3. Summary — 15
            4. Application — 15
            5. Evaluation — 15
        B. Teaching Methods — 15
            1. Lecture — 15
            2. Discussion — 15
            3. Demonstration — 16
            4. Performance — 16
            5. Which Method to Use — 16

PHILOSOPHY, PRINCIPLES, PRACTICES, AND TECHNICS
OF
SUPERVISION, ADMINISTRATION, MANAGEMENT AND ORGANIZATION

I. MEANING OF SUPERVISION

The extension of the democratic philosophy has been accompanied by an extension in the scope of supervision. Modern leaders and supervisors no longer think of supervision in the narrow sense of being confined chiefly to visiting employees, supplying materials, or rating the staff. They regard supervision as being intimately related to all the concerned agencies of society, they speak of the supervisor's function in terms of "growth", rather than the "improvement," of employees.

This modern concept of supervision may be defined as follows:

Supervision is leadership and the development of leadership within groups which are cooperatively engaged in inspection, research, training, guidance and evaluation.

II. THE OLD AND THE NEW SUPERVISION

TRADITIONAL
1. Inspection
2. Focused on the employee
3. Visitation
4. Random and haphazard
5. Imposed and authoritarian
6. One person usually

MODERN
1. Study and analysis
2. Focused on aims, materials, methods, supervisors, employees, environment
3. Demonstrations, intervisitation, workshops, directed reading, bulletins, etc.
4. Definitely organized and planned (scientific)
5. Cooperative and democratic
6. Many persons involved (creative)

III THE EIGHT (8) BASIC PRINCIPLES OF THE NEW SUPERVISION

1. *PRINCIPLE OF RESPONSIBILITY*
   Authority to act and responsibility for acting must be joined.
   a. If you give responsibility, give authority.
   b. Define employee duties clearly.
   c. Protect employees from criticism by others.
   d. Recognize the rights as well as obligations of employees.
   e. Achieve the aims of a democratic society insofar as it is possible within the area of your work.
   f. Establish a situation favorable to training and learning.
   g. Accept ultimate responsibility for everything done in your section, unit, office, division, department.
   h. Good administration and good supervision are inseparable.

2. *PRINCIPLE OF AUTHORITY*
The success of the supervisor is measured by the extent to which the power of authority is not used.
   a. Exercise simplicity and informality in supervision.
   b. Use the simplest machinery of supervision.
   c. If it is good for the organization as a whole, it is probably justified.
   d. Seldom be arbitrary or authoritative.
   e. Do not base your work on the power of position or of personality.
   f. Permit and encourage the free expression of opinions.

3. *PRINCIPLE OF SELF-GROWTH*
The success of the supervisor is measured by the extent to which, and the speed with which, he is no longer needed.
   a. Base criticism on principles, not on specifics.
   b. Point out higher activities to employees.
   c. Train for self-thinking by employees, to meet new situations.
   d. Stimulate initiative, self-reliance and individual responsibility.
   e. Concentrate on stimulating the growth of employees rather than on removing defects.

4. *PRINCIPLE OF INDIVIDUAL WORTH*
Respect for the individual is a paramount consideration in supervision.
   a. Be human and sympathetic in dealing with employees.
   b. Don't nag about things to be done.
   c. Recognize the individual differences among employees and seek opportunities to permit best expression of each personality.

5. *PRINCIPLE OF CREATIVE LEADERSHIP*
The best supervision is that which is not apparent to the employee.
   a. Stimulate, don't drive employees to creative action.
   b. Emphasize doing good things.
   c. Encourage employees to do what they do best.
   d. Do not be too greatly concerned with details of subject or method.
   e. Do not be concerned exclusively with immediate problems and activities.
   f. Reveal higher activities and make them both desired and maximally possible.
   g. Determine procedures in the light of each situation but see that these are derived from a sound basic philosophy.
   h. Aid, inspire and lead so as to liberate the creative spirit latent in all good employees.

6. *PRINCIPLE OF SUCCESS AND FAILURE*
There are no unsuccessful employees, only unsuccessful supervisors who have failed to give proper leadership.
   a. Adapt suggestions to the capacities, attitudes, and prejudices of employees.
   b. Be gradual, be progressive, be persistent.
   c. Help the employee find the general principle; have the employee apply his own problem to the general principle.
   d. Give adequate appreciation for good work and honest effort.
   e. Anticipate employee difficulties and help to prevent them.
   f. Encourage employees to do the desirable things they will do anyway.
   g. Judge your supervision by the results it secures.

7. *PRINCIPLE OF SCIENCE*
   Successful supervision is scientific, objective, and experimental. It is based on facts, not on prejudices.
          a. Be cumulative in results.
          b. Never divorce your suggestions from the goals of training.
          c. Don't be impatient of results.
          d. Keep all matters on a professional, not a personal level.
          e. Do not be concerned exclusively with immediate problems and activities.
          f. Use objective means of determining achievement and rating where possible.

8. *PRINCIPLE OF COOPERATION*
   Supervision is a cooperative enterprise between supervisor and employee.
          a. Begin with conditions as they are.
          b. Ask opinions of all involved when formulating policies.
          c. Organization is as good as its weakest link.
          d. Let employees help to determine policies and department programs.
          e. Be approachable and accessible - physically and mentally.
          f. Develop pleasant social relationships.

IV. WHAT IS ADMINISTRATION?

Administration is concerned with providing the environment, the material facilities, and the operational procedures that will promote the maximum growth and development of supervisors and employees. (Organization is an aspect, and a concomitant, of administration.)

There is no sharp line of demarcation between supervision and administration; these functions are intimately interrelated and, often, overlapping. They are complementary activities.

1. *PRACTICES COMMONLY CLASSED AS "SUPERVISORY"*
          a. Conducting employees conferences
          b. Visiting sections, units, offices, divisions, departments
          c. Arranging for demonstrations
          d. Examining plans
          e. Suggesting professional reading
          f. Interpreting bulletins
          g. Recommending in-service training courses
          h. Encouraging experimentation
          i. Appraising employee morale
          j. Providing for intervisitation

2. *PRACTICES COMMONLY CLASSIFIED AS "ADMINISTRATIVE"*
          a. Management of the office
          b. Arrangement of schedules for extra duties
          c. Assignment of rooms or areas
          d. Distribution of supplies
          e. Keeping records and reports
          f. Care of audio-visual materials
          g. Keeping inventory records
          h. Checking record cards and books
          i. Programming special activities
          j. Checking on the attendance and punctuality of employees

3. *PRACTICES COMMONLY CLASSIFIED AS BOTH "SUPERVISORY" AND "ADMINISTRATIVE"*
   a. Program construction
   b. Testing or evaluating outcomes
   c. Personnel accounting
   d. Ordering instructional materials

V. RESPONSIBILITIES OF THE SUPERVISOR

A person employed in a supervisory capacity must constantly be able to improve his own efficiency and ability. He represents the employer to the employees and only continuous self-examination can make him a capable supervisor.

Leadership and training are the supervisor's responsibility. An efficient working unit is one in which the employees work with the supervisor. It is his job to bring out the best in his employees. He must always be relaxed, courteous and calm in his association with his employees. Their feelings are important, and a harsh attitude does not develop the most efficient employees.

VI. COMPETENCIES OF THE SUPERVISOR

1. Complete knowledge of the duties and responsibilities of his position.
2. To be able to organize a job, plan ahead and carry through.
3. To have self-confidence and initiative.
4. To be able to handle the unexpected situation and make quick decisions.
5. To be able to properly train subordinates in the positions they are best suited for.
6. To be able to keep good human relations among his subordinates.
7. To be able to keep good human relations between his subordinates and himself and to earn their respect and trust.

VII. THE PROFESSIONAL SUPERVISOR-EMPLOYEE RELATIONSHIP

There are two kinds of efficiency: one kind is only apparent and is produced in organizations through the exercise of mere discipline; this is but a simulation of the second, or true, efficiency which springs from spontaneous cooperation. If you are a manager, no matter how great or small your responsibility, it is your job, in the final analysis, to create and develop this involuntary cooperation among the people whom you supervise. For, no matter how powerful a combination of money, machines, and materials a company may have, this is a dead and sterile thing without a team of willing, thinking and articulate people to guide it.

The following 21 points are presented as indicative of the exemplary basic relationship that should exist between supervisor and employee:

1. Each person wants to be liked and respected by his fellow employee and wants to be treated with consideration and respect by his superior.
2. The most competent employee will make an error. However, in a unit where good relations exist between the supervisor and his employees, tenseness and fear do not exist. Thus, errors are not hidden or covered up and the efficiency of a unit is not impaired.
3. Subordinates resent rules, regulations, or orders that are unreasonable or unexplained.
4. Subordinates are quick to resent unfairness, harshness, injustices and favoritism.
5. An employee will accept responsibility if he knows that he will be complimented for a job well done, and not too harshly chastised for failure; that his supervisor will check the cause of the failure, and, if it was the supervisor's fault, he will assume the blame therefore. If it was the employee's fault, his supervisor will explain the correct method or means of handling the responsibility.

6. An employee wants to receive credit for a suggestion he has made, that is used. If a suggestion cannot be used, the employee is entitled to an explanation. The supervisor should not say "no" and close the subject.
7. Fear and worry slow up a worker's ability. Poor working environment can impair his physical and mental health. A good supervisor avoids forceful methods, threats and arguments to get a job done.
8. A forceful supervisor is able to train his employees individually and as a team, and is able to motivate them in the proper channels.
9. A mature supervisor is able to properly evaluate his subordinates and to keep them happy and satisfied.
10. A sensitive supervisor will never patronize his subordinates.
11. A worthy supervisor will respect his employees' confidences.
12. Definite and clear-cut responsibilities should be assigned to each executive.
13. Responsibility should always be coupled with corresponding authority.
14. No change should be made in the scope or responsibilities of a position without a definite understanding to that effect on the part of all persons concerned.
15. No executive or employee, occupying a single position in the organization, should be subject to definite orders from more than one source.
16. Orders should never be given to subordinates over the head of a responsible executive. Rather than do this, the officer in question should be supplanted.
17. Criticisms of subordinates should, whoever possible, be made privately, and in no case should a subordinate be criticized in the presence of executives or employees of equal or lower rank.
18. No dispute or difference between executives or employees as to authority or responsibilities should be considered too trivial for prompt and careful adjudication.
19. Promotions, wage changes, and disciplinary action should always be approved by the executive immediately superior to the one directly responsible.
20. No executive or employee should ever be required, or expected, to be at the same time an assistant to, and critic of, another.
21. Any executive whose work is subject to regular inspection should, whever practicable, be given the assistance and facilities necessary to enable him to maintain an independent check of the quality of his work.

VIII. MINI-TEXT IN SUPERVISION, ADMINISTRATION, MANAGEMENT, AND ORGANIZATION

A. BRIEF HIGHLIGHTS

Listed concisely and sequentially are major headings and important data in the field for quick recall and review.

1. *LEVELS OF MANAGEMENT*

   Any organization of some size has several levels of management. In terms of a ladder the levels are:

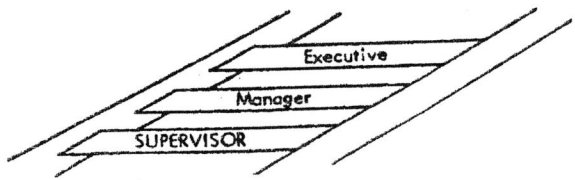

The first level is very important because it is the beginning point of management leadership.

2. WHAT THE SUPERVISOR MUST LEARN
A supervisor must learn to:
(1) Deal with people and their differences
(2) Get the job done through people
(3) Recognize the problems when they exist
(4) Overcome obstacles to good performance
(5) Evaluate the performance of people
(6) Check his own performance in terms of accomplishment

3. A DEFINITION OF SUPERVISOR
The term supervisor means any individual having authority, in the interests of the employer, to hire, transfer, suspend, lay-off, recall, promote, discharge, assign, reward, or discipline other employees or responsibility to direct them, or to adjust their grievances, or effectively to recommend such action, if, in connection with the foregoing, exercise of such authority is not of a merely routine or clerical nature but requires the use of independent judgment.

4. ELEMENTS OF THE TEAM CONCEPT
What is involved in teamwork? The component parts are:
(1) Members   (3) Goals   (5) Cooperation
(2) A leader   (4) Plans   (6) Spirit

5. PRINCIPLES OF ORGANIZATION
(1) A team member must know what his job is.
(2) Be sure that the nature and scope of a job are understood.
(3) Authority and responsibility should be carefully spelled out.
(4) A supervisor should be permitted to make the maximum number of decisions affecting his employees.
(5) Employees should report to only one supervisor.
(6) A supervisor should direct only as many employees as he can handle effectively.
(7) An organization plan should be flexible.
(8) Inspection and performance of work should be separate.
(9) Organizational problems should receive immediate attention.
(10) Assign work in line with ability and experience.

6. THE FOUR IMPORTANT PARTS OF EVERY JOB
(1) Inherent in every job is the *accountability* for results.
(2) A second set of factors in every job is *responsibilities*.
(3) Along with duties and responsibilities one must have the *authority* to act within certain limits without obtaining permission to proceed.
(4) No job exists in a vacuum. The supervisor is surrounded by key *relationships*.

7. PRINCIPLES OF DELEGATION
Where work is delegated for the first time, the supervisor should think in terms of these questions:
(1) Who is best qualified to do this?
(2) Can an employee improve his abilities by doing this?
(3) How long should an employee spend on this?
(4) Are there any special problems for which he will need guidance?
(5) How broad a delegation can I make?

8. PRINCIPLES OF EFFECTIVE COMMUNICATIONS
  (1) Determine the media
  (2) To whom directed?
  (3) Identification and source authority
  (4) Is communication understood?

9. PRINCIPLES OF WORK IMPROVEMENT
  (1) Most people usually do only the work which is assigned to them
  (2) Workers are likely to fit assigned work into the time available to perform it
  (3) A good workload usually stimulates output
  (4) People usually do their best work when they know that results will be reviewed or inspected
  (5) Employees usually feel that someone else is responsible for conditions of work, workplace layout, job methods, type of tools/equipment, and other such factors
  (6) Employees are usually defensive about their job security
  (7) Employees have natural resistance to change
  (8) Employees can support or destroy a supervisor
  (9) A supervisor usually earns the respect of his people through his personal example of diligence and efficiency

10. AREAS OF JOB IMPROVEMENT
The areas of job improvement are quite numerous, but the most common ones which a supervisor can identify and utilize are:
  (1) Departmental layout   (5) Work methods
  (2) Flow of work   (6) Materials handling
  (3) Workplace layout   (7) Utilization
  (4) Utilization of manpower   (8) Motion economy

11. SEVEN KEY POINTS IN MAKING IMPROVEMENTS
  (1) Select the job to be improved
  (2) Study how it is being done now
  (3) Question the present method
  (4) Determine actions to be taken
  (5) Chart proposed method
  (6) Get approval and apply
  (7) Solicit worker participation

12. CORRECTIVE TECHNIQUES OF JOB IMPROVEMENT

Specific Problems	General Improvement	Corrective Techniques
(1) Size of workload	(1) Departmental layout	(1) Study with scale model
(2) Inability to meet schedules	(2) Flow of work	(2) Flow chart study
(3) Strain and fatigue	(3) Work plan layout	(3) Motion analysis
(4) Improper use of men and skills	(4) Utilization of manpower	(4) Comparison of units produced to standard allowance
(5) Waste, poor quality, unsafe conditions	(5) Work methods	(5) Methods analysis
(6) Bottleneck conditions that hinder output	(6) Materials handling	(6) Flow chart & equipment study
(7) Poor utilization of equipment and machine	(7) Utilization of equipment	(7) Down time vs. running time
(8) Efficiency and productivity of labor	(8) Motion economy	(8) Motion analysis

13. A PLANNING CHECKLIST

(1) Objectives	(6) Resources	(11) Safety
(2) Controls	(7) Manpower	(12) Money
(3) Delegations	(8) Equipment	(13) Work
(4) Communications	(9) Supplies and materials	(14) Timing of improvements
(5) Resources	(10) Utilization of time	

14. FIVE CHARACTERISTICS OF GOOD DIRECTIONS

In order to get results, directions must be:
- (1) Possible of accomplishment
- (2) Agreeable with worker interests
- (3) Related to mission
- (4) Planned and complete
- (5) Unmistakably clear

15. TYPES OF DIRECTIONS

- (1) Demands or direct orders
- (2) Requests
- (3) Suggestion or implication
- (4) Volunteering

16. CONTROLS

A typical listing of the overall areas in which the supervisor should establish controls might be:

- (1) Manpower
- (2) Materials
- (3) Quality of work
- (4) Quantity of work
- (5) Time
- (6) Space
- (7) Money
- (8) Methods

17. ORIENTING THE NEW EMPLOYEE

- (1) Prepare for him
- (2) Welcome the new employee
- (3) Orientation for the job
- (4) Follow-up

18. CHECKLIST FOR ORIENTING NEW EMPLOYEES

	Yes	No
(1) Do your appreciate the feelings of new employees when they first report for work?	___	___
(2) Are you aware of the fact that the new employee must make a big adjustment to his job?	___	___
(3) Have you given him good reasons for liking the job and the organization?	___	___
(4) Have you prepared for his first day on the job?	___	___
(5) Did you welcome him cordially and make him feel needed?	___	___
(6) Did you establish rapport with him so that he feels free to talk and discuss matters with you?	___	___
(7) Did you explain his job to him and his relationship to you?	___	___
(8) Does he know that his work will be evaluated periodically on a basis that is fair and objective?	___	___
(9) Did you introduce him to his fellow workers in such a way that they are likely to accept him?	___	___
(10) Does he know what employee benefits he will receive?	___	___
(11) Does he understand the importance of being on the job and what to do if he must leave his duty station?	___	___
(12) Has he been impressed with the importance of accident prevention and safe practice?	___	___
(13) Does he generally know his way around the department?	___	___
(14) Is he under the guidance of a sponsor who will teach the right ways of doing things?	___	___
(15) Do you plan to follow-up so that he will continue to adjust successfully to his job?	___	___

19. *PRINCIPLES OF LEARNING*
    (1) Motivation   (2) Demonstration or explanation   (3) Practice

20. *CAUSES OF POOR PERFORMANCE*
    (1) Improper training for job
    (2) Wrong tools
    (3) Inadequate directions
    (4) Lack of supervisory follow-up
    (5) Poor communications
    (6) Lack of standards of performance
    (7) Wrong work habits
    (8) Low morale
    (9) Other

21. *FOUR MAJOR STEPS IN ON-THE-JOB INSTRUCTION*
    (1) Prepare the worker
    (2) Present the operation
    (3) Tryout performance
    (4) Follow-up

22. *EMPLOYEES WANT FIVE THINGS*
    (1) Security   (2) Opportunity   (3) Recognition   (4) Inclusion   (5) Expression

23. *SOME DON'TS IN REGARD TO PRAISE*
    (1) Don't praise a person for something he hasn't done
    (2) Don't praise a person unless you can be sincere
    (3) Don't be sparing in praise just because your superior withholds it from you
    (4) Don't let too much time elapse between good performance and recognition of it

24. *HOW TO GAIN YOUR WORKERS' CONFIDENCE*
    Methods of developing confidence include such things as:
    (1) Knowing the interests, habits, hobbies of employees
    (2) Admitting your own inadequacies
    (3) Sharing and telling of confidence in others
    (4) Supporting people when they are in trouble
    (5) Delegating matters that can be well handled
    (6) Being frank and straightforward about problems and working conditions
    (7) Encouraging others to bring their problems to you
    (8) Taking action on problems which impede worker progress

25. *SOURCES OF EMPLOYEE PROBLEMS*
    On-the-job causes might be such things as:
    (1) A feeling that favoritism is exercised in assignments
    (2) Assignment of overtime
    (3) An undue amount of supervision
    (4) Changing methods or systems
    (5) Stealing of ideas or trade secrets
    (6) Lack of interest in job
    (7) Threat of reduction in force
    (8) Ignorance or lack of communications
    (9) Poor equipment
    (10) Lack of knowing how supervisor feels toward employee
    (11) Shift assignments

    Off-the-job problems might have to do with:
    (1) Health   (2) Finances   (3) Housing   (4) Family

26. THE SUPERVISOR'S KEY TO DISCIPLINE

There are several key points about discipline which the supervisor should keep in mind:
1. Job discipline is one of the disciplines of life and is directed by the supervisor.
2. It is more important to correct an employee fault than to fix blame for it.
3. Employee performance is affected by problems both on the job and off.
4. Sudden or abrupt changes in behavior can be indications of important employee problems.
5. Problems should be dealt with as soon as possible after they are identified.
6. The attitude of the supervisor may have more to do with solving problems than the techniques of problem solving.
7. Correction of employee behavior should be resorted to only after the supervisor is sure that training or counseling will not be helpful.
8. Be sure to document your disciplinary actions.
9. Make sure that you are disciplining on the basis of facts rather than personal feelings.
10. Take each disciplinary step in order, being careful not to make snap judgments, or decisions based on impatience.

27. FIVE IMPORTANT PROCESSES OF MANAGEMENT
(1) Planning (2) Organizing (3) Scheduling
(4) Controlling (5) Motivating

28. WHEN THE SUPERVISOR FAILS TO PLAN
1. Supervisor creates impression of not knowing his job
2. May lead to excessive overtime
3. Job runs itself -- supervisor lacks control
4. Deadlines and appointments missed
5. Parts of the work go undone
6. Work interrupted by emergencies
7. Sets a bad example
8. Uneven workload creates peaks and valleys
9. Too much time on minor details at expense of more important tasks

29. FOURTEEN GENERAL PRINCIPLES OF MANAGEMENT
(1) Division of work
(2) Authority and responsibility
(3) Discipline
(4) Unity of command
(5) Unity of direction
(6) Subordination of individual interest to general interest
(7) Remuneration of personnel
(8) Centralization
(9) Scalar chain
(10) Order
(11) Equity
(12) Stability of tenure of personnel
(13) Initiative
(14) Esprit de corps

30. CHANGE

Bringing about change is perhaps attempted more often, and yet less well understood, than anything else the supervisor does. How do people generally react to change? (People tend to resist change that is imposed upon them by other individuals or circumstances.

Change is characteristic of every situation. It is a part of every real endeavor where the efforts of people are concerned.

A. Why do people resist change?
   People may resist change because of:
   (1) Fear of the unknown
   (2) Implied criticism
   (3) Unpleasant experiences in the past
   (4) Fear of loss of status
   (5) Threat to the ego
   (6) Fear of loss of economic stability

B. How can we best overcome the resistance to change?
   In initiating change, take these steps:
   (1) Get ready to sell
   (2) Identify sources of help
   (3) Anticipate objections
   (4) Sell benefits
   (5) Listen in depth
   (6) Follow up

B. BRIEF TOPICAL SUMMARIES

I. WHO/WHAT IS THE SUPERVISOR?
1. The supervisor is often called the "highest level employee and the lowest level manager."
2. A supervisor is a member of both management and the work group. He acts as a bridge between the two.
3. Most problems in supervision are in the area of human relations, or people problems.
4. Employees expect: Respect, opportunity to learn and to advance, and a sense of belonging, and so forth.
5. Supervisors are responsible for directing people and organizing work. Planning is of paramount importance.
6. A position description is a set of duties and responsibilities inherent to a given position.
7. It is important to keep the position description up-to-date and to provide each employee with his own copy.

II. THE SOCIOLOGY OF WORK
1. People are alike in many ways; however, each individual is unique.
2. The supervisor is challenged in getting to know employee differences. Acquiring skills in evaluating individuals is an asset.
3. Maintaining meaningful working relationships in the organization is of great importance.
4. The supervisor has an obligation to help individuals to develop to their fullest potential.
5. Job rotation on a planned basis helps to build versatility and to maintain interest and enthusiasm in work groups.
6. Cross training (job rotation) provides backup skills.
7. The supervisor can help reduce tension by maintaining a sense of humor, providing guidance to employees, and by making reasonable and timely decisions. Employees respond favorably to working under reasonably predictable circumstances.
8. Change is characteristic of all managerial behavior. The supervisor must adjust to changes in procedures, new methods, technological changes, and to a number of new and sometimes challenging situations.
9. To overcome the natural tendency for people to resist change, the supervisor should become more skillful in initiating change.

III. PRINCIPLES AND PRACTICES OF SUPERVISION
1. Employees should be required to answer to only one superior.
2. A supervisor can effectively direct only a limited number of employees, depending upon the complexity, variety, and proximity of the jobs involved.
3. The organizational chart presents the organization in graphic form. It reflects lines of authority and responsibility as well as interrelationships of units within the organization.
4. Distribution of work can be improved through an analysis using the "Work Distribution Chart."
5. The "Work Distribution Chart" reflects the division of work within a unit in understandable form.
6. When related tasks are given to an employee, he has a better chance of increasing his skills through training.
7. The individual who is given the responsibility for tasks must also be given the appropriate authority to insure adequate results.
8. The supervisor should delegate repetitive, routine work. Preparation of recurring reports, maintaining leave and attendance records are some examples.
9. Good discipline is essential to good task performance. Discipline is reflected in the actions of employees on the job in the absence of supervision.
10. Disciplinary action may have to be taken when the positive aspects of discipline have failed. Reprimand, warning, and suspension are examples of disciplinary action.
11. If a situation calls for a reprimand, be sure it is deserved and remember it is to be done in private.

IV. DYNAMIC LEADERSHIP
1. A style is a personal method or manner of exerting influence.
2. Authoritarian leaders often see themselves as the source of power and authority.
3. The democratic leader often perceives the group as the source of authority and power.
4. Supervisors tend to do better when using the pattern of leadership that is most natural for them.
5. Social scientists suggest that the effective supervisor use the leadership style that best fits the problem or circumstances involved.
6. All four styles -- telling, selling, consulting, joining -- have their place. Using one does not preclude using the other at another time.
7. The theory X point of view assumes that the average person dislikes work, will avoid it whenever possible, and must be coerced to achieve organizational objectives.
8. The theory Y point of view assumes that the average person considers work to be as natural as play, and, when the individual is committed, he requires little supervision or direction to accomplish desired objectives.
9. The leader's basic assumptions concerning human behavior and human nature affect his actions, decisions, and other managerial practices.
10. Dissatisfaction among employees is often present, but difficult to isolate. The supervisor should seek to weaken dissatisfaction by keeping promises, being sincere and considerate, keeping employees informed, and so forth.
11. Constructive suggestions should be encouraged during the natural progress of the work.

V. PROCESSES FOR SOLVING PROBLEMS
1. People find their daily tasks more meaningful and satisfying when they can improve them.
2. The causes of problems, or the key factors, are often hidden in the background. Ability to solve problems often involves the ability to isolate them from their backgrounds. There is some substance to the cliché that some persons "can't see the forest for the trees."
3. New procedures are often developed from old ones. Problems should be broken down into manageable parts. New ideas can be adapted from old ones.

4. People think differently in problem-solving situations. Using a logical, patterned approach is often useful. One approach found to be useful includes these steps:
   - (a) Define the problem
   - (b) Establish objectives
   - (c) Get the facts
   - (d) Weigh and decide
   - (e) Take action
   - (f) Evaluate action

VI. TRAINING FOR RESULTS
1. Participants respond best when they feel training is important to them.
2. The supervisor has responsibility for the training and development of those who report to him.
3. When training is delegated to others, great care must be exercised to insure the trainer has knowledge, aptitude, and interest for his work as a trainer.
4. Training (learning) of some type goes on continually. The most successful supervisor makes certain the learning contributes in a productive manner to operational goals.
5. New employees are particularly susceptible to training. Older employees facing new job situations require specific training, as well as having need for development and growth opportunities.
6. Training needs require continuous monitoring.
7. The training officer of an agency is a professional with a responsibility to assist supervisors in solving training problems.
8. Many of the self-development steps important to the supervisor's own growth are equally important to the development of peers and subordinates. Knowledge of these is important when the supervisor consults with others on development and growth opportunities.

VII. HEALTH, SAFETY, AND ACCIDENT PREVENTION
1. Management-minded supervisors take appropriate measures to assist employees in maintaining health and in assuring safe practices in the work environment.
2. Effective safety training and practices help to avoid injury and accidents.
3. Safety should be a management goal. All infractions of safety which are observed should be corrected without exception.
4. Employees' safety attitude, training and instruction, provision of safe tools and equipment, supervision, and leadership are considered highly important factors which contribute to safety and which can be influenced directly by supervisors.
5. When accidents do occur they should be investigated promptly for very important reasons, including the fact that information which is gained can be used to prevent accidents in the future.

VIII. EQUAL EMPLOYMENT OPPORTUNITY
1. The supervisor should endeavor to treat all employees fairly, without regard to religion, race, sex, or national origin.
2. Groups tend to reflect the attitude of the leader. Prejudice can be detected even in very subtle form. Supervisors must strive to create a feeling of mutual respect and confidence in every employee.
3. Complete utilization of all human resources is a national goal. Equitable consideration should be accorded women in the work force, minority-group members, the physically and mentally handicapped, and the older employee. The important question is: "Who can do the job?"
4. Training opportunities, recognition for performance, overtime assignments, promotional opportunities, and all other personnel actions are to be handled on an equitable basis.

IX. IMPROVING COMMUNICATIONS

1. Communications is achieving understanding between the sender and the receiver of a message. It also means sharing information -- the creation of understanding.
2. Communication is basic to all human activity. Words are means of conveying meanings; however, real meanings are in people.
3. There are very practical differences in the effectiveness of one-way, impersonal, and two-way communications. Words spoken face-to-face are better understood. Telephone conversations are effective, but lack the rapport of person-to-person exchanges. The whole person communicates.
4. Cooperation and communication in an organization go hand in hand. When there is a mutual respect between people, spelling out rules and procedures for communicating is unnecessary.
5. There are several barriers to effective communications. These include failure to listen with respect and understanding, lack of skill in feedback, and misinterpreting the meanings of words used by the speaker. It is also common practice to listen to what we want to hear, and tune out things we do not want to hear.
6. Communication is management's chief problem. The supervisor should accept the challenge to communicate more effectively and to improve interagency and intra-agency communications.
7. The supervisor may often plan for and conduct meetings. The planning phase is critical and may determine the success or the failure of a meeting.
8. Speaking before groups usually requires extra effort. Stage fright may never disappear completely, but it can be controlled.

X. SELF-DEVELOPMENT

1. Every employee is responsible for his own self-development.
2. Toastmaster and toastmistress clubs offer opportunities to improve skills in oral communications.
3. Planning for one's own self-development is of vital importance. Supervisors know their own strengths and limitations better than anyone else.
4. Many opportunities are open to aid the supervisor in his developmental efforts, including job assignments; training opportunities, both governmental and non-governmental -- to include universities and professional conferences and seminars.
5. Programmed instruction offers a means of studying at one's own rate.
6. Where difficulties may arise from a supervisor's being away from his work for training, he may participate in televised home study or correspondence courses to meet his self-develop- ment needs.

XI. TEACHING AND TRAINING

A. The Teaching Process

Teaching is encouraging and guiding the learning activities of students toward established goals. In most cases this process consists in five steps: preparation, presentation, summarization, evaluation, and application.

1. Preparation

    Preparation is twofold in nature; that of the supervisor and the employee.
    Preparation by the supervisor is absolutely essential to success. He must know what, when, where, how, and whom he will teach. Some of the factors that should be considered are:

(1) The objectives	(5) Employee interest
(2) The materials needed	(6) Training aids
(3) The methods to be used	(7) Evaluation
(4) Employee participation	(8) Summarization

Employee preparation consists in preparing the employee to receive the material. Probably the most important single factor in the preparation of the employee is arousing and maintaining his interest. He must know the objectives of the training, why he is there, how the material can be used, and its importance to him.

2. Presentation

In presentation, have a carefully designed plan and follow it.
The plan should be accurate and complete, yet flexible enough to meet situations as they arise. The method of presentation will be determined by the particular situation and objectives.

3. Summary

A summary should be made at the end of every training unit and program. In addition, there may be internal summaries depending on the nature of the material being taught. The important thing is that the trainee must always be able to understand how each part of the new material relates to the whole.

4. Application

The supervisor must arrange work so the employee will be given a chance to apply new knowledge or skills while the material is still clear in his mind and interest is high. The trainee does not really know whether he has learned the material until he has been given a chance to apply it. If the material is not applied, it loses most of its value.

5. Evaluation

The purpose of all training is to promote learning. To determine whether the training has been a success or failure, the supervisor must evaluate this learning.

In the broadest sense evaluation includes all the devices, methods, skills, and techniques used by the supervisor to keep him self and the employees informed as to their progress toward the objectives they are pursuing. The extent to which the employee has mastered the knowledge, skills, and abilities, or changed his attitudes, as determined by the program objectives, is the extent to which instruction has succeeded or failed.

Evaluation should not be confined to the end of the lesson, day, or program but should be used continuously. We shall note later the way this relates to the rest of the teaching process.

B. Teaching Methods

A teaching method is a pattern of identifiable student and instructor activity used in presenting training material.

All supervisors are faced with the problem of deciding which method should be used at a given time.

As with all methods, there are certain advantages and disadvantages to each method.

1. Lecture

The lecture is direct oral presentation of material by the supervisor. The present trend is to place less emphasis on the trainer's activity and more on that of the trainee.

2. Discussion

Teaching by discussion or conference involves using questions and other techniques to arouse interest and focus attention upon certain areas, and by doing so creating a learning situation. This can be one of the most valuable methods because it gives the employees 'an opportunity to express their ideas and pool their knowledge.

3. Demonstration

The demonstration is used to teach how something works or how to do something. It can be used to show a principle or what the results of a series of actions will be. A well-staged demonstration is particularly effective because it shows proper methods of performance in a realistic manner.

4. Performance

Performance is one of the most fundamental of all learning techniques or teaching methods. The trainee may be able to tell how a specific operation should be performed but he cannot be sure he knows how to perform the operation until he has done so.

5. Which Method to Use

Moreover, there are other methods and techniques of teaching. It is difficult to use any method without other methods entering into it. In any learning situation a combination of methods is usually more effective than anyone method alone.

Finally, evaluation must be integrated into the other aspects of the teaching-learning process.
It must be used in the motivation of the trainees; it must be used to assist in developing understanding during the training; and it must be related to employee application of the results of training.

This is distinctly the role of the supervisor.

SCHOOL BUS OPERATIONS

INTRODUCTION 1
- I. ADMINISTRATION 2
  - A. State Agency(ies) 2
  - B. Local Administrators 3
- II. PUPIL TRANSPORTATION DIRECTOR 3
  - A. State Pupil Transportation Director 3
  - B. Local Pupil Transportation Director and/or Private Operator 4
- III. DRIVER 5
  - A. Duties 5
  - B. Procedure for Selecting 5
  - C. Instructional Program 6
  - D. Driver's Handbook 6
  - E. Behind-the-Wheel Instruction 7
  - F. Driver Evaluation 7
- IV. BUS AIDE (See Special Education Section) 7
- V. MAINTENANCE AND SERVICE PERSONNEL 7
  - A. Staff 7
  - B. Instructional Program 7
- VI. PUPIL MANAGEMENT 8
  - A. Policy 8
  - B. Regulations 9
  - C. Behavior Control 9
  - D. Instruction 10
- VII. PROCEDURES 11
  - A. Policy 11
  - B. Site Selection and Plant Planning 12
  - C. Routing and Scheduling 12
  - D. Inspection of Equipment 14
  - E. Maintenance of Equipment 18
  - F. Records 19
  - G. Emergency Procedures 22
  - H. Communication 23

VIII.	EVALUATION OF THE PUPIL TRANSPORTATION OPERATION	24
	A. Plan for Operating	24
IX.	ACTIVITY BUS OPERATIONS	25
	A. Policies and Guidelines	25
	B. Vehicle and Equipment	27
	C. Training	28

SPECIAL EDUCATION OPERATION

INTRODUCTION		30
I.	GENERAL PRINCIPLES	30
II.	CHARACTERISTICS OF HANDICAPPED PUPILS	31
III.	CLASS PLACEMENT	33
IV.	DISCIPLINE AND BEHAVIOR CONTROL	34
V.	MEDICAL CONCERNS	36
VI.	EMERGENCY PUPIL MANAGEMENT	36
VII.	SUMMARY OF SUCCESSFUL PUPIL MANAGEMENT	37
POLICY DEVELOPMENT		38

NATIONAL MINIMUM STANDARD GUIDELINES FOR SCHOOL BUS OPERATIONS

INTRODUCTION TO OPERATIONS

A successful school transportation operation depends upon a high quality of dedication and performance by all those who are associated with it. This includes the school administrator, transportation director, supervisor, contractor, vehicle maintenance and service personnel, teachers, passengers, the public, and, most importantly, the driver of the school bus.

As school transportation operations expand, the driving environment becomes more complex. Also, inflation escalates the cost of vehicles and repairs and fuel becomes less available and/or more expensive. Therefore, school administrators must meet the challange to maintain increasingly high standards of safety and performance for all elements of the school transportation systems.

SCHOOL BUS OPERATIONS

I. ADMINISTRATION

A. The state agency(ies) responsible for pupil transportation should provide the following:

1. Leadership in the development of a comprehensive pupil transporation program for state-wide application.

2. A State Director of pupil transporation with the staff and other resources required to optimally perform the job.

3. A clear, concise pupil transportation policy.

4. A cost accounting system for all expenditures in the area of pupil transportation.

5. A state-wide management information system to accommodate pupil transportation data, i.e., costs, accidents and injuries, manpower availability, etc.

6. A promotion of pupil transportation safety program utilizing community, legislature, media, law-enforcement agencies and other state agencies concerned with pupil transportation.

7. A manual or handbook for local pupil transporation supervisors and school administrators containing detailed instructions for implementing the state's pupil transportation policies.

8. A manual or handbook for each school bus driver containing the state pupil transportation regulations.

9. A comprehensive school bus driver training program for both pre-service and inservice instruction.

10. A manual or handbook for school bus maintenance personnel.

11. Workshops, seminars and/or conferences for all pupil transportation personnel.

12. Encouragement for institutions of higher learning throughout the state to provide undergraduate and graduate courses in pupil transportation operation and safety. Instruction should be acceptable for certification purposes.

13. Safety and ridership curricula for pupil passengers.

14. Annual visits to local school systems to evaluate transportation systems and provide direction as necessary.

15. Bus and equipment standards that would be conducive to better and safer bus performance.

16. Coordination with other agencies having responsibility for pupil transportation services.

B. Local Administrators should:

1. Implement the state pupil transportation policy.

2. Become involved in the pupil transportation operation within their jurisdiction, including participation in training programs for all transportational personnel; review of school bus routes; provisions for supervision of loading and unloading areas at or near the school; investigation and reporting of accidents and other transportation problems and evaluation of the pupil transportation system. (Suggested action to be taken during and following observation of a school bus route appears at Appendix A.)

3. Provide resource material and require teachers to include instruction in passenger safety in the school curriculum, in compliance with Federal Standard 17.

4. Provide close continuous supervision of loading and unloading areas at or near the school and emergency evacuation drills.

5. Provide adequate supervision for pupils whose bus schedules require them to arrive at school before classes begin and/or remain after classes terminate.

6. Promote public understanding of, and support for, the school system's transportation program.

7. Develop local pupil transportation policies and regulations, including special education transportation policies.

II. PUPIL TRANSPORTATION DIRECTOR

A. State Pupil Transportation Director:

1. Specific duties include, but are not limited to:

    a. Assist in implementing basic pupil transportation policies throughout the state.

    b. Manage the state's pupil transportation program. This includes the ability to plan and budget for the operation and to forecast requirements.

    c. Supervise the preparation of manuals or handbooks for local transportation personnel, and for school bus contractors.

    d. Provide assistance to local school administrators upon request, and direction as may be necessary.

- e. Assist in evaluation of state and local operations and provide recommendations when appropriate.
- f. Plan and direct training for pupil transportation personnel.
- g. Assist local personnel in planning and conducting workshops for pupil passenger safety.
- h. Require and maintain appropriate reports and records.

B. Local Pupil Transportation Director and/or Private Operator:

1. Specific duties include, but are not limited to:
   - a. Provide assistance in planning, budgeting, and forecasting for the pupil transportation system.
   - b. Assist school officials in school site selection and plant planning.
   - c. Provide for chassis and body procurement when appropriate.
   - d. Develop and implement a plan for maintenance of equipment.
   - e. Recruit, select, instruct, and supervise personnel.
   - f. Route and schedule buses.
   - g. Assist in the development and implementation of safety instructional programs for pupils.
   - h. Work with administrators, teachers, transportation personnel, students, parents, and various public and private agencies to improve the quality of the transportation system.
   - i. Investigate and report accidents and other problems associated with the pupil transportation system.
   - j. Keep records and prepare reports.
   - k. Develop and supervise the implementation of an ongoing evaluation plan for the pupil transportation system.

2. The pupil transportation director and/or private operator should have an understanding of the educational process and the role of transportation in this process. Qualifications should include:
   - a. A satisfactory driving record as revealed through checks with the National Driver Register Service and the State Department of Motor Vehicles.
   - b. A satisfactory work history and a record free of criminal convictions. (The same type of checks should be made of the

applicant who seeks employment as a driver of a school bus.) Suggestions as to how this information may be obtained appear in Section III.

   c. An undergraduate degree or equivalent experience in one or more of the following major fields of study: education, business administration, management, transportation, or a related field.

   d. The ability to work effectively with a broad range of individuals and organizations.

   e. The ability to manage personnel and resources to achieve a desired objective.

3. The school transportation director and/or private operator should receive formal instruction in pupil transportation management. This training should include classroom work and field experience.

III. DRIVER

A. There are certain duties that all school bus drivers are required to perform. These may include:

   1. Safe and efficient operation of the vehicle.

   2. Conduct thorough pre-trip and post-trip checks on the vehicle and its special equipment.

   3. Maintain orderly conduct of passengers.

   4. Meet emergency situations in accordance with operating procedures.

   5. Communicate effectively with school staff and public.

   6. Complete required reports.

   7. Successfully complete training programs.

   8. Provide maximum safety for passengers while on the bus and during loading and unloading.

   9. Wearing seat belt when bus is in operation.

B. Procedures for selecting school bus drivers should include:

   1. A proper application form on which information of a personal and occupational history is requested. (An example of a form that the school district may want to use to seek personal and work history information appears at Appendix B.)

   2. A check of applicant's driving record. (Checks of the National

Driver Register and of the files of the State Department of Motor Vehicles are considered essential in the case of the individual who is applying for a position as a school bus driver.)

   NOTE: The applicant should be told that these checks will be made before being asked to complete the application for employment. Establish criteria for rejection of persons with unacceptable driving records.

3. A check to determine if an applicant has a record of criminal convictions. Establish criteria for rejecting those with unacceptable convictions.

4. One or more personal interviews. (A properly conducted interview can be one of the most important of the selection procedures.)

5. A physical examination administered by a School Board approved licensed physician. Tests for TB and other communicable diseases should be included. The physical examination should be conducted annually and at such other times as the school superintendent may deem necessary. (An example appears in Appendix C.)

6. A determination of educational attainment. An applicant for position as a school bus driver should demonstrate the ability to follow detailed written instructions and the ability to record and report data accurately.

C. Instructional Program for School Bus Drivers:

1. Adequate classroom and behind-the-wheel training in a state approved pre-service training program that enables the applicant to handle the vehicle in a safe and efficient manner prior to transporting pupils shall be required.

2. Annual state approved in-service training program shall be required.

D. Each state should develop and make available to each school bus driver a driver's manual or handbook at the time of hiring. (see Section I). This manual should include the following subjects:

1. The transportation policy of the school system.

2. Motor vehicle rules and regulations applicable to school bus operation.

3. Vehicle operation and maintenance.

4. Procedure following involvement in, or approaching, a highway crash.

5. Rudiments of basic first aid procedures. Local school systems should supplement the state-produced manual with information on local policy and practices that may vary from, but should not

conflict with, state level requirements.

E. Behind-the-wheel instruction should be given in the same type and size bus the driver will be operating. When the driver will be expected to operate more than one size and type of vehicle, instruction should be given in the specific handling characteristics of each different vehicle. This instruction should include:

   1. Familiarization with the bus and its equipment.

   2. Emergency exit drills. (see Appendix D)

   3. Use of the special warning and stop lamps and other traffic control devices.

   4. Procedures for loading and unloading pupils at bus stops.

   5. The necessity for cooperating with other highway users.

   6. Entrance to and departure from loading and unloading areas at school buildings.

   7. Entrance to and departure from the bus garage or other storage area.

   8. Procedure for reporting mechanical difficulties.

   9. Post-accident and post-road failure procedures.

   10. Procedure for performing pre-trip and post-trip inspections.

   11. Procedure for recognizing cause and effect relationship between driving habits and vehicle maintenance.

F. School bus drivers should be evaluated at regular intervals. These evaluations may include:

   1. Written tests.

   2. Road performance check.

   3. Evaluation interviews.

IV. **BUS AIDE:** (See Special Education Section)

V. **MAINTENANCE AND SERVICE PERSONNEL**

A. Adequate staff should be employed to perform maintenance functions on a timely basis consistent with safe transportation practices.

B. Instructional Program for Maintenance and Service Personnel.

   1. The transportation system should develop and make available to

maintenance and service personnel the required maintenance and service publications for the equipment being serviced.

2. The transportation system should arrange for pre-service and in-service training for maintenance and service personnel at regular intervals. They should also require or encourage maintenance personnel to attend state-sponsored workshops or training institutes. The training program should include instruction in:

   a. Preventive maintenance procedures.

   b. Repair procedures for each type of vehicle in the fleet and its special equipment.

   c. Service procedures for equipment.

   d. Inspection of the vehicle and its equipment.

   e. Recovery procedures for vehicles involved in an accident or breakdown.

   f. Preparation of maintenance records.

   g. A planned parts and equipment stock.

   h. Establishment of parts inventory control procedures.

VI. PUPIL MANAGEMENT

The program for pupil management should be developed cooperatively by responsible school administrators and transportation personnel. The program should be designed to insure the safety and welfare of all school bus passengers.

A. Policies should include but not be limited to:

   1. The bus driver's authority over, and responsibility for, pupils while in transit.

   2. The pupil's right to "due process" when disciplinary action is taken.

   3. The procedure for resolving problems when the driver needs assistance.

   4. The conditions under which a pupil might be temporarily suspended from the privilege of riding the bus.

   5. Procedures for handling emergencies.

   6. Use of bus monitors (or driver aides).

   7. Requirements and responsibility for school bus passenger and

pedestrian safety instruction.

8. Parental responsibility for damage to bus and/or equipment by their children.

B. Pupil Regulations:

Each school system should have a written set of regulations for transported pupils. These regulations should set forth standards of behavior and promote orderly conduct necessary for safe and efficient transportation. Regulations should include but may not be limited to:

1. Pupil shall arrive at the bus stop before the bus arrives.

2. Wait in a safe place, clear of traffic and away from where the bus stops.

3. Wait in an orderly line and avoid "horseplay."

4. Go directly to an available, or assigned seat when entering the bus.

5. Remain seated, keep aisles and exits clear.

6. Observe classroom conduct, and obey the driver promptly and respectfully.

7. Prohibit the use of profane language, eating and drinking of any type on the bus.

8. Prohibit the use of tobacco, alcohol or drugs and controlled substances.

9. Prohibit the throwing or passing of objects on, from or into buses.

10. Permit pupils to carry only objects that can be held on their laps.

11. Prohibit hazardous materials, objects and animals on the bus.

12. Respect the rights and safety of others.

13. Prohibit leaving or boarding the bus at locations other than the assigned home stop or assigned school.

14. Prohibit putting head, arms or objects out of bus windows.

15. Prohibit hooky-bobbing (hitching rides via rear bumper).

C. Behavior Control:

Proper pupil behavior is important. The distraction of the driver can contribute to accidents. Pupils and parents should be made aware of and abide by reasonable regulations to enhance safety. The consequences of unacceptable behavior should be clearly understood. The following procedures will protect the pupil's rights and maintain order on the bus:

1. The bus driver should establish proper rapport.

2. The bus driver should handle minor infractions through discussion with pupils and/or assignment of seats. (Sometimes a call to the parents will improve behavior.)

3. In case of serious or recurring misconduct, the bus driver must describe the violations in writing on the appropriate forms to the person designated to deal with discipline.

4. First offenses require at least a notification to the pupil and parent(s) either by phone or in person. Second or subsequent offenses may require a conference with the pupil, parents, driver, and school administrator(s) and could result in some period of suspension of pupil's riding privileges.

5. Suspend pupil's riding privileges when the safe operation of the bus is jeopardized.

D. Instruction:

Most pupils ride school buses to and from school or on activity trips. It is important that all pupils be taught safe riding and pedestrian practices. This instruction should be given as soon as practical at the beginning of the school year. Appropriate instruction should be developed for each grade level and should include:

1. Safe walking practices to and from the bus stop.

2. Wearing of light-colored or reflective clothing when going to and from bus stop in darkness.

3. How and where to wait safely for the bus.

4. What to do if the bus is late, or does not arrive.

5. How to enter and leave the bus. (use hand rail, etc.)

6. Safe riding practices.

7. Procedures for emergency evacuation. (See appendix D)

8. Safely crossing the highway before boarding and after leaving the bus.

9. Procedures to follow in emergencies.

10. Proper respect for the rights and privileges of others.

VII. PROCEDURES

A. <u>Policy</u>. The responsible state agency and the local school system should have clear and concise policies concerning the conditions for the operation of contractor and/or public-owned school buses within local school systems. Following are examples of the subjects that should be treated in the policy document:

1. Procedure for determining eligibility for pupil transportation service.

2. Procurement of equipment and supplies, maintenance and inspection procedures, and time period over which equipment will be depreciated.

3. Driver recruitment, selection, instruction, placement, and supervision.

4. Determination of areas in which the school will provide transportation services.

5. Principles of routing, establishing stops, and scheduling buses.

6. Use of special lighting and signaling equipment on school buses.

    a. Alternately flashing signal lamps shall be used when the bus is stopping or stopped for the purpose of taking on or discharging passengers, as follows:

    (1) Alternately flashing amber lamps are to be used to <u>warn</u> motorists that the bus is stopping to take on or to <u>discharge</u> passengers.

    (2) Alternately flashing red lights are to be used to <u>inform</u> motorists that the bus is stopped on the roadway <u>to take</u> on or discharge passengers.

    b. When a stop arm is used, it shall be operated simultaneously with the flashing red signal lamps.

    c. A white flashing strobe light may be used to increase the visibility of the school bus on the highway during adverse visibility conditions.

7. Policy with regard to standees, the length of time in transit and the type of supervision to be provided while pupils are on the bus and at school prior to the beginning and following the end of classes.

    a. Each occupant shall be properly seated and no standees will be permitted while the bus is in motion.

8. Policy with regard to the transportation of non-public school pupils.

   a. Such policy shall be determined by State statute and/or State regulations.

9. Policy relative to the supervision of pupils while loading and unloading at school sites and while enroute.

   a. Local school districts shall be responsible for such policy development.

10. Procedure to be observed in the employment of adult monitors to supervise the loading, transportation, and unloading of pupils requiring special care.

11. Procedure for evaluating the school transportation system and how frequently this should be done.

B. School Site Selection and Plant Planning. When school sites are being selected, consideration should be given to the safety of pupils riding school buses. School buses will be required to utilize the roads in and around the school site, plus public roadways leading into and from the school area. High density traffic flow near school exits and entrances should be avoided. Proper site selection and plant planning for improved school transportation is extremely important. (See Appendix E) More specifically, school officials should provide:

   1. Separate and adequate space for school bus loading zones.

   2. Clearly marked and controlled walkways through school bus zones.

   3. Traffic flow and parking patterns separate from the boarding area.

   4. A separate loading area for wheelchairs.

   5. An organized schedule of loading areas with stops clearly marked.

   6. A loading and unloading site to eliminate the backing of transportation equipment.

   See Appendix F, which may be used to evaluate school bus driveways in the vicinity of the school.

C. Routing and Scheduling. It is necessary to procure a map of the area served by a particular school or school system in order to establish bus routes that will adequately meet the needs of pupils in a particular area. Information on road conditions, railroad crossings, and other factors that might affect the particular operation should be recorded along with the location of homes and the number of school age children in each. (Recommended procedures for school bus drivers at railroad crossings appear in Appendix G.) Satisfactory school bus stops must be identified along streets and highways where buses can travel with the least amount of risk. The number of pupils to be transported and the distance to be traveled are primary factors in allocating equipment for a particular area. Pupils should be assigned to specific stops according to walking distances, grade level, and the school attended. Special attention must be given to the handicapped: there are a number of possible approaches to laying out school bus routes. Five routing techniques are among the most frequently used. They emphasize the necessity for pupil safety program efficiency, and operational economy.

1. Shoestring Routes. The shoestring route holds the number of miles a pupil must ride to a minimum and is the most economical if the driver lives in the vicinity of the first pupil pick-up and works in or near the attendance center during the day.

2. Circular Routes. "Circular" routes enable the first pupil who boards the bus in the morning to be the first one to disembark in the evening.

3. Retracing Routes. Retracing routes should be avoided, except when pupils would be subjected to greater than ordinary risk crossing the road after alighting from the bus. In these instances, retracing will eliminate the need for the pupil to cross the roadway.

4. Double Routing. Double routing permits one bus to transport more than one load of pupils, but requires careful planning, including school scheduling.

5. Emergency Routes. Emergency routing should be established in all school systems. When weather or road conditions dictate that it is not safe to travel on other than hard-surfaced roads, an announcement can be made by radio or other means that such routings will be used on that particular day or days.

A survey should be conducted by the pupil transportation director for the purpose of identifying factors that might indicate a route change. After the survey is completed a time study should be made by driving over the route in the same equipment that will be used in the actual operation. The driver(s) who will operate over the route(s) should regard the trip as a "dry run." All scheduled stops should be made "live" and "dead" mileage should be recorded; distance and time between stops should be indicated, etc. These data, if obtained accurately, will permit the development of a schedule which probably will need little revision once it is placed into effect. After the route has been definitely established, a schedule showing individual stops should be available in the bus for the information of substitute drivers.

Each request for new or additional service should be investigated thoroughly before making a change. This investigation often reveals characteristics about the area that would make a change in service unsatisfactory until certain conditions were corrected. It should be remembered that a stopped school bus presents a hazard when operating on thoroughfares where relatively high speeds or high traffic volume prevail. It is usually unwise for buses to take on or discharge passengers on main arteries.

Each stop should be established only after thorough investigation has revealed the location to be the most desirable in the area. It is considered poor practice to negotiate a "U turn" on main arteries of traffic even though provisions may have been made for such turns. The projection of the rear end of the bus into inside traffic lanes from medians that are too narrow to accommodate its length often create traffic interference that places the lives of transported pupils in jeopardy. Further, it is desirable to eliminate, insofar as possible, the necessity to turn the bus by backing. Bus stops should be located at a distance from the crest of a hill or curve to allow motorists traveling at the posted speed to stop within the sight distance. Additional precautions should include but may not be limited to the following:

    a. Determine the location and destination of all pupils to be transported.

    b. Provide the driver, the school of attendance, and the transportation office with the following information:

        (1) list of pupils on the bus(es).

        (2) approximate times for pick up and return of pupils.

        (3) map indicating routing of the bus and pupil locations.

    c. Provide the parents or guardians of all pupils with the driver's name, bus number, pick up and return times, school closing information, school calendar, etc.

    d. Determine the advisability of utilizing the concept of computerized scheduling.

    e. Plan bus routes that will permit optimum pupil safety, program efficiency and operational economy.

D. <u>Inspection of Equipment.</u> A thorough and systematic inspection procedure is the essence of a planned preventive maintenance program. Daily routine inspection will alert the driver to the need for minor repairs and adjustments. Failure to conduct such inspections for any sustained period of time could result in more extensive repairs at a later date. Inspection, therefore, is an indispensable factor in a safe school transportation system.

The school bus driver is the key to an effective daily inspection program. It is the driver's responsibility to make a planned and systematic inspection of the bus before each trip. A recommended procedure requires the conducting of both stationary and operating inspections. The following outline is not suggested as a model for use but is included as a guide for transportation personnel to use in developing a systematic inspection procedure.

1. Stationary Inspection

    a. Pre-starting inspection:

       (1) Observe the bus for evidence of oil, fuel, or water leaks, vandalism, etc.

       (2) Raise the hood and make sure the safety latch or hinge is in hold position, then check oil, water, belts, hoses, and wiring for frayed, cracked and/or deteriorated conditions.

    b. Walk-around inspection:

    Place the transmission in neutral and set the parking brake (fully depress the clutch pedal in manual transmission equipped vehicles). Start the engine and inspect the bus from top to bottom and end to end. Check for:

       (1) Tires: underinflated, flat, excessive wear or damaged.

       (2) Wheels: loose or missing nuts, excessive corrosion, cracks, or other damage.

       (3) Fluid leaks: evidence of wetness on inner wheels and tires.

       (4) Windshield and driver's side window: all school bus windows should be clean.

       (5) Mirrors: adequate view to the rear is essential for safety. They must be clean, properly aimed, and tightly adjusted.

       (6) Warning systems: running lights, back-up lights, all signals and signs, reflectors, turn signals, stop lights and warning flashers must be clean and working properly.

       (7) Exhaust system: sagging exhaust pipes, short and leaky tailpipes, and defective mufflers must be repaired and replaced.

       (8) Emergency exits: must be tightly sealed to prevent possible entrance of dangerous carbon monoxide fumes. (Check by opening and closing to keep hinges operational and to check functioning of warning buzzer.)

c. Inside safety check:

(1) The passenger compartment, seats, frames, emergency exits, and windows must be carefully checked.

(2) Inspect instruments and controls. With the engine operating, check the following:

(a) Vacuum or air pressure gauge or hydraulic indicator lights: these should indicate adequate capacity to operate brakes. Loss of air or hydraulic pressure or vacuum indicates a braking deficiency that must be corrected immediately.

(b) Oil pressure gauge: the engine should be turned off in the event of inadequate pressure and reported immediately.

(c) Warning lights:

1. Oil pressure warning light: prolonged displaying of the warning light is a signal of oil pressure problems and should be reported immediately.

2. Service brake warning light: a light on during the braking application indicates that the brake system is not operating properly.

3. Alternator/Generator warning light: a continuous light "on" after the engine is running indicates a malfunction in the charging system.

4. Ammeter and/or voltmeter: any continuous discharge should be reported immediately.

5. Water temperature gauge or warning light: the indicator should always read "cool" or "warm." If it indicates "hot" the engine should be stopped immediately. The same action should be taken if the temperature warning light goes "on."

d. Check each of the following for proper operation, adjustments, or condition:

(1) Directional signals.

(2) Stop lights and signals.

(3) Special warning lights.

(4) Emergency flashers.

(5) Clearance and marker lights.

(6) Headlights.

(7) Interior bus lights.

(8) Stop arm control, if so equipped.

(9) Windshield fan and defroster.

(10) Heaters.

(11) Horn.

(12) Service door and control.

(13) Rear view and side view mirrors.

(14) Fuses and emergency equipment.

(15) Driver's seat.

(16) Driver's seat belt.

(17) Fire extinguisher.

(18) First aid kit.

(19) Wipers/washers.

(20) Sanders, when equipped.

2. Operating Inspection. A planned road check enables the driver to evaluate the steering, suspension, clutch, transmission, driveline, engine, and brakes. The following items should be included when "road checking" the vehicle prior to transporting pupils:

   a. The Parking Brake: check by slowly engaging the clutch while the parking brake is "on." (In some air brake systems, the parking brake will remain applied if there is a partial or complete air pressure loss in the service brakes.)

   b. Transmission Operation: an automatic transmission should not slip and a manual transmission should allow for easy and smooth gear changes throughout the entire shifting range.

   c. The Clutch: the clutch should engage easily and smoothly without jerking, slipping excessively, or "chattering." A properly adjusted clutch should have some "free play" when the pedal is fully released.

d. Service Brakes: test at low speeds—bring the bus to a complete stop. It should stop in a "straight line" . . . without skidding, swerving, or pulling to one side.

e. The Engine: never race a cold engine. Instead increase speed slowly so that all parts may be properly lubricated.

f. The Steering: report any unusual ride or handling characteristics.

g. The Suspension: report any unusual ride or handling characteristics.

Not all drivers have the ability to spot every problem. But all school bus drivers, however, should make a thorough stationary and operating inspection of their bus each day. "Inspection" to them becomes an integral part of driving and they are always alert to any warning signal which tells them something is wrong. This continued alertness permits them to spot trouble and act accordingly before that trouble causes serious damage or contributes to an accident.

E. <u>Maintenance of Equipment.</u>

1. Teamwork and written policies are essential to a well organized maintenance program.

    a. Strong and reasonable school bus maintenance policies should be adopted that will provide efficient guidelines for the following:

        (1) director of transportation.

        (2) maintenance personnel.

        (3) operators of the vehicles.

    b. Such policies should include the maintenance responsibilities of each person involved and should provide for a planned maintenance program.

2. Planned maintenance may be defined as scheduled maintenance that involves making minor repairs and adjustments which, if neglected, may develop into major difficulties, thereby necessitating extensive and expensive repairs in addition to the costly "down time."

    a. Manufacturers' service manuals and warranty protection guidelines contain valuable information for successful preventative maintenance programs. These instructions and procedures should be carefully followed for maximum efficiency and safety in fleet operation. Vehicle manufacturers and component suppliers (transmission, electrical, etc. manufacturers) offer excellent training for fleet mechanics. Those interested in efficient operations will take advantage of these outstanding training programs.

    b. Objectives of a planned maintenance program:

        (1) keeping the vehicles in safe and efficient operating condition.

        (2) preventing road failures.

        (3) conserving fuel.

        (4) lowering the maintenance cost by reducing the need for major repairs or overhaul.

        (5) extending the useful life of the vehicle and its components.

        (6) enhancing the appearance of school buses.

3. School districts or private contractors should develop a system whereby written communication would allow interchange and feedback relative to maintenance work needed and maintenance work completed. An efficient system should include:

    a. Drivers report form to initiate needed maintenance.

    b. Mechanic certification of completed work.

    c. Method of permanently recording repairs and maintenance history of each vehicle.

F. Records

1. Accident records. The following should be included on all school bus accident report forms:

    a. A signed and dated statement from the driver concerning the particulars of the accident.

    b. A description and estimate of damage costs to all vehicles.

    c. A list of all persons injured, including home addresses and home phone numbers, a description of personal injuries, and appropriate narrative explanations.

    d. A list of passengers and witnesses, including addresses and phone numbers. A signed statement by witnesses is desirable, if obtainable. (Cards for witness signatures and statement should be carried in bus at all times.)

    e. A description of drivers involved including name, date of birth, sex, years of driving experience, license number, and occupation.

- f. Cost of repairs and other type follow-up information should be added to the accident report wherever it is filed, i.e., in federal, state, or local offices, so that the record of the accident is complete. Other pertinent information relating to the accident that should be added later includes:

    (1) disposition of any litigation.

    (2) disposition of any summonses.

    (3) net effects of all personal injuries sustained, including medical care, physician's fees, hospital expenses, etc.

    (4) amount of property damage other than to vehicles involved

    (5) action taken against the school bus driver, e.g., suspension or dismissal.

    (6) summation of the driver's total accident record so that each completed report form will contain a listing of the total number of accidents that the driver has experienced.

2. Personnel Records. The following types of information should be maintained on all employees:

    a. Employee

        (1) application, including occupational history, present occupation, previous employment, age, sex, vehicle driving experience, marital status, military service record (if applicable), and formal training. (see Appendix B)

        (2) confirmed work history.

        (3) driving record.

        (4) criminal record.

        (5) military record (if applicable).

        (6) physical examination (see Appendix C).

        (7) training and testing.

            (a) behind-the-wheel.

            (b) knowledge.

(c) hours of instruction.

(8) payroll record.

(a) absences, cause.

(b) current wages.

(c) years of service.

(9) complaints, commendations, evaluations, etc.

b. Organizational

(1) number employed.

(2) number of staff employed by job.

(3) wage scales.

3. Route records

a. Type of routes.

(1) number.

(2) designation.

b. Route description.

(1) pickups, by locations and times.

(2) route time.

(3) type of vehicle required.

c. Route miles.

d. Special education pupils information to include medical history, medical procedures, and emergency phone numbers.

4. Maintenance records

a. Type.

(1) line setting tickets.

(2) work orders.

(3) preventative maintenance records.

b. Vehicle depreciation.

c. Equipment specifications.

5. Cost Records

   a. vehicles.

   b. type.

G. <u>Emergency Procedures</u>. Each school system should have an emergency plan. This plan should be carefully thought through and developed in cooperation with all those whose services would be required in the event of various types of emergencies. The school transportation director, school administrators, teachers, drivers, maintenance and service personnel, pupils, and others should be instructed in the procedures to be followed in the event of:

   1. Accident. The plan should spell out precisely what is to be done, e.g., how to prevent further accidents; how to evacuate and control pupils; how to evaluate the need for medical assistance; how to get help from the police, the fire department, and the garage; and how to collect and record data essential to the preparation of the required accident reports. An operational plan to provide two-way communication with parents and/or guardians is imperative.

   2. Sudden Disability of Driver. Procedures for handling situations resulting in the fatal injury or disability of the bus driver should be established and communicated to appropriate persons.

   3. Road Failure. The emergency plan should cover the procedure for securing the bus, disposition and control of the passengers, diagnosing the cause(s) of the road failure, notification of school officials, securing alternate equipment, repair procedure and recovery of the disabled school bus.

   4. Inclement Weather Conditions. The emergency plan should provide procedures for when the schools are to be closed or when the schools are to be closed early; the person responsible for making these decisions; how decisions are to be relayed to parents, pupil, school officials and staff (including teachers and cafeteria manager), drivers, contractors, maintenance and service personnel, the news media, and others. Other natural phenomena that might affect the school bus operation should also be included in the plan under this general heading, e.g., floods, hurricanes, and tornadoes.

   5. Other Type of Emergency Situations. The emergency plan should cover such conditions and events as (a) civil defense drills; (b) strikes by school staff, teachers, drivers, or contractors; (c) road or bridge washouts and landslides that might block school bus routes; (d) bus hijacking. (Copies of the pre-emergency plan should be carried in each bus.) (See Appendix D for Instructions for Conducting Emergency Exit Drills.)

H. Communication. In the operation of a pupil transportation system, it is necessary to keep those who are in charge of the system as well as the parents and the pupils, informed regarding the operational procedures. The school system must ensure that the channels of communication are set up in such a way that any information that should be known about its transportation system and services can be disseminated quickly and effectively to reach everyone concerned. The school system must also ensure that all inquiries, requests, suggestions, and recommendations are given prompt and appropriate attention, and that they are handled efficiently. Some of the ways information regarding school bus systems can be disseminated satisfactorily, and examples of how each of these may be used to advantage are:

Method for Dissemination of Information	*Examples of Purposes for Which Used*
Bulletins:	To explain the school system's transportation policy to school administrators, teachers, drivers, parents, pupils, and others associated with the operation. To clarify new laws and safety policies so that everyone knows what is expected of them.
Meetings:	To provide an opportunity for those associated with the school transportation system to share their views to help build broad community support for safe pupil transportation.
Public Press:	To inform parents of policy, route, stop, and schedule changes; of the safety record of the operation; and positive driver achievement records.
Conferences:	To discuss with each driver, disruptive pupils and their parents, solutions to disciplinary problems that arise, new or revised policy decisions that affect drivers, contractors, pupils, and school administrators.
Letters:	To inform parents of all school and state regulations, new routes, etc. Reply to more urgent inquiries regarding pupil transportation safety, policy and procedures.
Telephone Calls:	To provide quick contact between bus drivers and the school, or between parents and the school in the event of urgent or emergency situations.
Radio, Television:	To inform the public of procedures the schools will follow in cases of severe weather conditions or other natural phenomena as well as new policies, laws, or controver-

	sial decisions regarding laws and specifications. Excellent for positive news, ideas, and achievement.
Public Address System:	Another tool the school personnel and drivers may utilize to communicate with pupils regarding all forms of safety reminders, rules, and school policy.

VIII. EVALUATION OF THE PUPIL TRANSPORTATION SYSTEM

A. Each school system should have a plan for evaluating its pupil transportation operation. (See Appendix H) There are several criteria which can be applied to obtain some estimates of the operation's effectiveness. These criteria relate to such factors as safety, efficiency, and economy.

   1. Safety criteria include, but may not be limited to:

      a. Injuries to pupils, the driver, and other highway users.

      b. Frequency and severity of property damage accidents in which buses are involved.

      c. Frequency and severity of moving traffic violations for which drivers are cited.

      d. Frequency and nature of complaints from parents, the motoring public, school administrators and the pupils.

      e. Frequency and nature of road failures and other emergency situations involving buses.

   2. Efficiency and economy criteria include, but may not be limited to:

      a. Route buses consistently operating within the framework of established school hours.

      b. Amount of driver layover time between routes. If, however, it can be scheduled, a brief layover period is desirable.

      c. Routes are equalized as nearly as possible and scheduled to minimize the actual time pupils are on the bus.

      d. Routes are designed to achieve maximum utilization, i.e., full capacity (within reason), and unnecessary mileage and duplication is eliminated.

      e. All routes and routing procedures including stops and times are reviewed annually.

      f. Written driver instructions, including pertinent information relative to mechanical operation and specifics, such as warm-up and idling times, braking practices, etc.

3. Problem identification criteria include, but may not be limited to comprehensive long and short range transportation plans, which include goals and a needs assessment. Information to assist school administration toward this end may be found in Appendix H, Needs Assessment Overview.

IX. ACTIVITY BUS OPERATIONS.

Each school system that provides activity bus transportation for pupils shall have comprehensive policies and guidelines regarding this type of transportation. In order to provide safe and efficient activity transportation, lines of responsibility and authority need to be defined. Persons involved in activity trips must have an understanding of their respective responsibilities. For the purpose of this section, activity trip is defined to include field trips which are extensions of the instructional program, and other trips such as athletic and other outings. This trips range from a few miles to trips extended over several days that cover large distances.

The following items need to be considered when developing criteria for activity trip transportation.

A. Policies and Guidelines

1. Purpose of trip—

    Instructional, athletic, pupil spectators' recreation, or other.

2. Funding source—

    District or individual school funds, individual charge, parent group or other.

3. Administrative approval—

    Person who has authority to approve or deny trip.

4. Advance notification—

    Allow adequate time for approval process, and for making driver and vehicle arrangements.

5. Methods of travel—

    District or contractor bus, commercial or local transit district equipment, air, boat, or combination of above, private or school passenger automobile.

6. Trip request form—

    This should include all necessary information from trip arrangements, payroll, reimbursement, and other local needs.

7. Chaperone—

   An adult chaperone should be required on all activity trips. Chaperone responsibilities include written authority to assist driver in maintaining passenger control. The drivers most always possess the final authority. Seating location for chaperones may also be a consideration.

8. Discipline procedures—

   Trip release signed by parents should include written procedures on handling of severe or difficult misbehavior problems, and emergency policies.

9. Communication—

   Drivers, pupils, chaperones and parents should be made aware of rules and regulations that apply on trip. Parents should have information on destination, mode of transportation, chaperones, departure and return times, and what the pupil is expected to wear and bring with them for the trip. A signed note from the parent or guardian is important.

10. Luggage—

    Method for transporting luggage or equipment forbidden to be carried in passenger compartment by state and/or local regulation. Loose luggage or equipment should never be transported in the passenger compartment which could cause injury or block passageways in the event of an accident or sudden maneuver.

11. Out-of-State Trips—

    Policy should detail if "out-of-state" trips are permitted and specific restrictions. Regulations for states to be visited should be reviewed prior to trip.

12. Insurance Policies—

    Should be checked or agents be contacted to determine if additional coverage is necessary. This is a necessity if a trip is scheduled to another state or country. If using transportation other than system owned vehicles, the board should set the minimum amount of insurance to be carried.

13. Road and Weather Check—

    Designate a person responsible for checking road conditions during months when adverse conditions could be encountered. State Patrol, Highway Divisions or auto clubs are generally cooperative in supplying road information. The Weather Bureau should also be contacted if warranted.

14. Contingency Plans—

    Policy should detail who has authority to make decisions if an unexpected occurrence happens during trip such as impassable roads, accident, or mechanical breakdown. Driver and chaperone should have phone number of local school person who has final authority. It is also advisable to obtain phone numbers of transportation personnel in various communities and school districts that trip buses travel through regularly. It is advisable to develop a Mutual Aid Directory for contacts within athletic league boundaries which could provide assistance in the event of a mechanical emergency. Drivers should have training on procedures and regulations if an accident occurs during trip.

15. Driving Hours—

    Schools should have regulations based on common sense and/or Bureau of Motor Carrier Safety manual: i.e., 15 hours of duty of which 10 are driving time; 8 hours continuous off-duty prior to long trip, no more than 60 hours driving in a week.

16. Driver Selection—

    Criteria for trip driver assignments is necessary to avoid conflict and confusion, knowledge, skill, experience, seniority and driver familiarity with trip vehicles. Driver knowledge of area to be traveled should also be a consideration. Driver assignment should take place at least 3 days in advance of trip date.

B. Vehicle and Equipment

   1. Trip vehicles should be selected taking into consideration the following.

      a. Miles to be traveled.

      b. Terrain and climatic conditions which may be encountered.

      c. Number and age group of pupils.

      d. Luggage and equipment to be transported.

      e. Driver familiarity with the vehicle and route to be traveled.

   2. Consideration should be given for specialized equipment needed such as:

      a. Luggage storage.

      b. Chains or sanders (chains should be prefitted prior to trip.)

c. Extra heaters.

   d. Public address system.

   e. Radio—A.M., C.B., or 2-way.

   f. Tires, off road tread or recaps (original tires on front required).

   g. Spare tire.

   h. Tool requirements.

   i. If an extended trip is planned, a phone call to transportation personnel at the destination is advisable to determine equipment requirements.

3. Inspection—

   a. All vehicles should pass the same inspections as regular route buses as well as detailed check prior to activity trips.

C. Training

1. Specialized training should be provided for activity trip drivers. Training should include but may not be limited to the following items:

   a. State laws and applicable policies and rules.

   b. Familiarity with trip vehicle and its components.

   c. Familiarity with specialized equipment and how to implement its use. (see B-2 above)

   d. Familiarity with local and state trip requirements.

   e. Route familiarization. This might include a dry run prior to the trip date, especially if extreme conditions, terrain or road difficulties may be encountered.

   f. Discipline procedures on trips.

   g. Driving under adverse conditions such as night driving, slippery road condition, or unfamiliar mountain driving.

   h. Destination location and parking areas. Maps should be made available to drivers.

   i. Destination parking if other than location of pupil destination.

   j. Provisions for bus security at destination.

k. Necessity to carry extra cash for items such as: bridge tolls, fuel, telephone, parking fees, and personal needs.

l. Emergency procedures including a thorough knowledge of contingency requirements.

m. Other items a driver should know prior to driving an activity trip, e.g., pupil counts, report form completion, convoy procedures, prohibiting non-required signs inside or outside of bus, etc.

n. All activity bus drivers should hold the same licenses and certificates as a regular school bus driver. This might be in addition to a chauffeur's license if vehicle is a commercial carrier.

SPECIAL EDUCATION OPERATION

INTRODUCTION TO
SPECIAL EDUCATION OPERATION

The purpose of this section of the report is to recommend minimum standard guidelines for those persons entrusted with the responsibility for transporting pupils requiring special care during the loading, unloading and transporting process. The term "special education" means specially designed courses of instruction and related support services, sufficient in both quantity and quality to meet the unique needs of handicapped children.

This section of the overall operations report is concerned with the identification of the multitude of practices and procedures that are relevant to the transportation of handicapped pupils. Special attention, for example, has been given to the development of general principles, the identification of the major characteristics of handicapped pupils, the noting of pupil needs relating to class placement, the behavioral actions that can be anticipated, the resulting corrective actions that must be taken, the types of medical concerns that must be dealt with in an efficient and professional manner, and the development of emergency pupil management procedures.

Few of the practices and procedures are discussed in detail. All, however, have been treated in sufficient depth to provide the administrator, the driver, and the aide with sufficient information to develop and administer a quality program service.

MINIMUM STANDARD GUIDELINES FOR
SCHOOL BUS OPERATION:
SPECIAL EDUCATION

INTRODUCTION

The term "special education" means specially designed instruction to meet the unique needs of a handicapped child. Transportation is one of the "related services" that is necessary to provide this instruction. The purpose of this document is to establish minimum standard guidelines of operation for those individuals involved in the transportation of the handicapped.

I. **GENERAL PRINCIPLES**

A. Pupil management encompasses all preparation and action taken to meet each pupil's needs while riding to and from school, in the interest of comfort and safety for all those aboard the bus. For the handicapped pupil, this means making a variety of adjustments to accommodate each one's individual needs without compromising the safety of the riders or the primary role of the driver—to drive the bus.

B. Transportation for handicapped pupils is a highly personalized service, requiring a thorough assessment of the pupils' physical, social, emotional, and intellectual capacities, and making allowances for existing handicaps.

C. Successful pupil management depends upon careful planning for each pupil's needs prior to placement and continued monitoring of the adjustments throughout the school year. Good pupil management techniques avoid the narrow, band aid approach of "What do I do when Johnny misbehaves on the bus?" by assessing needs and anticipating problems.

D. Mutual respect for, and communication and cooperation of drivers, parents, teachers, and other school officials will help to ensure safe, reliable, and comfortable transportation service. It is important to recognize that often the driver spends several hours a day with these pupils, thereby assuming a significant role in their lives.

II. CHARACTERISTICS OF HANDICAPPED PUPILS

A. The definition of the types of disabilities vary somewhat from State to State, but in general terms, the following behaviors are characteristic. Keep in mind that no one pupil is likely to manifest all of these behaviors.

1. Learning disabled pupils typically have average or higher intellectual ability, but suffer from disorders that prevent them from processing information, particularly language, in the usual manner. They may be disorganized or inefficient in solving problems. They may demonstrate impulsive or extreme emotional behaviors that seem out of proportion to the severity of the problem. Hyperactivity is also common among this population.

2. Emotionally disturbed pupils may have great difficulty controlling their own behavior. Emotional disturbance is characterized by very low self-esteem, and the pupil may either withdraw or act out his frustration and insecurity. Seemingly inappropriate types of duration of behavior may be observed, the seriousness of which should be discussed with the pupil's teacher. A limited number of clear, consistent rules will set goals for the pupil to regulate his own actions. Avoid angry outbursts and punishment, and never label a pupil "bad" when he/she misbehaves. Simply remind the pupil of what is expected and why, and reinforce proper behavior. A lack of stability from day to day in desirable behavior may be observed. This is not willful disobedience, but beyond the pupil's control.

3. Mental retardation encompasses a range of impairment from the mildly (educable) retarded through the trainable, and finally the severely and profoundly handicapped. Many pupils may have physical handicaps in addition to the mental handicaps, and may be afflicted by disorders involving poor motor coordination, seizures, and body tremors. Pupils may have few self-care skills,

and require aid in dressing, expressing themselves, and boarding the bus. They may be very friendly and affectionate. They need frequent reminders of bus rules because they have limited retention. Many pupils can understand what you tell them (possess receptive language) but cannot speak to you. You should insist that they use every mode of communication of which they are capable to make their needs known to you.

4. <u>Physical handicaps</u> can include deafness, blindness, paralysis, lack of head, trunk or back control, or erratic movement. These pupils may be of average or above intelligence, but are frequently behind in social and academic development due to their handicapping condition. Those with orthopedic handicaps often have leg braces, crutches, wheelchairs, or other supportive equipment. These pupils must be seated comfortably.

   a. Communication with pupils whose handicaps interfere with normal means of expression can pose a major challenge to the driver.

      (1) Visually handicapped pupils respond best when they are addressed by name, and when the events around them are described carefully. Remember that they cannot see facial expressions or other body language that constitutes a large part of communication for others. The visually impaired can develop self-sufficiency if their environment is structured in a stable and predictable way. They can fasten their own seat belts if they can find them on the same seat in the same position each day. They cannot easily recover them if they've fallen behind the seat, or if their seat changes and the seat belt is no longer there.

      (2) The deaf pupils use their visual skills to compensate for their hearing loss. Looking at them when you talk, and speaking clearly and distinctly will help them read your lips. Yelling does not help them understand. Facial expression and body language are very important; show them what you want. The drivers may wish to carry a pad and pencil to write down what the cannot otherwise convey. Those drivers who routinely transport deaf children may find a course in sign language valuable. Deaf children may find the noise level on their hearing aids uncomfortable, and turn them off. They will probably be most content if there are others on the bus with whom they can communicate. Hearing impaired children, along with visually impaired pupils, are unlikely to be much different from normal children in terms of behavioral problems.

B. Although the behaviors described above are characteristic of certain categories of disabling conditions, it is important to remember that each pupil is an individual, with his own distinct personality and that no label can completely or adequately describe any pupil. It should also be noted that all handicapped pupils are people, and can be expected to behave and misbehave very much like normal children. The driver of handicapped children needs to be more flexible, patient, and creative in his/her approach to managing these pupils.

III. CLASS PLACEMENT

A. Class selection should include a routine consultation with transportation personnel to avoid bus problems that may later develop into classroom problems.

   1. Some pupils may need to be transported in wheelchairs or specially designed car seats or vests to provide trunk and head support. The type of vehicle required must be ascertained in advance, and lead time may be needed to construct a device in which to transport the pupil.

   2. The last consideration in planning is the mixture of pupils on the vehicle. In sparsely populated areas, it may be virtually impossible to group pupils on vehicles by disability, but this may be desirable in some instances.

B. After the class assignment is determined, the transportation supervisor should research the details of the pupil's transportation needs.

   1. A thorough inventory of the pupil's needs should be taken by the school personnel in conjunction with the transportation director. This should include aspects of the pupil's personality and handicaps as they relate to the bus ride, and may determine such matters as seat assignments, order of stops, equipment needed, and techniques for effectively relating to the pupil. Seizures and other significant medical problems should be documented.

   2. At this time, any deviation from normal schedules should be noted.

   3. Arrangements should be made for alternate emergency drop-off points and telephone numbers. These last two points may seem more related to operations than pupil management, but not delivering the pupil to the right place at the right time can create anxiety in the pupil and his parents and undermine the driver's control of the situation.

   4. Arrangements for each pupil's transportation should be communicated to all involved parties, including parents, school personnel, driver, aide, and the other pupils on the bus. A smooth start for bus service will help make the pupil's first day of school a positive experience and will instill confidence in the parent that will reflect well on the entire school system.

IV. DISCIPLINE AND BEHAVIOR CONTROL

A. A driver recognizes that safety of passengers and respect for person and property are still needed when handicapped children are transported. A pupil cannot be allowed to behave in any manner which endangers others or causes serious harm enroute.

B. Lenience or pity for the pupils because of their handicaps is counterproductive to the development of self-sufficiency. Many pupils can sense this attitude and manipulate it to their own advantage. Pupils must be taught to accept responsibility for their own actions. This can usually be accomplished if the following rules are obeyed:

1. Always let the pupils know what is expected of them. Define terms and rules clearly, and enforce the rules fairly, firmly, and consistently.

2. Let the pupils know exactly what the consequences of their behavior will be. Always follow through on the disciplinary action you threaten, or the pupils will quickly learn that your authority is not to be taken seriously.

3. Demonstrate, using as many modes as possible, what you want them to do. Don't just tell them to fasten their restraining devices, show them how to do it.

4. Accentuate the positive. Continually telling the pupils "don't do this" and "don't do that" leaves them wondering what they can do. On long bus rides that can be a tiring and boring experience, suggest methods of acceptable behavior.

C. Behavior modification is a technique that requires pupils to behave in an appropriate way before they are given some reward, thereby increasing the likelihood they will behave as desired. To be effective, such a program must take into consideration the ages of the pupils aboard, the nature of the reward, and a clear definition of what constitutes acceptable behavior.

1. It is generally a good policy to develop a simple reward system for good behavior. Liberal amounts of praise should be given as a general rule, but behavior modification techniques can be a more concrete, consistent way of maintaining control.

2. The driver can develop a chart to keep track on a weekly basis of who has behaved well and who has not, and a reward given to those with satisfactory ratings. This may be something simple like a smile face or a gold star on the chart, giving the pupil a preferred seat on the bus, or, with permission of both parent and teacher, some candy or other treat.

3. Some disruptive pupils respond well when given responsibility, such as leading the others in singing or a quiet game. This may channel excess energy into some more constructive although

limited activity that can be pursued safely on the bus ride.

D. Other techniques of behavior control involve relatively simple methods such as rearranging seating or isolating the troublemaker.

   1. Seating arrangements on the bus can be important in managing handicapped pupils. A good driver will learn to know his/her pupils and seat those who get along well near each other.

      a. The seat closest to the front of the vehicle may be used either as a reward or as a punishment, depending on the attitude of the pupils. Younger pupils often perceive sitting near the driver as a privilege, and this may be granted as a reward for good behavior. Older pupils are more likely to view a front seat as undesirable, and it may then be used to isolate a troublemaker.

      b. An insightful choice of seat partners can help the driver manage pupils. For instance, a young hyperactive pupil may be seated with an older, well-behaved pupil. The older pupil is made to feel important by looking after his young charge, and the younger pupil may look up to the elder and behave better to impress him. A more advanced pupil may be able to sit with one who is easily distractible to "entertain" the other by talking or looking at a book.

      c. Very young or fragile pupils should be seated away from older, larger pupils who might harm them if they become angry or frustrated.

   2. In cases of serious misbehavior, temporary suspension of bus privileges may be in order. This should only be done after consultation with parent and teacher, because in some cases this may mean a pupil might be left home unsupervised, or an adolescent may spend the day out on the streets getting into trouble rather than being in school. Suspension from the bus is usually most appropriate when the safety of other pupils is threatened by the pupil in question.

   3. Most pupils respond best to rules if they have a voice in developing them. The driver may be able to tell the pupils that the bus is "their bus" and to encourage pride in making it a clean, safe, and enjoyable place to be. For those pupils who are able, the driver may have them suggest rules for the bus and the means of enforcing them. Often the pupils will be more strict in determining regulations that the driver would have been.

   4. Cases of serious misbehavior which do not respond to any of the above methods may require referral to a school counselor or psychologist to develop a more personalized behavior management scheme for that pupil.

   5. Behavior management systems will be most effective if developed

after consultation with the parents and teachers. It can be confusing and frustrating to the pupils if they are allowed to behave one way on the bus but not that way in the classroom. Cooperation of all concerned parties is the ideal way to achieve a safe bus environment.

V. MEDICAL CONCERNS

A. Handicapped pupils are often more susceptible to illness than regular pupils, and therefore miss school more often. They are often on medication for their disability. Normally, a driver should never administer this medication. It is strongly recommended that drivers of handicapped pupils enroll in a first-aid course to prepare themselves for medical emergencies that may arise along the route.

B. A change in the type of dosage of medication can dramatically alter a pupil's behavior. Sudden personality changes should be reported to the parent and teacher at the earliest possible time.

C. There are certain medical problems that may arise routinely on the bus ride, for which a driver should be prepared.

   1. Many handicapped children are subject to convulsive disorders, or seizures. These can vary in intensity from a few-second (petit mal) blackout, often not even noticeable, to severe grand mal seizures, involving thrashing of arms, and body rigidity. Normally, seizures are self-limiting, and the driver's primary role should be to see that the pupil does not harm him/herself and rests comfortably afterward. Nothing should be placed in the pupil's mouth, nor should the limbs be restrained in any manner—this could result in broken bones. Extended seizures constitute a medical emergency, and medical help should be summoned.

   2. Some pupils may be inclined toward respiratory difficulties and drooling, and may occasionally choke on their own saliva or foreign objects. The method of dealing with these problems should be discussed with the parent, teacher and medical personnel. Pupils may become nauseated on the bus ride so it is recommended that materials for clean-up be kept on the vehicle.

D. Most medical incidents on the bus ride, while requiring special attention of the driver or aide, will not necessitate summoning professional medical attention. Extended seizures and other serious medical matters may require either diverting the run to a medical facility or summoning an ambulance. In any event, all medically related incidents should be reported to the school and parents at the earliest possible moment.

VI. EMERGENCY PUPIL MANAGEMENT

A. It may be useful to educate those pupils who are capable of comprehending and retaining such information about emergency procedures.

It is possible that the driver may be incapacitated in an accident and a pupil may have to take over.

B. In those emergencies where the driver is not injured, it is important to assure the pupils that the situation is under control.

C. The most important preparation for pupil management in an emergency is preplanning.

   1. Assess the abilities and handicaps of each pupil, and determine what each pupil's needs may be in an emergency.

   2. Plan how to evacuate each pupil if this becomes necessary, determine what special attention might be needed after evacuation. For instance, those pupils normally tense and insecure may require special reassurance than what would be required for most pupils under such circumstances. The appearance of confidence on the part of the driver will help calm the pupils.

VII. **SUMMARY OF SUCCESSFUL PUPIL MANAGEMENT**

A. Take a conscious inventory of the abilities and handicapping conditions of each pupil, and gear the rules of the bus to each individual bus load of pupils.

B. Continuity and consistency of expectations by those in authority at home, in the classroom, and on the bus, will do much to aid the pupil in his social development, independence, self-esteem, and recognition and respect for the rights of others.

POLICY DEVELOPMENT

Develop pupil, driver and aide policies.

PUPIL POLICY:

1. Develop a written list of do's and don't's that you <u>expect</u> pupils to be aware of to ensure a safer, more enjoyable ride.

    A. Post in the bus.

    B. Print in pupil handbook.

    C. This may be written into an overall policy package that should have board approval.

DRIVER POLICY:

1. List all requirements that must be fulfilled prior to pupil transportation (license, physical, driving exam, written exams, license check, etc.).

2. List all requirements placed on the driver by the school system. Examples:

    A. Pre-trip inspection.

    B. Discipline.

    C. Records keeping.

    D. Contract provision, if any.

    E. Pupil safety.

    F. Knowledge and use of safety equipment.

3. List all requirements placed on the driver by state and/or federal legislation. Examples:

    A. School bus stop laws.

    B. Speed limits.

    C. Railroad crossing laws.

    D. Etc.

An entire policy package should be developed, approved and adopted by the Board of Education and implemented.

AIDE POLICY:

Aides should:

1. Be selected for their physical and emotional ability to cope with the situation(s) making the assignment of an aide to that particular bus necessary.

2. Receive special training regarding the needs of handicapped pupils and their role in caring for those needs in transit.

3. Work under the bus driver's direction to provide care and assistance to pupils as needed when entering and leaving the bus and during the bus ride.

4. Be sure that protective safety devices are properly fastened at all times.

5. Have available to them in the vehicle confidential data including:

    A. Pupil's name and address.

    B. Nature of pupil's handicap.

    C. Emergency health care information.

    D. Name and the phone number of pupil's physician, parent, or other person to be contacted in case of an emergency.

    E. Provisions for pupil's welfare if and when pupil is not met at the designated bus stop.

6. Be well versed in emergency procedures in the event the driver is incapacitated.

ROUTING AND SCHEDULING

1. Determine location and destination of all pupils to be transported.

2. Obtain information pertaining to individual needs for additional specialized equipment such as safety harnesses, seat belts, wheelchair, pupil safety seat, etc.

3. Plot the safest, most efficient route available avoiding high traffic areas, high accident areas, and road hazards.

4. Provide the drivers, the attending school, and the transportation office with the following information:

    A. List of pupils on the bus(es).

    B. Approximate times for pick-up and return of pupils.

C. Map indicating routing of the bus and location of pupils.

D. An identification form for each pupil with information such as pupil's name, parent or guardian name, address, phone number, location and description of home, medication, picture, etc.

5. Provide the parents or guardians of all pupils with the driver's name, bus number, pick-up and return times, school closing information, school calendar, etc.

6. Transportation of pupils in certain cases may require a contract between school systems and/or specifications of transportation in the pupil's I.E.P. (Individual Education Plan).

7. If computer scheduling is available, it should be assessed for possible utilization.

8. The goal of pupil transportation is to economically and efficiently operate with the optimum pupil safety and consistency.

COMMUNICATION

1. Determine what your schools needs are for communications.

2. Determine the geographical area to be covered and topographical features to contend with.

3. Determine which type of two way radio system, if used, will be functional.

SCHOOL BUS FLEET OPERATIONS

Contents

Chapter		Page
1	**Planning for Safety** Choosing pickup and delivery points. Planning special activity trips. Supervisor responsibilities.	1
2	**Establishing the Safety Program** Developing safety guidelines.	4
3	**Providing Local Direction** The role of the local school board. The role of the school superintendent.	6
4	**Supervising the School Bus Fleet** Qualifications of a supervisor. Supervising drivers. Purchasing and maintaining vehicles. The supervisor's role in public relations. Keeping up-to-date.	9
5	**Selecting the School Bus Driver** Who should screen applicants? What type of person makes a safe school bus driver?	15
6	**Training the School Bus Driver** What to include and where to find it. Types of training: initial, refresher, and remedial. Psycho-physical testing.	20
7	**Motivating the School Bus Driver** Set a good example. Show real interest. Use competition effectively. Recognize good work.	26

SCHOOL BUS FLEET OPERATIONS

CHAPTER 1

Planning for Safety

More than a quarter million school buses operate over three billion miles annually. They carry more than 21 million elementary and secondary pupils each day. School transportation, therefore, is a giant in the U.S. transportation industry.

This giant is made up of many divisions. Most school transportation is operated by the school district or by a contractor-operated school bus service.

Getting and keeping uniform, adequate, standards of vehicle and driver operation pose a tremendous challenge to the public and private sectors of the industry. The needs of school systems vary because the needs of the population centers they serve vary.

Although responsibility for guidance and results lies at the state level, supervision of school bus service involves the county, city, and local school districts. As a result, problems can arise from incomplete communication or lack of direction.

In addition to the normal problems of transportation, there are parental and political influences to consider. Whether school transportation is a function of the school system or is provided through contract service, basic standards must be met to protect pupil passengers.

Conflicting traffic laws and differences in local operating policies and practices confuse the motoring public. They can impede the normal traffic flow and imperil the lives they were designed to protect. Uniform national standards are necessary to guide local regulation of school bus operating conditions and schedules in the traffic stream.

Choosing Pickup and Delivery Points

In rural districts, pickup locations are scattered and frequently far apart. Routes and pickup points should be planned for the least interference with the normal traffic flow. Traffic delays caused by frequent bus stops, or by the need to allow pupils to cross the highway, should be kept to a minimum. When the school transportation system repeatedly interrupts traffic, other drivers grow impatient and may be tempted to violate local conditions of control.

Political pressure for special privileges or unusual, frequent, personalized bus stops should not be permitted by school authorities or local traffic officials.

In suburban districts, the school system should follow the pattern of transit operations, creating minimum interference with traffic on arterial or collector streets. Corner pickups at traffic-controlled locations should be encouraged. When possible, the young passengers should cross streets at locations where crossing protection is a community responsibility instead of the bus driver's. To reduce interference with the normal traffic flow, lightly traveled streets should be used for pupil pickup points in suburban operations.

Uniform operating policies also must be established to regulate transportation by special activity buses. Area discharge points away from the heavy traffic of arterial and collector streets should be designated. Parents should understand that they must pick up their children at these points or permit them to make their own arrangements to get home.

Planning Special Activity Trips

When school buses are scheduled for special events and activities outside the community, "protection routes" should be mapped out and drivers should be required to follow them. Supervisors should plan routes with these factors in mind: traffic volume on the available alternate routes; dangerous intersections; railroad crossings; sharp curves; steep hills; one-lane bridges; and narrow pavements.

Pupils on special activity trips should be supervised and controlled by a person *other* than the bus driver. Principals should assign one or more staff members to each bus who have demonstrated their supervision and control of pupils under special circumstances. The bus driver should be free to concentrate on driving duties.

Supervisor Responsibilities

Supervisor responsibilities are varied. Among them is having a written set of specifications for new vehicle purchases. The person responsible for the specifications should consider the number of pupils to be transported, the general climatic conditions in the area, and the type of terrain in which the vehicle will be used.

Special training is needed to be an effective supervisor. Also, continuous in-service training is necessary to update knowledge and maintain competence.

Knowing the operating policies and procedures is essential. Each employee is entitled to a detailed description of his or her duties, and should know who can provide special instruction and assistance when the unexpected or unusual occurs.

Vehicle accidents do not "just happen." They are usually the cumulative result of poor environmental conditions and faulty driving habits or attitudes. Although most adverse environmental factors cannot be controlled, they can be compensated for by teaching drivers the principles of defensive driving. It also would help to recognize bad driving habits as they develop, and correct them before they contribute to accidents.

The experience of bus, truck, and passenger fleet operators demonstrates that drivers need help and encouragement to be safe. Management must formulate and enforce specific policies to regulate vehicle operation and maintenance. (See Chapter 3, "Providing Local Direction.") Drivers need constant in-service training in safe driving techniques and attitudes. Drivers are motivated to perform safely when they feel that their safety records are important and that good safety performance is recognized and appreciated.

CHAPTER 2

Establishing the Safety Program

Safety programs must begin at the top. If top management is not genuinely interested in the safety program or is unwilling to provide supervisory time and funds for implementation, the program will fail. In many cases, it will not even get started.

Increasing attention has been focused on highway safety by the creation of the National Highway Traffic Safety Administration within the federal government, and by establishment of guidelines covering the vehicle, the driver, and the highway.

To assure their constituents that these guidelines are met, state governments must establish standards and regulations and provide leadership and direction in training.

The role of most state Departments of Education is to help schools provide education for safe and efficient living in our society. An extension of this role lies in the area of pupil transportation. State Departments of Education must take the lead in establishing criteria for driver selection and training, and promulgate rules and regulations governing the transportation of pupils. States must provide guidelines for obtaining funds for both transportation and instruction.

Developing Safety Guidelines

Leadership must provide comprehensive safety programs for school transportation. Minimum standards must be established for safety and efficiency.

1. Standards must be established for buses and equipment. In many instances they should exceed the established national minimums.
2. Maintenance standards must be set and enforced by rigid, periodic vehicle inspections, made by competent personnel, to guarantee that vehicles are maintained in safe operating condition, consistent with standards for new vehicles. Superficial annual inspection by un-

trained personnel cannot meet this need.
3. Driver qualifications must be established, and mental and physical standards and strict licensing procedures must be set and adhered to, for the protection of the pupils who ride the buses.
4. Mandatory driver training schools or workshops should be established.
5. Basic rules and regulations governing transportation of pupils should be established. They should state the extent of transportation services provided, who has authority at various levels of responsibility, and expected safe pupil behavior.

These minimum requirements should apply to all public and private school transportation in the state. Personnel and funds must be available to implement these programs and provide for supervision and inspection.

Leadership at the state level should maintain liaison with the departments of public instruction, public safety, motor vehicles, and state highways. It also should provide for adequate training facilities, seminars, and specialized courses to be conducted for individuals at all levels of responsibility.

CHAPTER 3

Providing Local Direction

The top officials of the school administration must want a safe transportation system in order to achieve it. They must be thoroughly familiar with the mechanics of good fleet safety programs and must apply proven principles of driver selection, training, and supervision.

Driver interest is a direct reflection of the degree of interest the administration shows. For this reason, members of the school board, the school superintendent, and other school officials must demonstrate their sincere interest in the safety program. They must convince newly hired drivers that they demand safe, efficient operation at all times. They should personally present safe driving awards to deserving drivers to let them know that everyone in the school district appreciates their professional achievement.

The Role of the Local School Board

Local school board officials must decide that they want safe, dependable pupil transportation, and channel that determination through the school administration and the driver safety supervisor to the school bus drivers. They must show their interest by participating in such safety program activities as driver award dinners and meetings.

Because local conditions and situations vary, school boards need to establish local policies that are within the framework of policies established at the state level. Definite policies will elevate the system's safety and efficiency and enlist the understanding and cooperation of other school personnel and the public. Policy statements should define areas and the extent of responsibility. They should specify the following:
1. The supervisor's qualifications, responsibilities, and authority, which includes attendance at safety seminars, training courses, and national, regional, and state safety meetings that are important for the fleet safety supervisor's development and efficiency;
2. The extent of the supervisor's responsibility for liaison with other administrators, the public, the schools, the Department of Public

Safety, and the news media;
3. Minimum requirements for driver selection and training;
4. The extent of the driver's responsibility and authority for the safety and conduct of pupils using school bus transportation (e.g., research and experience indicate that school board policy should prohibit pupils from standing in any part of the bus while it is moving);
5. The extent of service, including who is entitled to transportation, and conditions under which it will be provided;
6. Provisions for extracurricular transportation and its relation to the regular transportation program policy. (These should provide for minimum interference with the normal traffic flow on arterial or collector highways and streets and for preplanning of routes by the supervisor, so that hazardous routes and areas are avoided.)
7. Equipment replacement schedule (or basis), defining standards and stating who is responsible for writing specifications for the purchase of new buses;
8. Standards for bus maintenance and the facilities needed to accomplish a maintenance program;
9. Budget allocated to cover the services that are demanded.

The Role of the School Superintendent

The school superintendent should:
1. Recommend transportation needs to the school board and provide a factual basis for establishing transportation policies.
2. Show interest in a good accident control program, and expect continuing interest from all employees; the superintendent should attend some of the driver safety meetings and participate in safe driver award presentations.
3. Outline authority and responsibilities of all participants in the transportation system and require strict conformance with policies.
4. Provide specific guidelines for driver recruitment, training, and supervision, and for maintenance control.
5. Involve schools and parents in the transportation safety program by requiring schools to teach pupils how to ride safely and by including transportation discussion in P.T.A. meetings. (Parents can play a vital role in the safety program. They can learn about the program and demonstrate their interest by requiring their children to obey safety rules and to cooperate fully with the school transportation system.)

NOTE: In parochial school transportation systems, the school superintendent, or the person in charge of the diocese or parish, should provide this stimulus and guidance.

Top administrative interest and continuity are equally essential for public school-, parochial school-, and contract-operated fleet safety program. Administration must demand constant emphasis on accident prevention from all transportation system employees.

CHAPTER 4

Supervising the School Bus Fleet

The superintendent should appoint a school transportation safety supervisor in each school district. Supervision might be a part-time job in small fleets, but in many fleets, supervision requires much time and ability. In some large fleets, more than one person may be needed to provide adequate supervision.

The vehicle, its maintenance, and the driver are the factors that determine the safety and efficiency of the school transportation program. It is impossible to avoid accidents when any of these ingredients are neglected. The supervisor is the catalyst that makes these factors produce results. The right individual, with proper training and adequate support, will produce the safety and efficiency necessary for pupil passenger protection.

The checklists that follow treat the qualifications, responsibilities, authority, and performance of the school transportation supervisor.

Qualifications of a Supervisor

Here is a checklist to help evaluate the experience and training needed for a school transportation supervisor. Individual supervisors may find areas in which they need to increase their efforts.

1. Has the supervisor had formal training in fleet supervision? Did he or she attend a school or have in-service training?
2. Does he or she have previous experience in fleet safety supervision? Supervising a commercial fleet, a bus fleet, a delivery service fleet, or another type of fleet?
3. Does he or she have an aptitude for and an interest in the work? What can the supervisor offer to the job?
4. Does he or she have the ability to get along well with other people?
5. Does he or she have public speaking experience?

Supervising Drivers

How does a supervisor's job responsibilities and authority to carry them out compare with other supervisors in similar positions? Consider his or her authority and responsibility in the supervision of your drivers.

Is your supervisor:
1. Authorized to take charge of the drivers?
2. Allowed ample time for proper supervision?
3. Responsible for selection of new drivers?
4. Responsible for planning and implementing the driver training program?
5. Responsible for transportation records?
6. Responsible for accident investigation including the following?
    a. Establishing preventability
    b. Establishing an accident review committee

Here is a brief self-test for the driver supervisor:

How do you rate your own performance in the supervision of your drivers?
1. Do you use the accident report to counsel the driver involved in an accident?
2. Are you able to use accident reports in remedial training of drivers?
3. Can you recognize substandard performance and symptoms of accidents-in-the-making? Such as the following:
    a. Errors in the performance of work
    b. Changes in everyday behavior and manners
    c. Changes in simple habits of a routine nature
    d. Near-accidents
4. Are you alert in your personal observations of driver performance?
5. Do you carefully check reports received from drivers, pupils, school authorities, parents, police, and others involved, to determine the validity of the report and the need for counseling?
6. Can you check reasons for substandard performance?
7. Do you spend your time helping your drivers to drive safely, instead of merely determining preventability after an accident?
8. Are you capable of establishing a program of counseling and retraining?
9. Do you know all the laws and regulations that are applicable to school bus fleet operation?
10. Do you keep posted on innovations, research, and new techniques in school transportation?

11. Have you built "flexibility" into your operation so it can handle unexpected emergencies?

How to spot driver errors

Drivers are capable of committing any number of errors that can have serious consequences. The supervisor should know what these errors are, how they can be spotted, and how to prevent them. Supervision is more than the art of getting things done through people—it is the art of getting them done well.

There are a number of specific driving errors that frequently lead to accidents. A list of these errors was compiled from a survey of more than 150 of the nation's top fleet safety professionals. To help the supervisor recognize these errors and head off accidents *before* they occur, review the errors that are listed in the section, "Driving Errors."

Because each fleet of school buses transports pupils and uses the public streets and highways, its drivers have a special obligation to operate within the law. Violations of traffic laws cannot be condoned. Violations may not only expose the pupil passengers to serious hazards, but may also reflect badly on the school system. Repeated violations by individual drivers should be cause for their dismissal.

Purchasing and Maintaining Vehicles

The supervisor's authority and responsibility for vehicles usually includes both purchasing and maintenance.

Purchasing

School buses must be properly selected and equipped to assure the safe and efficient operation of the school transportation program. The supervisor's knowledge of bus routes, pupils to be transported, special environmental or operational conditions, and maintenance factors qualifies him or her to prepare specifications for bus purchases or to assist another person who is knowledgeable about school buses and components to prepare specifications.

The school board should provide guidelines to help make the best selection. The following questions will help to evaluate purchasing procedures:

1. Are local minimum standards in effect?
2. Are needs in excess of minimum standards considered?
3. Are local vehicle specifications written?
4. Are specifications carefully explained to each prospective bidder?
5. Does policy require rejection of any bid that does not meet specifications, even when it is the lowest bid?
6. Do specifications reflect consideration of the required bus capacity and the environmental factors affecting the operation—such as hills, average temperature, and type of roadway?
7. Do specifications reflect careful evaluation of safety factors such as horsepower, tires, service brake effort, special emergency and parking brakes, defrosters and windshield washers?
8. Are the advantages of power steering and automatic transmissions (with built-in retarders) considered?
9. Do specifications rule out, on the basis of size or performance, components that have previously caused problems or concern in vehicle operation and maintenance?
10. Does the transportation supervisor prepare vehicle specifications, or assist in their preparation?

Maintaining

Preventive maintenance plays a vital part in the safety and efficiency of the school transportation program. It is as much a part of the safety supervisor's responsibility as other facets of the program. School buses must be kept in top mechanical condition.

Proper vehicle maintenance ensures dependability, maximum life, peak performance, and safety. Both sound operating policies and adequate maintenance will help control fleet accidents and costs. Efficient supervision makes the safe method a part of everyday operations.

The following questions will help you to determine whether you have what is necessary for good maintenance:
1. Are you in charge of maintenance facilities, vehicles, and mechanics?
2. If your school district operates the school bus fleet, are the facilities adequate to maintain today's school buses? If a contractor operates the fleet, is maintenance quality high?
3. Do you have the financial support necessary to keep shop equipment up-to-date and to retain well-trained, experienced mechanics?

If you are responsible for maintenance, answer the following ques-

tions to determine the quality of your maintenance operation:
1. Are buses scheduled for regular mileage or time-interval preventive maintenance inspections?
2. Are drivers required to make pretrip inspections?
3. Are drivers required to report all defects in writing?
4. Is immediate attention given to all reported defects?
5. Are mechanics required to sign each repair order and be responsible for maintenance quality?
6. Are drivers required to road test completed repairs before loading pupils?
7. Are individual drivers held personally responsible for vehicle abuse?

8. Are mechanics fully qualified?
9. Do they receive periodic instruction and in-service training?
10. Do they keep abreast of the latest equipment maintenance procedures and the techniques? (Much of this information is available from manufacturers and suppliers at little or no cost to the mechanics or the fleet.)
11. Are the buses and equipment, including warning devices, maintained so they operate as originally intended?
12. Does inadequate maintenance ever prevent a bus from operating or contribute to irregular schedules?
13. Has lack of adequate maintenance ever contributed to an accident —or near accident—in your fleet?

The Supervisor's Role in Public Relations

The school transportation supervisor also is responsible for the fleet's public image. The supervisor should make the drivers feel they share the responsibility for good public relations. Courtesy and safety are inseparable in the operation of motor vehicles. They are an important part of the school bus operator's job.

The following checklist will serve as a guide for combining the efforts of the fleet service, school, pupils, and parents for a safe and efficient school transportation program.
1. Are bus routes planned to eliminate as many traffic hazards as possible, including traffic interference, sharp curves, and railroad crossings?

2. Are routes planned to provide minimum time on the bus?
3. Are the smallest children given the most consideration in keeping to a minimum the distances they have to walk?
4. Are school authorities asked to cooperate with staggered school hours for greater fleet utilization and less pupil time away from home?
5. Are pupils taught the safe way to approach, ride, and leave a bus? Are emergency drills conducted?
6. Does the supervisor actively seek parental cooperation by participating in P.T.A. and civic club meetings?
7. Does the supervisor and other school authorities explain transportation policies and problems to parents and teachers?
8. Are influential parents and civic-minded persons given the opportunity to observe the driver training program and bus maintenance facilities?
9. Does the supervisor take advantage of opportunities for favorable publicity through news media?
10. Do drivers extend driving courtesies to other motorists?
11. Are buses kept clean and painted?

Keeping Up-to-Date

Although a supervisor's initial qualifications and experience may be excellent, his or her safety education must be continuous to do a good job. Every school transportation supervisor must keep professionally up-to-date.

The following checklist focuses on some important factors of a supervisor's in-service training. Does the supervisor:
1. Keep current on school bus safety research?
2. Have adequate funds to obtain publications and papers giving research results and conclusions?
3. Apply these findings to upgrading the safety and efficiency of the fleet?
4. Maintain contact with bus and bus equipment manufacturers?
5. Use fleet operation safety innovations as they are proven and become available?
6. Keep abreast of the latest techniques and programs for the selection, training, and supervision of drivers and maintenance of vehicles?
7. Attend state, regional, and national safety meetings?
8. Attend fleet and safety supervision seminars?
9. Periodically attend courses in safety supervision?

CHAPTER 5

Selecting the School Bus Driver

The goal in driver selection should be to provide the highest possible transportation service quality and safety by selecting school bus drivers who will improve the fleet's record and performance.

Few occupations involve a greater need for good safety attitude. The school bus driver has both the responsibility of a professional driver and responsibility for the well-being of every pupil who rides the school bus.

Driver selection, training, and motivation must be designed to prevent accidents. Before discussing the qualities to look for when seeking applicants, we must examine the qualifications of the person responsible for hiring.

Who Should Screen Applicants?

Personnel selection is a demanding task requiring skill, tact, and training. It must be performed by a qualified person who can exercise good judgment and take the time and trouble to screen applicants thoroughly. If no staff member is trained in personnel selection, it is advisable to send a staff member for training to fill this role.

Even individuals with "natural ability" in this area should be encouraged to enroll in refresher courses, seminars, and workshops to hone their skills and to acquire current personnel recruitment techniques. Recruitment sources, methods and channels of communication must be thoroughly explored and understood. Such training would be valuable not only for selecting drivers, but also for other jobs that need filling over a period of time.

If possible, the transportation supervisor should be the person responsible for driver selection.

What Kind of Person Makes a Safe School Bus Driver?

A school bus operator does not need the stature and endurance of a professional athlete, but certain physical and mental characteristics are required for good job performance.

Physical characteristics

Because of the configuration of the driver's compartment in school buses, the size of the driver should be considered. The driver needs sufficient height to reach the hand- and foot-operated controls, and to see easily both inside and outside the vehicle.

Requirements should be determined by the school bus fleet supervisor, the contractor, the school district, and the state director of public transportation.

The following Bureau of Motor Carrier Safety requirements are a minimum for commercial truck drivers. Minimums for school bus drivers should be no less stringent.

1. No loss of foot, leg, hand, or arm.
2. No mental, nervous, organic, or functional disease that is likely to interfere with safe driving.
3. No impairment in the use of foot, leg, fingers, hand, or arm, or other physical defect or limitation likely to interfere with safe driving.
4. Visual acuity not less than 20/40 (Snellen), in both eyes with or without glasses; a field of vision, not less than 140 degrees in a horizontal plane; and the ability to distinguish the colors red, green, and yellow.
5. Hearing should be such that, measured by an audiometric device, there is an average hearing loss in the better ear no greater than 40 dB at 500 Hz, 1000 Hz, and 2000 Hz with or without a hearing aid.
6. Not addicted to narcotics or habit-forming drugs, or to excessive use of alcoholic beverages.

DISQUALIFYING CONDITIONS

Emotional instability	Hernia
Convulsion disorder	Back injuries
Diabetes	Cardiovascular disease

Some states have physical requirements that equal or exceed the Bureau of Motor Carrier Safety Regulations. If your state is one of these, see that your drivers meet those requirements. If physical requirements in your state are less stringent, have your local school board establish adequate physical qualifications to provide the reasonable safeguards you need.

Mental characteristics

The American Medical Association's Committee on Medical Aspects of Automobile Injuries and Deaths reports that persons with an intelligence quotient (IQ) below 70 are more susceptible to accidents than are individuals with an average IQ of 100 or higher. This is especially true when they are faced with emergency situations requiring accurate judgment or decisive action. Low-IQ drivers might also be difficult to supervise and could make poor witnesses in case of an accident.

It is also known that highly intelligent drivers are likely to have accidents—not because they do not drive well, but because their minds are so active they find it difficult to concentrate while driving a vehicle. To these drivers, personal mental distraction can be more dangerous than external physical distraction.

Obeying traffic regulations and extending courtesies to pedestrians and other motorists is essential for both safe driving and good public relations. Conversely, there is a close correlation between repeated traffic violations and repeated accidents.

The driver must be able to find satisfaction in the job and get along well with others. A new employee brings to the job skill, aptitude, and, sometimes, negative personality traits. The new driver who gets along well with others contributes to the morale of the entire group, helps keep pupil discipline problems at a minimum, and is valuable in maintaining the fleet's good public image.

Other considerations

Drivers differ in the degree that they maintain or abuse their vehicles. Because many school transportation systems operate on limited budgets, evidence of this trait in an applicant should be carefully evaluated. Conservation of the vehicle reduces the expense of maintaining it in a safe and operable condition, extends its useful life and service, and contributes to a more accurate schedule. The vehicle that is abused breaks down more often on the route and is frequently in the shop for repairs. As a consequence, schedules are delayed. Frequent schedule irregularities disrupt school teaching programs, antagonize parents and students and lower the fleet's service image. No school district can afford an unreliable and irregular bus schedule.

The emotionally mature employee makes the best and safest driver. Permitting an immature person to operate school buses is dangerous. Maturity does not always correspond directly with the age of a driver. Safe drivers of any age recognize and accept their full responsibility for the operation of the bus and the safety of their pupil passengers.

Another important point to consider is the employee's emotional health. Family and other personal problems and responsibilities often can affect on-the-job performance. Personal troubles can distract one's attention from driving. Anger, carried to the job, can cause a driver to disregard common sense, courtesy, and caution.

The applicant's maturity is reflected in his attitude. An immature person blames others for past accidents and always is ready to blame the other party for disagreements or misunderstandings. The mature person shows an interest in people's opportunities, needs and interests. Interest in the problems and welfare of others contributes to a driver's ability to get along with pupils. The immature person is easily irritated, and cannot be expected to act for the safety and best interest of the pupil passengers and others at all times. Patience and understanding indicate a person can be responsible for the transportation of pupils.

Therefore, check an applicant's past record carefully. If there are discrepancies between the applicant's statements and previous employment records, try to reconcile the differences. Try to learn about the person's attitude, health, dependability, and loyalty during this check.

Traffic convictions and reportable accidents are usually on file in the state where they occur. It is worth the time and effort to check with the motor vehicle department in any state where the applicant has lived or has been licensed to operate a motor vehicle. Request that the department check the applicant's record at the National Driver Register Service. Checking the register will enable you to find any instances of license suspension or revocation, regardless of where they have occurred. A driver's real attitude toward safety and authority often is reflected in the records of the person's violations and accidents.

In summary, careful driver selection consists of seeking the following qualities in each applicant:
1. Physical fitness.
2. Good adjustment and emotional stability.
3. Size and stature to fit the job.
4. Impeccable references.

5. Neat appearance.
6. Congenial personality.
7. Acceptable driving skill, or capability of being trained.
8. No record of repeated traffic violations or preventable vehicular accidents.
9. Honesty, punctuality, and dependability.

CHAPTER 6

Training the School Bus Driver

The most important ingredient in an efficient school transportation service is safe driving. The skill, attitude, and knowledge necessary for safe driving and control of pupils must be developed through a driver training program. The training program must cover everything the driver needs to know to do the job well.

Driver instruction begins with the first contact with the supervisor, whose attitude toward the total safety program will be reflected in the driver's performance. Effective training establishes a standard of performance in all areas, including safe driving.

Three types of driver training are essential: initial training, refresher training, and remedial training. However, before discussing them, let us discuss the subject areas that should be included in training and the sources for training materials.

What To Include and Where To Find It

There are many approaches to training. In developing a fleet training program, be sure to include management policies, all the functions of the fleet, local laws and ordinances, state laws and regulations, and pertinent *Bureau of Motor Carrier Safety Regulations.*

Material is available from many sources. Be sure the material chosen covers the subject thoroughly and in an interesting manner. Because it will be presented to new drivers, it must be revised to keep it up-to-date. Some of the factors determining the extent and frequency of any revision are audience reaction, the subsequent performance of trainees, changing needs of the fleet, changes in administrative policies, changes in the extent and type of service rendered by the fleet, and changes in local and state laws and regulations.

Resources

. Films and selected video tapes are available either by purchase or rental to help the supervisor or other instructor teach proper driving techniques, including defensive driving.

Defensive Driving Course

The Defensive Driving Course emphasizes the six positions of the two-car crash. Each year, one of 12 drivers is involved in a two-car accident. This represents over 80 percent of the total number of accidents annually.

A two-car crash may involve you with another vehicle (*a*) ahead of you, (*b*) behind you, (*c*) meeting you head on, (*d*) meeting you at an intersection, (*e*) passing you, or (*f*) being passed by you. The Defensive Driving Course teaches a simple defense to prevent accident involvement in any of these six situations. Application of these principles can help each school bus driver avoid accidents.

The films that teach the six positions of the two-car crash can be purchased for your training materials library and used to teach defensive driving to your fleet for years to come.

Accidents may have many contributing factors, but in almost every instance, one or more driving errors trigger the accident. The well-trained operator understands his vehicle's limitations, the effect of his physical and mental condition, interaction with others, and the environmental conditions that can contribute to accidents. Drivers must be taught to compensate for such factors to prevent accidents.

Backing

Because of the high frequency of backing accidents, this subject also belongs in the driving training program. Although the results of backing accidents usually are minor in terms of vehicle and property damage, they can have serious personal injury consequences. The implications are that the driver involved has failed to exercise proper caution and has an attitude toward safety that could contribute to many serious incidents and accidents. Any time another vehicle or object is hit in a backing accident, the driver must be aware that a pupil could just as easily have been struck. Drivers should be taught that backing is to be avoided when possible, and should learn how to back safely when it becomes necessary.

Procedures to stress include: (*a*) getting out of the bus before beginning the maneuver and carefully noting the available clearance and all objects or obstructions, (*b*) backing from the driver's side, (*c*) backing slowly, (*d*) checking both sides continually as you back, and (*c*) using a reliable person to guide you.

New drivers should practice the driving techniques they are taught. The supervisor can only observe driving habits and respond to traffic situations by riding with them. By putting the driver behind the wheel and observing his driving performance over a prescribed course, the supervisor can evaluate the trainee's progress and readiness to transport pupils.

No transportation director should allow any driver to transport pupils until that driver has fully demonstrated an understanding of the principles of defensive driving and has acquired the driving skills necessary for safe, efficient operation.

Types of Training: Initial, Refresher, and Remedial

Before assembling any training material, the instructor should list the points trainees should learn and decide on their relative importance. The objectives of the training program should be to provide the driver with the knowledge needed to do the job, the skill necessary to do it properly, and an appreciation of the importance of the job and the need to do it safely.

Safe driving is not a simple skill. It requires the ability to make driving decisions quickly which should be acquired through planned training—not picked up haphazardly.

Each new driver must be thoroughly trained by a good training program that provides for development of driving skills to a high performance level. Good supervision will further refine and improve such skills.

The driver who completes the training course should:
1. Be able to maintain control over pupils on the bus;
2. Know procedures to deal with pupils who disobey established rules and regulations;
3. Understand schedules and know the flexibility permitted during adverse conditions or emergencies;

4. Be able to cope with emergencies that may arise during the course of duty;
5. Be qualified to administer first aid if needed;
6. Be able to operate a fire extinguisher effectively;
7. Know what to do if involved in an accident.

The amount of time needed for initial training depends on the selection program, the person employed, and the amount of usable skill and experience the person has. Adequate time must be allowed to develop the new driver's knowledge and skill to the degree necessary for effective job performance.

Refresher training

Periodic refresher training reinforces a driver's understanding of the policies, rules and regulations pertinent to operations. Also, it helps keep their performance efficient and safe.

Material covered in these classes will vary, but, in general, it should include the following:
1. Review of initial material as experience indicates it is needed;
2. Instruction covering the operation of new equipment;
3. Handling of new operating problems;
4. Changes in policies, laws, and regulations;
5. Periodic first aid refresher training;
6. Periodic fire extinguisher training;
7. Review of emergency evacuation procedures;
8. Review of vehicle inspection procedures;
9. Review of procedures to follow in the event of accident or emergency.

Remedial training

Remedial training can improve the performance of drivers whose records indicate that they have problems. The discussion technique is useful in such training. A description of an accident involving one member of the class, followed by a group discussion of defensive measures that could have prevented it, will help all to learn from the accident.

This type of training is indicated for any driver who:
1. Becomes involved in preventable accidents;
2. Fails to solve pupil behavior problems;
3. Abuses the vehicle;

4. Is discourteous;
5. Fails to operate reasonably close to schedule;
6. Is the subject of frequent complaints about attitude or performance;
7. Shows changes in personal habits that indicate personal problems;
8. Experiences changes in physical fitness because of the aging process or the consequences of illness or disease.

Psycho-physical Testing

Many psycho-physical and other tests are available and should be used to demonstrate to drivers their personal limitations or handicaps. Several qualities treated by these tests are discussed next.

Reaction time

Often, drivers do not realize the reaction time or distance that makes adequate following distance so important. This test emphasizes the importance of keeping an adequate distance between moving vehicles. A great help in preventing accidents is a visual demonstration of the distance a vehicle travels between the time the need to stop occurs and the time that braking effort actually begins. It is also useful to point out to older drivers that their reaction time may have increased and they must allow additional following distance to compensate for this change.

Distance judgment

A test of judgment of distance helps drivers recognize how well they can estimate the distance to approaching vehicles by comparing their positions with other objects. The ability to evaluate the distance and speed of approaching vehicles accurately is essential in such traffic maneuvers as passing a vehicle going in the same direction and entering a thoroughfare from a side road.

Glare recovery

Glare recovery is an important test for anyone who drives at times when headlights must be used. It reveals the time it takes for full vision to return after being subjected to the direct beams of car headlights at night. The distance traveled while the driver cannot see can be computed to emphasize this factor. Many drivers do not realize this hazard exists.

Tunnel vision

Some people have limited peripheral vision, called "tunnel vision." They can be taught to compensate for this limited sight by increased side-to-side head movement to observe all possible traffic conditions.

Such driver testing is needed to enable the supervisor to help each driver develop the compensating habits needed to drive safely. Drivers also should be impressed with the need to keep in good physical condition and to avoid things such as drugs, drug combinations and fatigue since they can adversely affect driving ability.

CHAPTER 7

Motivating the School Bus Driver

Motivation is the key to any safety program's success. Drivers must be motivated to police their own driving because their work environment makes direct supervision difficult.

The true test of the supervisor's skill is the ability to provide conditions that motivate the driver to maintain high standards. The following motivational methods and techniques can be used effectively by supervisors:

1. Make drivers aware of the high degree of skill they must acquire before qualifying to drive in your fleet.
2. Require remedial training for drivers involved in preventable accidents, and limit the number of accidents a driver can have and remain in your employ.
3. Demand that buses be cleaned inside each day, and cleaned outside as needed. Hold each driver responsible for any failures in this area.
4. Require neat appearance at all times. Drivers present a neat appearance and command more respect from both pupils and the public when uniforms are required.
5. Require drivers to be courteous at all times.
6. Appeal to the spirit of competition and publicly recognize those who do superior work.

High standards are challenging. Meeting them gives the driver a sense of pride in the job. Personal pride in their own skill makes drivers enjoy working in a fleet that is known for its high standards.

Set a Good Example

The supervisor should radiate dedication, pride, and enthusiasm in the transportation system. Your attitude and conduct should stimulate the safety consciousness of the drivers. Never do or say anything that might suggest you are not loyal to the system and its objectives.

Show Real Interest

Impart a sense of belonging to the drivers. Keep them informed of plans that involve them. Let them know periodically that they are meeting their objectives. Make them feel they are part of the team and that their personal efforts are necessary to achieve the goals of safety and efficiency. Let them know you welcome their suggestions. If their ideas cannot be used, explain the reasons; give them recognition for ideas that are used.

Encourage top management to use every opportunity to show personal interest in the drivers and the fleet safety program. Keep management aware of the importance of good buses, up-to-date maintenance facilities, and comfortable, adequate driver-room facilities.

Show your interest in the drivers by offering counsel and help if they come to you with personal problems. Let them know that you are always available for discussion of any problem.

Use Competition Effectively

Create job interest by appealing to the spirit of competition. Encourage each driver to compete with his or her own record to improve skills and performance. Many drivers enjoy the competition

Recognize Good Work

Most people appreciate recognition when they seriously devote themselves to their work. Drivers are no exception. Individual recognition of achievement through safe driver awards is a powerful incentive to good driving performance.

PREVENTIVE MAINTENANCE OF THE BUS

TABLE OF CONTENTS

	Page
OBJECTIVES	H-2
OVERVIEW	H-3
BUS COMPONENTS	H-9
PREVENTING MAJOR PROBLEMS BY DETECTING EARLY SIGNS OF TROUBLE	H-13
WHAT YOU SHOULD DO TO PROLONG THE LIFE OF THE BUS	H-17

OBJECTIVES

1. Use their senses to detect symptoms of possible trouble.

2. Describe basic bus components.

3. Identify driving actions which avoid undue wear on the bus.

OVERVIEW

INSTRUCTOR GUIDELINES	CONTENT
	Preventive maintenance is the scientific care of a vehicle that will guarantee the dependability and maximum life from the various parts. It is a carefully organized system of inspections made at regular mileage and/or time intervals, combined with immediate attention to all reported defects. These inspections are made up of a series of well-balanced checking procedures combined with the process of cleaning, tightening, lubricating, and adjusting of parts and units. It is the best known, simplest, and most economical means of protecting the original investment in a fleet of motor vehicles.
Refer to Figures 1 and 2 for sample inspection forms. Substitute your own forms if more appropriate. Explain why and how forms are filled out. Provide an example form filled out. ⬇	A regular periodic inspection program is the key to a good preventive maintenance program. (For sample inspection forms refer to Figures 1 and 2.)

Provide examples of symptoms they can detect through their senses. For example, smelling burning insulation, feeling a shimmy in the steering, hearing a knock or rattle, seeing a loose wire or connection, etc. Ask them for other suggestions of defects they might detect. Provide feedback.	You have a responsibility in this field, in addition to the inspection program carried out by a trained mechanic. You are on the road with the bus for a number of hours each day. You and you alone are in a position to observe its performance under all conditions. You should learn to recognize defects and immediately report the symptoms to the maintenance department. Don't attempt to diagnose the trouble but report anything unusual that you HEAR, SEE, SMELL, and FEEL. Remember, defects cannot be repaired if they are not reported.
	
	1. Listening for trouble.
	   a. Sharp knock when picking up speed.
	   b. Light knock when engine is running at idle speed.
	   c. Dull regular knock.

SCHOOL BUS MONTHLY OR 1000 MILE INSPECTION REPORT

Bus. No. _____   Driver _____   Inspection Date _____

Speedometer Reading _____

BODY		ENGINE	
1 Check all instrument panel gauges		27 Inspect motor supports: front, rear	
2. Check all lights, signals, and wiring		28 Check oil and air filters	
3 Check horn; first aid kit		29 Check muffler, manifold and exhaust line	
4 Check flares; fusees; flags; axe		30 Inspect fan belt	
5 Inspect heater and defroster equipment		31 Inspect generator and distributor	
6 Inspect fire extinguisher		32 Check battery and starter	
7 Inspect windshield wipers		33 Check cooling system	
8 Check and adjust rear view mirrors		34 Check carburetor and fuel line	
9 Check cleanliness: Interior; Exterior		35 Others	
10 Inspect windows; windshield; door glass			
11 Check seats and upholstery (seats must be tight to floor)			
12 Inspect emergency door, latches, warning signal			
13 Inspect service door, controls, steps			
14 Check stop arm			
TIRES			
15 Check for cuts, bruises, uneven wear, air pressure			
FRONT END			
16 Check spindles; wheel alignment; tie rods; drag links			
17 Check springs; clamps; shackles			
18 Check steering mechanism			
REAR AXLE			
19 Check springs; clamps; shackles			
CLUTCH			
20 Check pedal clearance & adjustment			
21 Check clutch for slipping or dragging			
TRANSMISSION			
22 Check shifting for noise			
23 Check for leaks and cracks		I certify that I have completed the inspection of this bus as indicated above.	
BRAKES			
24 Check pedal clearance and pressure			
25 Check fluid			
26 Check emergency brake			

_____   _____
Date   Mechanic

NOTE: Place a check mark (✓) in the column when each item is completed. If an item is unsatisfactory, leave column blank until repairs are made. If there is more than one item on a line, circle the ones that are unsatisfactory. A check mark in the column will indicate that the circled items have been completed.

Figure 1. Sample School Bus Monthly or 1000 Mile Inspection Report

SCHOOL BUS ANNUAL INSPECTION SHEET

Bus Number _____ Make _____ Year Model _____ Driver _____

Date of Inspection _____ Speedometer Reading _____

MOTOR		BRAKES	
1 Inspect for oil or grease leaks and any unusual noises		41 Remove wheels, inspect lining, linkage, drums, wheel bearings, hydraulic cylinders and lines	
2 Tighten cyclinder head bolts			
3 Tighten manifolds--stop leaks		42 Inspect booster and hoses	
4 Inspect muffler and exhaust line		43 Check air compressor, governor, gauge	
5 Inspect and adjust fan belt		44 Check emergency relay valve	
6 Tighten engine block to base		45 Check chambers, travel & adjustment	
7 Tighten engine support bolts		46 Inspect emergency brake lining, ratchet and pawl	
8 Tighten lower crankcase bolts			
9 Adjust valves and tappets		CHASSIS	
10 Inspect ignition cables		47 Check all wheels for trueness	
11 Check battery: clean, tighten, refill		48 Tighten rim lugs, check studs	
12 Clean and adjust distributor points		49 Tighten body bolts and clips	
13 Inspect and adjust carburetor		50 Tighten fenders, bumpers	
14 Check and clean generator and starter		51 Inspect universal joints and flanges; tighten all bolts	
15 Oil generator and starting motor			
16 Check voltage regulator, connections and charging rate		52 Check propeller shaft center bearing	
		53 Check & adjust radius rods	
17 Clean fuel pump; air cleaner		BODY	
18 Clean or replace oil filter		54 Inspect windshield wipers; test horn	
19 Clean and adjust spark plug gaps		55 Check seats and upholstery (seats must be tight to floor)	
COOLING SYSTEM			
20 Drain and flush radiator		56 Inspect and adjust rearview mirrors	
21 Inspect & tighten hose connections		57 Inspect heater & defroster equipment	
22 Inspect water pump & cooling system		58 Inspect fire extinguishers	
23 Tighten radiator stay rods and hold-down bolts		59 Inspect windshield, windows, glass	
		60 Inspect emergency door, latches, hinges, warning signal	
STEERING AND FRONT END			
24 Check wheel bearings, knuckle pins bushings, spindles, steering arms, tie rod ends, drag link; align front wheels		61 Inspect service door, controls, rubber	
		62 Check stop arm	
		63 Check all instrument panel gauges	
25 Tighten steering housing to frame		64 Flares, fusees, flags, first aid kit, axe (replace when necessary)	
26 Tighten pitman arm			
27 Adjust play in steering post		65 Check floor covering, safety shield	
28 Inspect springs for faulty leaves		66 Inspect body mounting sills & bolsters	
29 Tighten spring clips & U-bolts		67 Tighten tank support bands	
30 Tighten spring shackles & hangers		68 Check visibility of all signs and lettering	
CLUTCH			
31 Check pedal clearance & adjustment		69 Check all lights, signals, wiring	
32 Check clutch for slipping or dragging		TIRES	
TRANSMISSION		70 Check for cuts, bruises, uneven wear	
33 Check shifting and for noise		71 Check tread (replace if smooth)	
34 Check for leaks and cracks			
REAR END		CHANGE OIL AND GREASE	
35 Inspect differential for leaks		LUBRICATE ACCORDING TO CHART	
36 Inspect differential pinion for play			
37 Tighten differential housing bolts			
38 Tighten rear axle flange bolts			
39 Tighten spring clips & U-bolts			
40 Tighten spring shackles & hangers			

I certify that I have completed the annual inspection of this bus as indicated above.

NOTE: Place a check mark (✔) in column when each item is completed.

_____ _____
Date Mechanic

Figure 2. Sample School Bus Annual Inspection Sheet

INSTRUCTOR GUIDELINES	CONTENT

Emphasize:
 	
<u>listening</u>
 	
<u>feeling</u>
 	
<u>looking</u>
 	
<u>smelling</u>
	d. Clicking or tapping noises.
	e. Continuous or intermittent squeal or squeak.
	f. Loud exhaust noise.
	g. Engine backfiring, missing, popping, spitting, or overheating.
	h. Steaming or hissing.
	2. <u>Feeling for trouble.</u>
	   a. Excessive vibration.
	      (1) Engine compartment
	      (2) Steering wheel
	      (3) Drive line
	   b. Low speed or high speed shimmy.
	   c. Hard steering and steering wander.
	3. <u>Looking for trouble.</u>
	   a. Sudden drop in oil pressure.
	   b. Low oil pressure.
	   c. No oil pressure.
	NOTE: *If any of the above exist, the vehicle shall not be driven until corrected.*
	   d. Excessive oil consumption.
	   e. Smoke coming from under dash.
	   f. Smoke coming from under hood.
	   g. Scuffed tires or spotty wear.
	4. <u>Smelling trouble.</u>
	   a. Odor of gasoline.
	   b. Odor of burning rubber.

INSTRUCTOR GUIDELINES	CONTENT
	c. Odor of burning oil.
	d. Odor of burning rags.
	e. Exhaust fumes.
Stress that anything they notice that is out of the ordinary should be reported. There is a danger of thinking that an unusual noise, etc., is nothing to worry about, especially if a driver has mechanical experience. It's better to report <u>any</u> unusual condition and have it be something minor, than not to report it; it could be a very costly and even dangerous defect. Stress that they <u>don't</u> need to know what is wrong before they report something "suspicious."	<u>Any other unusual conditions should be reported immediately to the proper authority.</u>

BUS COMPONENTS

INSTRUCTOR GUIDELINES	CONTENT
Discuss each component briefly. Avoid long technical explanations. Complete comprehension of mechanical operation is <u>not</u> the purpose here. Provide line drawings of each part and show the flow of the process from ignition to bus motion.	You should have a basic knowledge of the school bus components to know generally how these will affect the bus' operation. There will be times when this knowledge will be useful to you in adjusting your driving performance and in detecting trouble while on the route. Proper driving habits will increase the efficiency and economy of the bus operation. Brief explanations of the basic bus components are provided on the next few pages. Bus components included are: • Braking System • Engine • Transmission and Driveshaft • Clutch • Steering • Electrical System • Suspension Your instructor will discuss how each bus component works.

INSTRUCTOR GUIDELINES	CONTENT
	BUS COMPONENT HOW IT WORKS
	BRAKING SYSTEM Pressing on brake pedal causes fluid or air to flow into brake cylinder. Cylinder moves brake shoes outward against brake drum (inner surface of metal wheel). This pressure of shoes against drum causes wheel to slow and stop.
	· Hydraulic
	· Vacuum-Hydraulic
	· Air
	ENGINE
	· Carburetor Takes fuel in gas tank, mixes it with air in carburetor. Mixture is fed into combustion chamber where it's ignited by spark plugs. The exploding mixture causes pistons to move. The motion of the pistons causes the crankshaft to turn. The rotating crankshaft connects the final power from the engine to the transmission. The power is then carried to the driveshaft, the differential, the rear axles, and the rear wheels.
	· Combustion Chambers
	· Pistons
	· Crankshaft
	TRANSMISSION AND DRIVESHAFT A system of gears which allows you to change the ratio of number of engine revolutions to number of wheel revolutions. For example, in low gear, engine might turn 100 times for one wheel turn. In a

INSTRUCTOR GUIDELINES	CONTENT
	higher gear, the engine might turn 10 times for one wheel turn. Driveshaft connects transmission to rear wheels, making them turn.
	CLUTCH — When depressed, disconnects engine from transmission so you can change transmission gears.
	STEERING — Steering wheel and column connects to gears and linkage mechanism which changes direction of front wheels.
	ELECTRICAL SYSTEM — Supplies power for primary engine functions and auxiliary functions:

Primary Engine Functions

- Power generation and storage (battery, generator/alternator, and voltage regulator)
- Power distribution (engine wiring)
- Timing (distributor)
- Spark generation (spark plugs and coil)

Auxiliary Functions

- Inside/outside lighting (headlights, amber/red flashing warning lights, turn

INSTRUCTOR GUIDELINES	CONTENT
	signals, instrument panel lights, etc.)
	· Air/heat circulation (heater, defroster, blowers)
	· Horn
	SUSPENSION Springs and shock absorbers which enable driver to handle bus properly on rough terrain and sharp curves, etc.
Have trainees volunteer answers to the questions. Provide feedback. Correct answers are:	Answer these questions: 1. Which bus component is made up of a system of gears?
1. Transmission	
	2. Which component is responsible for the way the bus handles and rides on rough terrain and sharp curves?
2. Suspension	
	3. Which bus component works on fluid or air pressure?
3. Brakes	
	4. Which component disconnects the engine from the transmission so you can change gears?
4. Clutch	
Answer any questions trainees ask. Lead discussion.	Your instructor will answer any questions <u>you</u> may have on how the bus works.

PREVENTING MAJOR PROBLEMS BY DETECTING EARLY SIGNS OF TROUBLE

INSTRUCTOR GUIDELINES	CONTENT

OPTION: You may want to have one of your bus mechanics on hand to answer questions. The intent here is a basic knowledge of the operations so trainees can spot troubles early. Do not lead them to believe they are being trained to be mechanics.	1. BRAKING SYSTEM--EARLY SIGNS OF TROUBLE
	
	   a. Air pressure drop (air brakes only)
	
	   b. Brake pedal low (hydraulic or vacuum-hydraulic brakes)
	
	   c. Pedal spongy (hydraulic or vacuum-hydraulic brakes)
	
	   d. Smell or see brake fluid (hydraulic or vacuum-hydraulic brakes)
	
	   e. Brake drum very hot (all types)
	
	   f. Bus swerves when brakes are applied (all types)
	
	2. ENGINE--EARLY SIGNS OF TROUBLE
	
	   a. Engine miss at low speed
	
	   b. Engine miss at high speed
	
	   c. Ping when accelerating
	
	   d. Dull "clunk" at idle
	
	   e. Sharp loud knocking. <u>SHUT OFF ENGINE IMMEDIATELY</u>
	
	   f. Heat gauge indicates temperature rising higher than normal
	
	   g. Oil pressure dropping below normal. <u>SHUT OFF ENGINE IMMEDIATELY</u>
	
	   h. Engine stalls or runs sluggish on cold damp morning

INSTRUCTOR GUIDELINES	CONTENT

	3. TRANSMISSION AND DRIVESHAFT--EARLY SIGNS OF TROUBLE
	
	   a. Hard shifting
	
	   b. Slipping out of gear
	
	   c. Clunk or jerk when power is applied or released
	
	   d. Unusual sounds when power is applied
	
	4. CLUTCH--EARLY SIGNS OF TROUBLE
	
	   a. Motor revving with clutch engaged and vehicle moving and in gear
	
	   b. Odor of burning clutch lining
	
	   c. Gear clash
	
	   d. Squealing sound when clutch pedal is depressed, with engine running
	
	   e. Clutch "chattering"
	
	5. STEERING--EARLY SIGNS OF TROUBLE
	
	   a. Steering very difficult
	
	   b. Wheels shimmy
	
	   c. Bus veers one way or the other
	
	   d. Bus wanders on roadway
	
	6. ELECTRICAL SYSTEM--EARLY SIGNS OF TROUBLE
	
	   a. Ammeter indicates a discharge. <u>WATCH OUT FOR FIRE</u>
	
	   b. Smoke appearing around wires, switches, etc. <u>DISCONNECT BATTERY IMMEDIATELY</u>
	
	   c. Ammeter indicates heavy charging
	
	   d. Lights dim

INSTRUCTOR GUIDELINES	CONTENT
	7. SUSPENSION--EARLY SIGNS OF TROUBLE
	a. Bus bounces or rolls from side to side easily
	b. Bus out of alignment as it travels along road
	c. Bus "bottoms" on bumps
Describe in detail your local procedures for <u>reporting</u> any of these symptoms. Provide your own forms that drivers are to use. Explain how to fill them out.	NOTES:

WHAT YOU SHOULD DO TO PROLONG THE LIFE OF THE BUS

INSTRUCTOR GUIDELINES	CONTENT
Explain the reasons for "WHAT YOU SHOULD DO." Avoid long, technical explanations. For example, you might describe the wearing action on the discs when a driver "slips the clutch." OPTION: If you have access to actual worn brake shoes, clutch plates, etc., pass them around for examination by the class. Explain what is meant by "lugging"--e.g., trying to go up a hill in too high a gear which causes a strain on the engine.	You can develop good driving habits that will avoid undue wear on each specific bus component. BRAKES • Do not jam brakes on hard. Apply them smoothly and steadily. • Do not depress clutch until engine stall speed is reached so engine can assist in stopping the bus. • Do not drive with your foot resting on the brake pedal. • Drain water out of air reservoir on buses equipped with air brakes. (If board policy permits.) • Pump the brakes (once or twice) on long hard stops and on hills to aid heat dissipation and reduce brake fade. ENGINE • Don't race engine during warm-up. • Don't over-speed engine at any time. • Don't lug engine; this causes engine and drive-line damage. • Don't allow engine to operate beyond established oil change and maintenance intervals. • Don't accelerate harshly; this causes extreme stress during periods when oil pressure is low; therefore, excessive wear.

INSTRUCTOR GUIDELINES	CONTENT
	• Don't attempt to operate engine when oil pressure is low, temperature is high, or ammeter indicates a continuous discharge.
	• Do not add water to over-heated engine.
	• Use caution when removing radiator cap on a hot engine.
	TRANSMISSION AND DRIVE SHAFT
	. Usually you shouldn't skip gears when upshifting or downshifting.
	• Do not lug the engine.
	• Do not speed in any gear.
	• Do not release the clutch quickly.
	• Transmit power smoothly (coordination).
	• Shift smoothly.
	• Avoid fast acceleration on rough surfaces.
	• Avoid jerky movements of any kind.
	CLUTCH
Explain what "riding the clutch" means, e.g., keeping foot on clutch pedal and leaving pedal part way depressed when not shifting gears.	• Don't "ride" the clutch, it partially disengages the clutch causing excess heat or wear.
	• Don't upshift at low engine speed. Permit engine to speed up enough in one gear so that when the shift is made to the next gear, the engine won't lug.
	• Usually, you shouldn't skip gears when upshifting or downshifting; this causes undue engine lugging and shock-loading of clutch and driveline.
	• Don't speed.

INSTRUCTOR GUIDELINES	CONTENT
	• Usually, you shouldn't skip gears when down-shifting, this causes the clutch components to turn at very high speeds.
	• Don't coast with the clutch disengaged; the asbestos clutch disc will spin at a very high speed and may disintegrate.
Explain what is meant by "slipping the clutch," e.g., keeping the clutch partially engaged with the accelerator also partially depressed to the point where the bus can hold on the hill without the use of the brake pedal.	• Don't hold the bus on a hill by slipping the clutch. <u>Nothing wears out a clutch faster</u>. Adjust shifting speeds to accommodate load and terrain. STEERING • Avoid potholes--slow up! (Drive around if possible.) • Have mechanic inspect steering if you hit a bad bump or pothole. ELECTRICAL SYSTEM • Don't drive when ammeter indicates discharge. • Don't start engine when lights and/or heaters are on. • Don't forget to check belt tension and battery water level. • Don't allow heaters and lights to remain in operation when bus is not moving or engine is stopped for an extended period. • Make sure polarity is correct when using jumper cables (+ to +, - to -). SUSPENSION • Don't travel fast on rough roads.

INSTRUCTOR GUIDELINES	CONTENT
	· Don't cross rough areas at an excessive rate of speed.
	· Avoid "potholes" when possible (but don't turn out of your lane. It's better to slow down.)
Administer Unit Review Questions. Provide feedback. Provide review discussion for any trainee who does not meet criterion.	· Don't accelerate harshly on rough surfaces.
	· Check wheel alignment of bus that is on a rough road frequently.

ANSWER SHEET

TEST NO. _____ PART _____ TITLE OF POSITION _____
(AS GIVEN IN EXAMINATION ANNOUNCEMENT - INCLUDE OPTION, IF ANY)

PLACE OF EXAMINATION _____ DATE _____
(CITY OR TOWN)   (STATE)

RATING

USE THE SPECIAL PENCIL. MAKE GLOSSY BLACK MARKS.

	A B C D E		A B C D E		A B C D E		A B C D E		A B C D E
1	⋮ ⋮ ⋮ ⋮ ⋮	26	⋮ ⋮ ⋮ ⋮ ⋮	51	⋮ ⋮ ⋮ ⋮ ⋮	76	⋮ ⋮ ⋮ ⋮ ⋮	101	⋮ ⋮ ⋮ ⋮ ⋮
2	⋮ ⋮ ⋮ ⋮ ⋮	27	⋮ ⋮ ⋮ ⋮ ⋮	52	⋮ ⋮ ⋮ ⋮ ⋮	77	⋮ ⋮ ⋮ ⋮ ⋮	102	⋮ ⋮ ⋮ ⋮ ⋮
3	⋮ ⋮ ⋮ ⋮ ⋮	28	⋮ ⋮ ⋮ ⋮ ⋮	53	⋮ ⋮ ⋮ ⋮ ⋮	78	⋮ ⋮ ⋮ ⋮ ⋮	103	⋮ ⋮ ⋮ ⋮ ⋮
4	⋮ ⋮ ⋮ ⋮ ⋮	29	⋮ ⋮ ⋮ ⋮ ⋮	54	⋮ ⋮ ⋮ ⋮ ⋮	79	⋮ ⋮ ⋮ ⋮ ⋮	104	⋮ ⋮ ⋮ ⋮ ⋮
5	⋮ ⋮ ⋮ ⋮ ⋮	30	⋮ ⋮ ⋮ ⋮ ⋮	55	⋮ ⋮ ⋮ ⋮ ⋮	80	⋮ ⋮ ⋮ ⋮ ⋮	105	⋮ ⋮ ⋮ ⋮ ⋮
6	⋮ ⋮ ⋮ ⋮ ⋮	31	⋮ ⋮ ⋮ ⋮ ⋮	56	⋮ ⋮ ⋮ ⋮ ⋮	81	⋮ ⋮ ⋮ ⋮ ⋮	106	⋮ ⋮ ⋮ ⋮ ⋮
7	⋮ ⋮ ⋮ ⋮ ⋮	32	⋮ ⋮ ⋮ ⋮ ⋮	57	⋮ ⋮ ⋮ ⋮ ⋮	82	⋮ ⋮ ⋮ ⋮ ⋮	107	⋮ ⋮ ⋮ ⋮ ⋮
8	⋮ ⋮ ⋮ ⋮ ⋮	33	⋮ ⋮ ⋮ ⋮ ⋮	58	⋮ ⋮ ⋮ ⋮ ⋮	83	⋮ ⋮ ⋮ ⋮ ⋮	108	⋮ ⋮ ⋮ ⋮ ⋮
9	⋮ ⋮ ⋮ ⋮ ⋮	34	⋮ ⋮ ⋮ ⋮ ⋮	59	⋮ ⋮ ⋮ ⋮ ⋮	84	⋮ ⋮ ⋮ ⋮ ⋮	109	⋮ ⋮ ⋮ ⋮ ⋮
10	⋮ ⋮ ⋮ ⋮ ⋮	35	⋮ ⋮ ⋮ ⋮ ⋮	60	⋮ ⋮ ⋮ ⋮ ⋮	85	⋮ ⋮ ⋮ ⋮ ⋮	110	⋮ ⋮ ⋮ ⋮ ⋮

Make only ONE mark for each answer. Additional and stray marks may be counted as mistakes. In making corrections, erase errors COMPLETELY.

	A B C D E		A B C D E		A B C D E		A B C D E		A B C D E
11	⋮ ⋮ ⋮ ⋮ ⋮	36	⋮ ⋮ ⋮ ⋮ ⋮	61	⋮ ⋮ ⋮ ⋮ ⋮	86	⋮ ⋮ ⋮ ⋮ ⋮	111	⋮ ⋮ ⋮ ⋮ ⋮
12	⋮ ⋮ ⋮ ⋮ ⋮	37	⋮ ⋮ ⋮ ⋮ ⋮	62	⋮ ⋮ ⋮ ⋮ ⋮	87	⋮ ⋮ ⋮ ⋮ ⋮	112	⋮ ⋮ ⋮ ⋮ ⋮
13	⋮ ⋮ ⋮ ⋮ ⋮	38	⋮ ⋮ ⋮ ⋮ ⋮	63	⋮ ⋮ ⋮ ⋮ ⋮	88	⋮ ⋮ ⋮ ⋮ ⋮	113	⋮ ⋮ ⋮ ⋮ ⋮
14	⋮ ⋮ ⋮ ⋮ ⋮	39	⋮ ⋮ ⋮ ⋮ ⋮	64	⋮ ⋮ ⋮ ⋮ ⋮	89	⋮ ⋮ ⋮ ⋮ ⋮	114	⋮ ⋮ ⋮ ⋮ ⋮
15	⋮ ⋮ ⋮ ⋮ ⋮	40	⋮ ⋮ ⋮ ⋮ ⋮	65	⋮ ⋮ ⋮ ⋮ ⋮	90	⋮ ⋮ ⋮ ⋮ ⋮	115	⋮ ⋮ ⋮ ⋮ ⋮
16	⋮ ⋮ ⋮ ⋮ ⋮	41	⋮ ⋮ ⋮ ⋮ ⋮	66	⋮ ⋮ ⋮ ⋮ ⋮	91	⋮ ⋮ ⋮ ⋮ ⋮	116	⋮ ⋮ ⋮ ⋮ ⋮
17	⋮ ⋮ ⋮ ⋮ ⋮	42	⋮ ⋮ ⋮ ⋮ ⋮	67	⋮ ⋮ ⋮ ⋮ ⋮	92	⋮ ⋮ ⋮ ⋮ ⋮	117	⋮ ⋮ ⋮ ⋮ ⋮
18	⋮ ⋮ ⋮ ⋮ ⋮	43	⋮ ⋮ ⋮ ⋮ ⋮	68	⋮ ⋮ ⋮ ⋮ ⋮	93	⋮ ⋮ ⋮ ⋮ ⋮	118	⋮ ⋮ ⋮ ⋮ ⋮
19	⋮ ⋮ ⋮ ⋮ ⋮	44	⋮ ⋮ ⋮ ⋮ ⋮	69	⋮ ⋮ ⋮ ⋮ ⋮	94	⋮ ⋮ ⋮ ⋮ ⋮	119	⋮ ⋮ ⋮ ⋮ ⋮
20	⋮ ⋮ ⋮ ⋮ ⋮	45	⋮ ⋮ ⋮ ⋮ ⋮	70	⋮ ⋮ ⋮ ⋮ ⋮	95	⋮ ⋮ ⋮ ⋮ ⋮	120	⋮ ⋮ ⋮ ⋮ ⋮
21	⋮ ⋮ ⋮ ⋮ ⋮	46	⋮ ⋮ ⋮ ⋮ ⋮	71	⋮ ⋮ ⋮ ⋮ ⋮	96	⋮ ⋮ ⋮ ⋮ ⋮	121	⋮ ⋮ ⋮ ⋮ ⋮
22	⋮ ⋮ ⋮ ⋮ ⋮	47	⋮ ⋮ ⋮ ⋮ ⋮	72	⋮ ⋮ ⋮ ⋮ ⋮	97	⋮ ⋮ ⋮ ⋮ ⋮	122	⋮ ⋮ ⋮ ⋮ ⋮
23	⋮ ⋮ ⋮ ⋮ ⋮	48	⋮ ⋮ ⋮ ⋮ ⋮	73	⋮ ⋮ ⋮ ⋮ ⋮	98	⋮ ⋮ ⋮ ⋮ ⋮	123	⋮ ⋮ ⋮ ⋮ ⋮
24	⋮ ⋮ ⋮ ⋮ ⋮	49	⋮ ⋮ ⋮ ⋮ ⋮	74	⋮ ⋮ ⋮ ⋮ ⋮	99	⋮ ⋮ ⋮ ⋮ ⋮	124	⋮ ⋮ ⋮ ⋮ ⋮
25	⋮ ⋮ ⋮ ⋮ ⋮	50	⋮ ⋮ ⋮ ⋮ ⋮	75	⋮ ⋮ ⋮ ⋮ ⋮	100	⋮ ⋮ ⋮ ⋮ ⋮	125	⋮ ⋮ ⋮ ⋮ ⋮

ANSWER SHEET

MAY - - 2016

TEST NO. _____ PART _____ TITLE OF POSITION _____
(AS GIVEN IN EXAMINATION ANNOUNCEMENT - INCLUDE OPTION, IF ANY)

PLACE OF EXAMINATION _____ DATE _____
(CITY OR TOWN)   (STATE)

RATING

USE THE SPECIAL PENCIL. MAKE GLOSSY BLACK MARKS.

Make only ONE mark for each answer. Additional and stray marks may be counted as mistakes. In making corrections, erase errors COMPLETELY.